DATE DUE

MAR 2 5 2002	

BRODART   Cat. No. 23-221

WORK, SELF AND SOCIETY

Changes currently occurring in the world of work are large-scale, affecting what people do every day and altering our relations with one another and with the physical world. There is a shift in the nature of industrial work, from a materiality of labor and product, and specialization of function, to forms of production that are discursive, or symbolic, and highly integrated. Among the far reaching implications of a post-industrial condition is a dissolution of traditional and modern bonds of social solidarity and a metamorphosis of the character of the modern self.

Work, Self and Society examines the relationships between the institutional practices of work under post-industrial conditions and the formation of the self. Drawing on data from field work in a multi-national corporation, the book critically analyzes organizational and cultural practices in contemporary corporate work. The author interprets the deliberate construction of "designer cultures" as a response to the broad crisis in industrial production, work organization and culture. The book also develops a critical social psychology of corporate work. It analyzes the production of "designer employees" and other effects of contemporary corporate culture, and describes and analyzes self-strategies effected by the discursive practices of corporate work.

The author argues that a "post-occupational" condition, an event precipitated and facilitated by new technologies and organizational change, is emerging in corporate organizations. "Post-occupational" work has significant implications for self-identity and social cohesion within the work place, and more broadly, in society. The relationships between the institutional processes of the new work in post-industrial corporate culture, and changes in social organization and self formation have not yet been described. *Work, Self and Society* offers original analyses of these relationships, and proposes some important new categories by which to interpret the work–self–society relation.

Catherine Casey is a lecturer in the School of Commerce and Economics at the University of Auckland, New Zealand.

WORK, SELF AND SOCIETY

After industrialism

Catherine Casey

London and New York

First published 1995
by Routledge
11 New Fetter Lane, London EC4P 4EE

Simultaneously published in the USA and Canada
by Routledge
29 West 35th Street, New York, NY 10001

© 1995 Catherine Casey

Typeset in Times by J&L Composition Ltd, Filey, North Yorkshire

Printed and bound in Great Britain by Mackays of Chatham PLC, Chatham, Kent

British Library Cataloguing in Publication Data
A catalogue record for this book is available from the British Library.

Library of Congress Cataloging in Publication Data
A catalogue record for this book has been requested

ISBN 0–415–11202–8 (hbk)
ISBN 0–415–11203–6 (pbk)

For my parents, Hazel and Norbert Casey

CONTENTS

ACKNOWLEDGEMENTS

The support and assistance of many people helped make writing this book, and conducting the earlier field work, both possible and worthwhile. The part of this book that describes work, life and culture in a multi-national corporation took me for an academic year into the everyday working life of a corporation. Although the people at the company, and the company itself, must remain anonymous, I wish first to thank them for allowing me to be among them. The generosity and openness which they afforded me made my role as observer and analyst a relatively comfortable one. I thank them all for their time, their stories and their forbearance.

I wish to thank most especially Philip Wexler, my teacher and friend, and the late Christopher Lasch. I am deeply indebted to them both for encouraging and facilitating this work. Among others who have read, criticized and commented on chapters or ideas in this book I thank especially Michael Powell and Barry Smart for their criticism and comments on the chapters, and their warm encouragement. I thank also David Barry and Bruce Luske for their helpful comments at various stages of this research. For many stimulating conversations over ideas and themes in this book, and about much else, I thank Stephen Appel, Roger Booth, Gill and John Denny, Nicola Armstrong, Lynn Vacanti and Doug Noble. And I wish also to thank Brett Warburton, Ilene Wexler, Stephanie Doyle, Trevor Mallard, Flan Lynch, and my family.

INTRODUCTION

Eschatological interests have flourished at the end of centuries before now, and the imminent end of the twentieth century is no exception. It might be that the current interest among a number of social observers in endings and our proclivity toward transformations and beginnings is an effect of some vast cosmic season. On the other hand, the passing of industrialism simply coincides with the passing of the century. What comes after does not begin neatly on a date in our conventional measure of time. The old decays unevenly. It is sometimes repaired and revived and sometimes destroyed and discarded. The new is generated by both the living and the dead. Like Weber still, we do not know what social life beyond industrialism will be like. Without the certainties and hopes of modern thought our readings of this juncture are only modest and reasonable offerings for thinking about the present and the future. And hence I prefer to retain the limited concept of "post-industrial" to describe the changes in modern industrial society we can readily see around us. Post-industrial society provides a way of thinking about these changes as we seek new categories for theorizing a new social formation after industrialism. It is an interim term for an interim condition.

In typical, western industrial society, as Marx, Durkheim and Weber analyzed, the social bases of society were organized around the productive economic activities of human beings. An extensive division of labor, the rationalization of economic and social processes and deep tensions between *gemeinshaft* and *gesellschaft* characterized modern society. Our modern forms of social solidarity, in which we became increasingly interdependent, existed amid a complex struggle between classes and power elites, exacerbating conflicts between individualism and community. The increasing rationalization of all spheres of life characterized modern industrial society. Unifying "grand" narratives of social meaning and behavior demanded and achieved, by and large, social conformity to the values and practices of western modernity.

Since the early 1970s social analysts have been proposing that a range of technological and social developments occurring in western societies is

1

bringing about vast social and cultural changes that are challenging the meta trends of modern industrialism. Although there are evidently continuities in many social practices these post-industrial events are effecting changes in many areas of modern industrial society and not just, although fundamentally, in production, or the postmodern turn in the cultural sphere. Among the far-reaching implications of a post-industrial condition is a dissolution of traditional and modern bonds of social solidarity and a metamorphosis of the character of the modern self. The changes occurring in work and production are large-scale. There is a shift in the nature of industrial work, from a materiality of labor and product, and specialization of function, to forms of production that are discursive, or symbolic, and highly integrated. These practices affect what people do every day, and they are altering relations among ourselves and with the physical world.

The advent of advanced electronic technologies, based upon microprocessor and integrated-circuit technologies, is changing how we produce and exchange both material and discursive commodities. It is also precipitating and facilitating the emergence of new products and practices in service, knowledge, information and images, as well as the globalization of communications and financial transactions. The "global world" is a technological phenomenon. In the midst of these profound changes in the productive sphere, including increasing and persisting unemployment, can work continue to be a primary basis of social organization, and a primary constituent of self formation, as it has been throughout the modern industrial era? Will work and production endure as central organizing elements at this post-industrial juncture, and beyond?

This book offers a critical social analysis of the transformations occurring in the world of work and of the effects of contemporary institutional practices of work on self formation. As we move beyond modern industrialism I imagine that work, as conventionally understood, will no longer remain a primary basis of social organization. But in the meantime, the deep industrial legacy of the predominance of work lingers ominously at this juncture. It is an ominous lingering because we are creating a world in which it seems work for many will be scarce, unrewarding and sporadic as society has the capacity, through technological and organizational developments, to produce more and more (the dream of industrialism) with fewer and fewer workers. Growth without work is a decidedly post-industrial condition. The industrial legacy of the centrality of production and work in social and self formation hovers precipitously with the post-industrial condition in which work is declining in social primacy. Social meanings and solidarity must, eventually, be found elsewhere.

SELF

Talking about the "self" is currently fraught with difficulty. A number of analysts now prefer to emphasize identity processes (Aronowitz 1992,

Giddens 1991, Hall 1987, 1990, Hewitt 1989, Lash and Friedman 1992) although these are usually intertwined with notions of self. Others, in postmodern vein, reject a notion of self (Deleuze and Guatarri 1979, Derrida 1982, Lyotard 1984). For the past twenty years much of social and cultural theory in the West has been influenced by the French philosophers Derrida, Foucault, Lacan, Lyotard, Baudrillard, and Kristeva. Their influence, and also that of the American philosopher Richard Rorty, has prompted a contestation of and departure from what they consider to be a modern or humanist view of the self.

It has been argued that the modern view conceives of the self as a fixed, irreducible "solid" entity – the essential core of one's being. Whether or not this is actually the modern view of self, and there are some, importantly Charles Taylor (1989) who propose that the self, while indeed a modern concept, has always been more contingent and ephemeral than modernity's critics suggest, it is a commonly held view that is now criticized and rejected by many contemporary and postmodern thinkers. There has been a theme in the modern tradition in which the self is conceived as historically specific and socially and culturally patterned. Marx, Durkheim and Freud each held, variously, the idea that the self is a social construction shaped by institutional processes. Other modern thinkers, notably Mead (1934), Goffman (1959, 1961) and Berger and Luckman (1966), never held the view of self as "fixed entity", preferring to emphasize the social construction of self through constitutive elements, dialectical processes, self-narratives and displays. The unresolved debate on selfhood continues. I offer from the outset an explanatory note on my usage of the concept of self.

The self may be a convenient fiction, a narrative construct that gives some coherence and continuity to a process of mind–body sensations, conscious and unconscious experiences and meaning-making. To agree with the postmodern critics that the self is not a fixed and solid entity does not require an outright rejection of the concept. Rather, recognizing the self as a pattern or a constellation of constituent events and processes (particles and waves in Zohar's (1990) quantum physics metaphor) can still enable an understanding of the person who experiences, as we western moderns do, a sense of agency, inwardness and individuality (cf. Taylor 1989). One might hold the "contingency of selfhood" (Rorty 1989) and at the same time, like Sartre and Foucault, espouse the existential project of self creation and self care in the world as it is for us. The self is the fluid locus of one's subjective experience, it is where affect and reason are experienced and the capacity to act beheld.

The self is the name we have given to the process of modern identity and, therefore, it is often regarded (in the language of industrialism) as an outcome or a social product. If, however, we can take a view of self that encompasses both identity-making processes (including multi-linear biological, psychological and cultural processes) and outcomes (self-strategies), the self remains not only a useful term in understanding the person, but a worthy project of human endeavor that endures into post-modernity's pursuit of free play, *différance* and plurality. The tensions between social production of identity and the existential project of self creation are at the heart of this matter. The emphasis in this book is upon the effects of social and institutional practices, specifically the practices of work and production, on self formation. The discursive constitution of subjectivity manifests itself in the strategies of self that individuals devise and practice within and against the ineluctable constraints of social and cultural conditions. These strategies are processes and representations that are not fixed or essential, rather dynamics in flux and open to multiple configurations.

The dynamics of the various institutional processes of modern society and their relation to self formation have seldom been described and analyzed. In recent decades there have been some important efforts to understand the construction of the modern self (Lasch 1978, 1984, Rose 1990, Taylor 1989) and to describe the dynamics of self processes (Foucault 1988a, 1988b, Gergen 1991, Hewitt 1989, Wexler 1992, Probyn 1993) and identity formation (Aronowitz 1992, Giddens 1991, Hall 1990). Most of them offer a cultural analysis of self dynamics and few attempt to describe the relation of these dynamics to institutional processes. The earlier efforts of Goffman (1961) and of Becker *et al.* (1968) to study institutions and persons were not widely shared but there are echoes of these symbolic interactionist works in Wexler's (1993) more recent critical study of institutional processes, in particular schooling, in relation to self formation. Studying the connections between the institutional processes of work and the formation of the self is an even less common endeavor. There are some studies on the relationship between work and personality (Kohn and Schooler 1983, O'Brien 1986). Maccoby (1976), Baum (1987) and LaBier (1986) have studied the relationship between the psychostructure of workplaces and the self, and Hirschhorn (1988) has contributed to this theme in his examination of the "post-industrial" workplace and its organizational psychology. Kunda (1992), Powell and DiMaggio (1991) and Martin (1992), as recent examples, explore organizational cultures and offer critical analyses of new organizational forms and practices. Kondo's (1990) study of "power, gender and discourses of identity in a Japanese workplace" focuses an anthropological gaze on self processes and western images of work in Japanese society.

Notwithstanding these contributions, the connections between the vast technological and organizational changes currently taking place in production in advanced industrial societies, and their affect on societal changes in self formation and social solidarity need further investigation and interpretation. Work in virtually all sectors has changed in a number of aspects.

4

The "new" work is characterized by advanced technological developments including in the first instance automation, advanced computer and information technologies in production, and the restructuring of work tasks, occupations and organizational practices. The relationships between the institutional processes of the new work in post-industrial corporate culture, and changes in social organization and self formation have not yet been described.

Work, Self and Society explores the effects on the self of the social relations and institutional practices of a sector of work in post-industrial capitalism. In the 1991–2 academic year I undertook an extensive field study of advanced technological work in a multi-national corporation based in the United States of America (see Appendix). The findings of that study are reported and analyzed in chapters 4–6 of this book, while the first three chapters discuss the problematics of work and self. The book offers a complement to the work of others studying self development now (Gergen 1991, Giddens 1991, Hewitt 1989, Wexler 1992) and also to those studying organizational life (Hirschhorn 1988, Kunda 1992, LaBier 1986, Martin 1992). Its distinctive focus is to analyze the relationship between the "discursive practices" (the communication and cultural practices) of the new production and work organization and self development.

I share with Kunda's recent book (1992) a focus on corporate culture and advanced technology, but, unlike Kunda, I make a particular effort to explore questions of self formation and social solidarity that arise from the discursive practices of work. Kunda offers an analysis of corporate culture that emphasizes normative control. I interpret the advent of deliberately designed corporate cultures as a post-industrial condition. I propose that "designer cultures" are being constructed in response to the broad crisis in industrial production, work organization and culture. I offer too an interpretation of the technological changes in work in an analysis of what I call an emergent "post-occupational" condition. From such an interpretation, I offer an analysis of self-strategies effected by the discursive practices of corporate production. Finally, I attempt to sketch theoretical propositions of post-industrial, or what I call "post-occupational" solidarity.

The transformation of occupation has implications beyond creative flexibility and enhanced dispensability in the workplace. It is not simply a matter of multi-skilling and job re-design. Rather, "post-occupational" work in large corporations has significant implications for social cohesion within the workplace, and more broadly, in society. The method of the empirical study from which the analyses are drawn is in the ethnographic genre. But I admit that I take, perhaps, a greater risk than is usually taken by ethnographers – away from ethnographic reluctance to attempt broad theoretical statements, to the critical theorist's passion for them. The reader will decide on the validity of the persuasion.

My objective is to describe and analyze the relationships between the new work (material and discursive) and self formation and societal changes. I attempt, by bringing critical theory back to work, to develop a critical social psychology of contemporary corporate work. The book offers interpretations of the changes in institutional work practices and their implications for social organization, social solidarity and social life, after industrialism. As all social theory is inevitably political, I declare my implicit value position in an ultimate interest in transformed social organization. It is my (modern) hope that social and cultural life after industrialism will be qualitatively better for selves than that under the iron embrace of industrialism. In this time of postmodern uncertainty, or at least modesty, the interventionary voice of modern radicalism is somewhat quieter, but not yet relinquished. I wish in this book, as primarily a scribe of the end of industrialism, to describe and make some sense of the conditions of this time and to discern spaces of possibilities for self and social creation in the imminent future.

Chapter 1 introduces the problematic of work in contemporary social theory. I discuss the major theoretical responses to political and production changes and consider the place of work in contemporary social theory. I argue for a renewed critical theorizing of work as a path to understanding the self–society relation in contemporary social conditions. Chapter 2 describes and reviews the changes in industrial production and work in the latter decades of the twentieth century. It contextualizes the study of contemporary corporate work developed in subsequent chapters. Chapter 3 similarly traces the historical production of the self through modern thought and contemporary self psychology. It introduces a critical self psychology from which I elaborate a critical social psychology of corporate work in Chapter 6. Chapter 4 examines the working self through the formative experiences of modern forms of work. In Chapter 5 I report and discuss an empirical field study of contemporary corporate work that I conducted in a large multi-national company in the United States of America. The chapter describes the "discursive practices" of corporate work and develops a concept of "post-occupational" corporate work that is emerging in the practices of advanced technological production and organizational reform. Chapter 6 discusses the effects of the discursive practices of work on the self and develops a typology of self types that are being patterned by these discursive practices of work in the corporation. I describe "designer employees" and analyze the relationships between self strategies and corporate culture. Finally, in Chapter 7 I consider the problem of "post-occupational" social solidarity and the globalization of the effects of advanced technological production and corporate culture. I develop in this chapter some propositions for understanding the present juncture as western societies move beyond modern industrialism.

1

CRITICAL ANALYSIS AND THE PROBLEM OF WORK

INTRODUCTION

An earlier generation of critical theorists, influenced by Marxism, regarded work and production as primary sites of social analysis and social change. The abiding influence of Marxist thought, and of Durkheim's, upon thinkers up until the last decades of the twentieth century ensured that the productive sphere was at least implicitly addressed in the attempts to understand social structure and character, and to proffer practical sources of social transformation. As Weber pointed out, the logic of industrial technology, production and social organization made possible the increasing rationalization of all spheres of human life. The processes of industrialism were abetted and legitimated by the dominant "modern" religion of the age. Mechanization, standardization and routinization in industrial production required comparable processes in the cultural sphere. Accordingly, the methodical, reliable, disciplined bourgeois citizen became the ideal industrial worker in a rational bureaucratized society.

Although none of these processes came about without contestation and disruption, the triumph of modern industrialism in the twentieth century seemed, to critical observers of the 1940s and 1950s, virtually complete. The influential Frankfurt School critical theorists, and their descendants, having witnessed the "technocratic rationality" of Nazism, the Soviet gulag and the atomic bomb, exaggerated Weber's foreboding prognosis and despaired of all possibilities for social and psychic life. Repression and totalitarianism were the social products of modern industrial technocratic rationality that deadened the emancipatory hopes and visions of modernity's espoused project. We have now been irrevocably affected by what Aronowitz (1981) neatly terms "the crisis in historical materialism." That crisis, and that of modern thought more broadly, has triggered a reluctance to pursue analyses of sites we once believed harbored the seeds of social transformation. The failing efficacy of historical materialism to adequately interpret and effectively change the world prompted Marcuse's pronouncement of the "integration of the working class" (Marcuse 1964) into the industrial capitalist apparatus. After the apparent confirmation of that view following the events in Paris in May, 1968, there began a search among critical intellectuals for sources of social transformation in sites other than production and by agents other than the working class. The abandonment of production and workers' movements as fruitful sites of social analysis and political action is now, by and large, taken for granted among contemporary social and cultural analysts. Production, it seems, was modernity's concern. Nowadays, the cultural arena is the favored site for critical analyses.

Coinciding with these historical and academic events, technological and social developments were afoot in production and work that would launch a transformation of considerable magnitude in that domain by the end of the twentieth century. I address in this chapter the theoretical problematic of work during these transformations of modern industrial capitalism. I discuss the current neglect of work in critical social theory, since the post–1960s crisis in historical materialism, and I argue that the contemporary transformations occurring in that domain require renewed critical attention. In addition, I review briefly the discourses of occupation and solidarity which provide the conventional modern understandings of these categories as a preface to my later challenging of these modern categories in subsequent chapters. I conclude this chapter with a discussion on self and society.

For some readers already, or still, convinced of the importance of work, these discussions may seem superfluous and digressionary. However, as so much of the emphasis of critical theorizing is now on cultural phenomena, I feel I must argue the case for a renewed attention to work. I am wary of allegations of Marxist productionism, modern progressivism, or from the feminists, "masculinist" and essentialist convictions. But I argue that a critical social analysis of work, that is not a nostalgic reinvocation of modern radicalism and privileged subjectivity, opens possibilities for understanding self and social processes in post-industrial conditions that might otherwise be neglected. I am, simply, looking again at work as modern industrialism decays. Are embryonic patterns for social life after industrialism emerging there? It is premature and mistaken, notwithstanding the currently popular rejection of the grand modern theories and metanarratives and the apparent failure of modernist radicalism, to reject the serious critical analysis of those old sites in favor of the brighter lights of postmodern signs. A renewed analysis of what happens to the person under new conditions of work (that includes permanent structural unemployment) advances our understanding of the self–society relation at the end of industrialism, and enables some informed imagining of social life beyond the industrial epoch.

BACK TO WORK: RETURNING THE SOCIAL TO CRITICAL THEORY

The shift in emphasis to the cultural sphere among contemporary analysts was prompted in part by the early Frankfurt School's effort to understand psychic and cultural processes in capitalist society. The Frankfurt thinkers' exploration of cultural and psychic phenomena emphasized the connections of these phenomena with capitalist social relations in the productive sphere. But the more recent emphasis in cultural studies, since the 1970s, has adopted an interpretation of the French "new philosophers" (Foucault, Derrida, Lyotard, Baudrillard, and Barthes) that not only recognizes the limits of modern totalistic theory but facilitates a departure from economic emphases altogether. The French philosophers' call for a "freedom from political forms of life", a rejection of the "tyranny of reason" and a welcoming of what some (Lyotard 1984) called postmodern forms of life was intended to expose the totalism in modern thought and to seek ways to liberate the modern project from ossification by technocratic rationality. The French theorists' rejection of modern grand narratives and universal categories for their tendency to become totalistic, dominating social and psychic practices inspired a focus among their followers on the fragmented, the immediate, the marginal and the subjective. The playful *jouissance*, discontinuity and micro-contextuality of postmodern thought have captured the imagination of a new generation of thinkers in the academy. Analyses of diverse subjectivities, sexuality and cultural phenomena – television, film, advertising, "style," and theory itself – are now popular arenas in critical theoretical debate.

However, for many of this generation of thinkers, the attraction to the spectacle of postmodern impulses and manifestations has frequently rendered the neglect of postmodernism's serious challenges, that the French thinkers offered, through disruption, disjuncture and disunity, to modernism. The possibilities for renewed social analyses and counter-practices beyond the personal and the particular are seldom sought in most contemporary critical theorizing. By the 1990s this neglect has left the world of work and associated social relations largely the monopoly of traditional economic, management and labor relations analysts, few of whom are equipped or oriented to critically, socially analyze the transformation of production practices and to read their broader implications for self and social life.

Of course sociologists continue to study work and there are some welcome recent efforts, notably the collections by Pahl (1988) and Eriksen and Vallas (1990) that address the transformation of work practices as well as more conventional work related topics. But efforts to critically analyze broader social implications associated with these developments are rare (Offe 1992). In the traditional disciplines postmodern ideas and approaches

9

are often rejected outright and conventional methods and analytical categories reinvoked. It is neither critical theorists nor sociologists of work who are producing the provocative new readers about work and society. Rather it is the business analysts such as Drucker (1993), Reich (1991), and Handy (1989, 1990) whose works are found in the world's libraries, airport bookstores, and liberal arts and commerce curricula, and whose authoritative words are freely quoted in university graduation speeches.

The focus on the cultural sphere in recent decades, although initially sparked by the crisis in historical materialism that the New Left experienced in the 1970s and fueled by the actual rise in importance in significatory practices (as Baudrillard describes the post-industrial condition), has been facilitated by developments in literary theory, particularly post-structuralism, deconstruction, and feminism. These developments have enabled attention to cultural practices, especially language and other symbolic rituals, to be conducted in abstraction from the former modernist attachment to social or economic practices. Among the insights gained from such attention is Jean Baudrillard's notion that, the "social" has been absorbed by the cultural, and "there is no longer any social signified to give force to a political signifier" (Baudrillard 1983: 19). Again, although Baudrillard was indicating the new importance of signfication and symbolic production as a post-industrial condition that departs from the primacy of materiality, his ideas were interpreted by many cultural analysts to mean that production and materiality are no longer important. Baudrillard added that the death of the social is also that of theory, a view that although not broadly taken up, gave license to some who would propose that theorizing is a masculinist endeavor (Marks and de Courtivron 1981) that feminists, apparently, should abandon.

Baudrillard's (1988) view of the present post-industrial condition is that it is a consumer culture, in which we consume no longer products but signs – the signs of advertisements, of television, of the material product, and of promised libidinal gratification. The symbols of those products become objects of consumption themselves and have value for us. The "triumph of consumption" in the present era is the reification of the sign, as itself a commodity, that represents the displacement of beings and things by symbols and signs. This, for Baudrillard, is the post-industrial condition. Many social theorists now argue (Baudrillard 1983, Finlay-Pelinski 1987, Habermas 1987, Harvey 1989, Kroker and Cook 1986, Luke 1991, Wexler, 1987) that we are at an historical moment when significatory or knowledge processes are of crucial importance and the dominant conditions of production have become discursive. Further, according to Baudrillard, domination (of the masses) is effected through discourse – through communications in the sphere of production. Workers are consumers and producers of that discourse, and in Baudrillard's view, now fully integrated into the processes of domination through an implosion of the old meanings

10

of "signifier and signified," subject and object, producer and consumer. In his view, there is not much prospect for meaningful collective practice, because such referents are imploded, and the condition is now one of hyper, simulated reality, that cannot be "known" outside itself.

If we are looking for transformative, collective practices in work of the type once envisaged by critical intellectuals and modern radicals then indeed Baudrillard and Marcuse are likely to be right. The integration and domination of "the masses" is well in place and sites of production are unlikely arenas for social and cultural transformation. But that does not relegate all activities of work to an archeology of industrialism. Self constituent events and processes occur in everyday practices of work which in turn affect the social relations and organizational practices of society. Although Baudrillard eschews the idea of social practices as a separate domain his analysis is a useful one. It points again to the importance of the sphere of production (albeit symbolic) and consumption for the constitution of individual and collective identity. It exposes the practice of new, disguised, forms of domination through the discourses of new production practices. Others, including Finlay-Pelinski (1982, 1987) and Wexler (1987), similarly stress the importance of significatory and information production processes. Their approaches direct attention to what I call "discursive practices of work" in addition to physical practices of work. By "discursive practices of work" I am referring to communicational and symbolic relations in production and work organization that include organizational cultural programs and the psychodynamics of the workplace. I argue that a focus on symbolic practices that are linked with material social practices, enables a renewed analysis of the practices of work and may illuminate new understandings of self-formation processes.

The postmodern attempt to avoid the essentialism and progressivism inherent in the categories of modern social theories favors an approach to social analysis that celebrates the "free play of signifiers without reference," the blurring of boundaries and the fragmentation of former universal categories. The new emphases and insights enabled by Baudrillard's and others' observations of the disintegration of separate domains and the primacy of signs and images in postmodern conditions that have absorbed social life into a commodified culture are vital challenges to modern thought and analytical methods. Yet that welcome effort is often coupled with the rejection of the modern privileging of economic analyses and has resulted in a dismissal of many of the institutions of modern industrial society and sites of modern social analysis, including work, as irrelevant in contemporary postmodern conditions. The flight into cultural studies as the current arena for postmodern "social" analyses is, for many, a defense against the confusion and dislocation of modern industrialism's demise and the dissolution of the programmatic certainty of Marxist social analysis.

11

This is manifested in the new privileging of micro-contextual cultural phenomena, marginality, fragmentation and diffusion.

I wish to turn away again from culture, or at least from its privileging, and return the social to critical theory. The institutional practices in everyday life in this postmodern juncture continue to affect the constitution of individual and collective identity. Production endures. But rather than reviving a conventional modern social analysis which necessarily privileges the material social relations of work, I recognize that work is both a social practice and a cultural practice. The discursive practices of work are constituent processes of self formation which occur through the everyday, institutional experience of work. My return to the materiality of production, as it is experienced by workers, this time encompasses the discursive and cultural dimensions of work practices. Self-constituent processes other than those of work are implicitly recognized but they are not the focus of this particular gaze and study at this particular time. The approach, summarily, is that the social structures and discursive practices of production and consumption are discursive constituents of contemporary western selves.

CONTEMPORARY CRITICAL SOCIAL THEORY

Within critical social theory today fierce struggles are occurring over the nature of theory, discourse, subjectivity, knowledge and politics, a condition, in large part, bequeathed by the prolonged crisis in historical materialism, the rise of French post-structuralist theory and of cultural studies and feminism. There have been, of course, good reasons to doubt the validity and universal relevance of Marxist theory in view of the lived experience of western history over about the last fifty years, especially after the events in Europe in 1968, and more recently in Soviet Europe since 1989. The crises in modern thought and in historical materialism in particular concern intellectuals of various persuasions. The triumph of capitalism as a mode of production and a social system is hailed by some as the "end of history" (Fukuyama 1989) or the "end of ideology" (Bell 1988). Some have reinvoked classical Marxist positions (Aglietta 1979, Braverman 1974, Lefebvre 1976, Mandel 1978, Offe 1985, O'Connor 1973, Poulantzas 1975). Others have begun a process of rethinking the old tradition, retaining or rejecting, variously and uncertainly, some of its categories (Anderson 1976, Aronowitz 1985, Gouldner 1970, Harvey 1989, Kellner 1989, Laclau and Mouffe 1985, 1987, Lash and Urry 1987, Smart 1992).

The emergence of the French philosophers and the timely influence of their work after the 1960s has influenced a new generation of critical analysts many of whom reject the old masters altogether in despair of their totalizing discourses or their embedded patriarchicalism.[1] The Enlightenment-inspired project of modernity is now trenchantly criticized and its validity questioned. Modernity's primary monolithic categories of Reason, Truth, Science, the idea of progress and the centrality of the human subject are variously rejected or challenged. The rejection of Hegelian historicism and the insistence on "the base," in which production is accorded primacy in shaping human social, cultural and political development is commonly accepted. Most of the new cultural analysts concentrate on what classical Marxist theory called the "superstructure" – the cultural sphere, where language, knowledge, meanings and identities are formed.

The French philosophers, adapting concepts from literary theory on deconstruction and representation, developed a post-structuralist theory of subjectivity. They rejected bourgeois humanism in which the conscious human subject is regarded as the agent of history by decentering the human subject into a dispersion of arbitrary reference points. They viewed history as discontinuous and fragmented rather than as a longitudinal totality. They argued for a suspension and interrogation of unities and for a recognition of the specificity of phenomena, and of "subjugated knowledges" (Foucault 1972). Michel Foucault excavated what he identified as the "power/knowledge episteme" of the modern era in which the power relations, structures and institutions of modern industrial society produce the "configuration of knowledge forms" of contemporary life. These knowledge forms operate through discourses that reproduce, legitimate and render invisible their dominance. Persons and political possibilities are positioned by discourses and their domination is obscured by the "system of right and truth" established as knowledge throughout western history.

Foucault's theory of power represented a paradigmatic departure from the classical Marxist and Freudian understandings of power, in which power was viewed respectively as primarily located in the economic base and as repression. Foucault viewed the individual as constituted by power, and the relations of power cannot be "established, consolidated nor implemented without the production . . . and functioning of a discourse" (Foucault 1980: 93). The primary site of operation of power is the human body, which, for Foucault, is a priori to the concept of self. From the moment of birth the human body is shaped, subjugated and disciplined. The individual's sense of self is acquired through the experience of power relations in which it is immersed. The project of self creation and self care is enunciated within those discourses of power. Foucault conceived of power as a multiplicity of "networks" that operate spatially and discursively. This notion directed attention to multiplicities of power relations, subjectivities, and sites of practice, and away from the emphases of structural analyses on the primacy of the productive sphere.

The postmodern turn inspired by the French new philosophers has had a profound impact on contemporary social theory. Many contemporary theorists see new arenas for theorizing and action in the move away

13

from humanism and from structuralism. For some, following Foucault, the effort is to retrieve that which was left out of the totalizing discourses of modern thought, and attention is focused on the marginal and the subjugated.[2] Earlier critical theory sought to conceive of societal construction as a composite of psychological, cultural and economic activities – not as primarily (although ultimately) determined by the base (Horkheimer and Adorno 1972, Marcuse 1964). Post-structuralism goes further than this effort by abandoning the idea of universals, holisms and composites, in favor of fragmentation and discontinuity.

Post-structuralism has especially attracted the interest of feminists, cultural analysts and theorists of race and ethnicity who find in the freedom from Enlightenment Truth and universal categories spaces to articulate positions and politics of difference. For some writers influenced by Derrida and a selective interpretation of Lyotard and Foucault their intentions include a rejection of the modernist interest in politics and rationality as the avenue for social and cultural change. Like Foucault, they reject the Enlightenment notion that freedom is inextricably linked to reason and political forms of life. They adopt a disinterest in politics, as conventionally understood, and look to spontaneity and immediacy and for possibilities in multiple positionings and specific strategies. Since the 1980s, for many analysts who have adopted post-structuralism and a focus on significatory practices, the predominant arena of interest has been an exploration of cultural practices and "images and things" (Hebdige 1989): subjectivity, identity, representation and signification (Hebdige 1989, Hall 1980, Grossberg and Nelson 1989, Grossberg, Nelson and Treichler 1992, Nicholson 1990, Sheridan 1988).

Among feminist theorists some are also exploring renewed possibilities in psychoanalytic theory (Benjamin 1987, 1988, Flax 1989, Kristeva 1980, Butler 1990) while others have adopted post-structuralism as the theoretical alternative to the universalism of Marxism or liberal humanism. Their effort is to reconfigure women's subjectivity, identity and feminist political practice in the spaces of multiple positionings and power dispersions. Theorists of race and ethnicity also see possibilities in post-structuralism for analyses of difference, other, and subjectivity (Hall 1987, Hooks 1992, Said 1993, Wallace 1990). Post-structuralism has generally enabled deconstructionist approaches to the grand universal theories of modernity. The task of theory work beyond deconstruction is problematic to all of these post-structural projects. None the less, the challenges to modern totalism and certainty in contemporary thinking, and the Marxist engagement with post-structuralism's categories and the postmodern turn are producing a vital arena for theory, self and social possibilities in the 1980s and 1990s.

14

Marxist responses

The problematic of the postmodern has implications that are broader and more serious than a move in theoretical methods. The varied responses from Marxist thinkers to post-structuralism and postmodernism take two general approaches. Habermas (1981, 1987) criticizes the theories of postmodernity and postmodernism on the basis that they necessarily indicate the end of the Enlightenment and the "project of modernity" in which a more rational and moral organization of everyday life would be brought about. Habermas argues that the Enlightenment's project in which "objective science, universal morality and law" and the "tradition of reason" (1981, 1987) enable society to be rationally and cohesively organized, should not be abandoned for their incompletion in the late twentieth century. Rejecting the progress of modernity, Habermas argues, amounts to the "repudiation of modern forms of life" and the truncation of social and personal emancipation. He points to a conservatism and anti-modern reactionary impulse inherent in the postmodern rejection of modern politics and the celebration of its dissolution. Habermas rejects Foucault's and Lyotard's equating the grand vision and emancipatory hope of modernity with totalizing theories and political practice. Other writers from the Marxist tradition have developed similar perspectives, particularly Anderson (1984) and Berman (1983, 1991), while still others reassert classical Marxist analyses to theorize the endurance of capitalism and the failure of socialism (Burawoy 1989).

Jameson shares Habermas' wish to retain the project of modernity and a concern that rejecting emancipatory projects would lead to the occlusion of opposition and resistance. But he recognizes that we are already in a culture of postmodernism (Jameson 1984a) that must be analyzed. Jameson argues that the rise of postmodernism is a cultural project of a "restructuration of capitalism" (1984a). Post-structuralism has arisen as the partial critical theory of the postmodern condition which he identifies as the "cultural logic of late capitalism" (Jameson 1984b), following Mandel's (1978) periodizing of capitalist development. Again, others recognize the disruptive contribution of post-structuralism but argue that post-structuralism is too closely connected to the structuralism from which it came and is thus limited in its capacity to construct theory and analytical methods beyond those conventionally regarded as modern. Post-structuralism remains constrained by its origins in literary theory and linguistic structuralism. Feminists such as Fraser and Nicholson (1990), Harding (1990), Flax (1989), while sometimes employing post-structuralist methods, argue that privileging of discursive practices renders problematic the material political project of power sharing and social reorganization of historically dominant groups and discourses. There remains ambivalence among feminists about the validity of post-structuralism for the

15

modern feminist project (Modleski 1991) although few argue for a revival of Marxist economism.

Another group of thinkers from the Marxist tradition, sometimes called "post-Marxist" (Smart 1992), associated with Laclau and Mouffe (1985) and Foster (1985) argue for possibilities for an oppositional postmodernism in a post-industrial capitalist condition. This group recognizes the erosion of the grand modern narratives – Marxism and liberalism – and attempts to theorize postmodern conditions without complete rejection of Marxist categories or orientations (Laclau and Mouffe 1985, Harvey 1989, Smart 1992) but with a recognition of the end of certainties, totalities and privileged vantage points. For Foster (1985), following Foucault, a postmodernism that deconstructs modernism may operate as a "counter-practice" in which a politics of resistance is developed. Political counter-practices take the form of challenging all taken-for-granted knowledge forms and practices as the grand theories and their vestiges everywhere are made continually problematic. Resistance is practiced in the struggle for everyday liberties against the multifarious operation of dominant power networks. The postmodern Marxists seek to devise a vantage point from which to practice social analysis that recognizes the endurance of the problematic of capitalism (now global) and the exhaustion of modern theory, and to offer possibilities for transformatory politics (Foss and Larkin 1986, Fraser 1989, Kellner 1989, Lash and Urry 1987, Luke 1991, Langman 1991). Like Jameson (1984a), they call for a recognition of the postmodern condition that we are now in, and rather than railing against postmodernism in refutation or denial, they suggest that contemporary conditions need to be analyzed and possibilities discovered.

The post-structural "free-play of the signifiers" has opened up possibilities for a multiplicity of analyses of power, of sites of identity formation, and of sites of organizational and political possibilities. By appropriating some elements of post-structuralist thought, and turning it away from its attachment to the text from which it came, a renewed analysis of the social conditions of our post-industrial era may be practiced.

New social movements

Accompanying the postmodern problematic is the view of many contemporary critical theorists that the "old" struggles of the left and the sites around which it was once organized are faded remnants of an old meta-discourse whose historical dissolution is now evident. The failure of socialism and the demise of the working class and its historical political movement, organized labor, has been followed by the rise of "new" social movements with a plurality of interests and agendas. Many now argue that the main sites of crisis and conflict are in non-economic domains, and the major oppositional groups are not social classes, but heterogeneous social movements (Alberoni 1984, Foss and Larkin 1986, Habermas 1981, Laclau and Mouffe 1985, Touraine 1981, Melucci 1980). The new social movements that are organized around issues of identity, subjectivity, ecology, community, regional and urban issues and so forth, have emerged out of the sediment of the old movements (Foss and Larkin 1986). The new social movement theorists point to the inability of the classical Marxist tradition to adequately develop categories to explain social dynamics concerned with personal and social identity formation, social integration and solidarity. Classical Marxism could neither foresee nor account for the domination of the working class, its subsequent integration and the totally administered society.

Touraine (1981) and Melucci (1980) argue that the new social movements are sites of struggle for "self-production" – for individual and collective identity in a contested social and cultural arena. The new social movements struggle for control and influence over the symbolic realm in cultural production, seeking the possibility to negotiate (at least some of) the conditions for individual and collective life. The new social movements are post-Marxist efforts to contest hegemonic power networks and they are manifestations, for Touraine, of social action for the production of society. They act in implicit recognition that society "has neither nature nor foundations; it is neither a machine nor an organization; it is action and social relations" (Touraine 1981: 25). The new social movements recognize the contingency rather than the totality of the political and cultural arena in which they struggle.

Habermas interprets the new social movements as reactions to the industrial-capitalist system's assault on the "lifeworld." The new social movements, for Habermas, are efforts to resist the "colonization of the lifeworld" (Habermas 1984). He argues for a practice of "communicative action" as the coordinating agency of the lifeworld that would counter colonization by the instrumental logic of the industrial-capitalist system. For Laclau and Mouffe (1985) the new social movements represent efforts to develop a new politics of "radical democracy" that recognizes the multiplicity of subordinate interests and struggles; as such they are the new sites of transformative political practice.

In theorizing the new social movements as multiple arenas for individual and collective identity formation, of struggle for transformative action and social production, the new social movement theories, although not necessarily post-structuralist (Habermas, Touraine and Melucci), have both recognized and assisted the shift of focus away from the economic foundations of the traditional social movements. The new social movements do not include the sites of production and the old political movements and struggles there practiced. The new social movement theories have tended to have little to say about the rise of revamped versions of old and conservative social movements, in particular the resurgence of fundamentalist

17

religious and nationalist movements. These manifestations of struggle over the symbolic realm and over identity may be interpreted as a reactionary postmodern event in that they defy the completion of modernity's rationalizing project and the emancipatory endeavors of new social movements. The shadow of the localism and tribalism of premodern identificatory movements in postmodern conditions competes with the liberal and radical impulses in the new social movements regarded by many as the politically appropriate transformative agents at this fragmented juncture.

Furthermore, the inclusion of women's, racial minorities' and indigenous peoples' movements in the category "new social movements" reveals the modernist gaze behind this category. These movements have been struggling for generations and are not really "new." But they are new only in respect to the universalism inherent in classical Marxist thought in which the one true struggle and the project of history was class struggle.

The focus of the new social movement theories on transformatory struggles evokes a modernist continuity with radical visions of agency, struggle and social and cultural transformation. Yet at the same time the focus on cultural and identity movements and the retreat from economic issues and work provides some with an opportunity to both admonish the working class, however fragmented and reconfigured, for its conservatism and integration, and to ignore its interests in favor of the identity and political interests of the middle class. Many middle-class "liberal" interests have now become the domain of "left" political struggles carrying those old modernist left hopes without the impediment of class and labor issues. Possibilities for workplace political action and self struggles are either ignored or dismissed as remnants of former political ideologies and practices. Many new-social-movement theories, oblivious of their class-specificity, carry within them an old, familiar bias against working-class knowledge and struggles. Yet the working life of the professional middle class is hardly so free from oppression and personal pain (Ehrenreich 1989, LaBier 1986), as we shall see in Chapters 5 and 6, as to warrant the middle class's rejection of work as a site of political and educational practice.

Yet, again, the plurality of resistances and assertions are themselves a manifestation of the dissolution of universal discourses that would once have seen these diversities united in a common struggle against a unitary "enemy" – capitalism. Diverse struggles against domination may also be seen as a continuation of the project of the New Left for personal emancipation and for further democratization of everyday life, that does not necessarily exclude workplace struggles. The multiple positionings and social agents in the political arena require a moving beyond the categories of modern Marxism and the privileged essential positions of the working class and the economic base. In short, there is no "privileged position" from which to conduct social analysis or radical practices in social transformation. As Laclau and Mouffe (1985) argue: "all struggles, whether those of workers or other political subjects have a partial character" (1985: 169). Recognizing this partial character and relinquishing the category and project of the unified subject allows for the possibility of multiple "disorganized" struggles of other subordinated social subjects and "subjugated knowledges" (Foucault 1972). A persistence to privilege *any* subject position, including workers, displays not only a denial of the fragmented, diverse, plural and contingent condition of our postmodern world, but a failure of modern theory to comprehend and analyze the realities of the present time. I argue, therefore, for a critical postmodern position that embraces uncertainty and contingency, and does not abandon production and work as old Marxist concerns for the attractions of the "new" and the fantastic. Like Laclau and Mouffe (1985) I offer a post-Marxist theoretical orientation in this book that accommodates my earlier Marxist gaze to postmodern, and post-industrial conditions.

Critical theorists abandoned an analytic focus of work and production just as the emergence of a post-industrial economy was transforming production and work. Initially, as advanced technologies displaced working-class jobs, perhaps the diminished size of the old site of production added fuel to the rejection of the centrality of production in modern projects of social transformation. But the conditions of the post-industrial economy are such that the middle-class is now at risk of losing its relatively stable position, especially as many middle-class jobs, particularly in middle management, become redundant (see Chapter 2). Work has been the primary locus of social organization in modern industrial society. The transformations now occurring in that domain suggest that work may no longer be primary in society truly beyond industrialism. The present juncture indicates an *emergence* from industrialism which is far from complete. Many legacies of industrial culture endure. But the transformations currently occuring in technology, production, culture, and social organization present immense implications for the imminent organization of social and cultural life, as well as for the character of a post-industrial self. They require renewed awareness and analysis. The popular focus in much contemporary critical theory on micro-cultural issues has somewhat neglected theorizing on the transformations occurring in the material practices of work and production at this post-industrial juncture. Attention to significatory practices can ignore the concrete existence of the material world.

With the demise in historical materialism, the compensatory rise of post-structuralism and various postmodern cultural analyses, and the focus on the new social movements, few "social" theorists, other than traditional Marxists (Burawoy 1985, Callinicos 1989, Frank 1980), and business and economic analysts (Drucker 1993, Piore and Sabel 1984, Zuboff 1988, Reich 1991) are concerned with the world of work. With the recognition of the current precariousness, if not end, of modern meta-theory, the political crises following the failure of socialism and the implosion (in theory) of the social sphere into the cultural as modernity comes to a close, "privileging" work and production again as a site of social analysis may seem nostalgic. But the intention behind my critical theoretical emphasis on work as a dominant arena in people's lives, and the workplace as an everyday site of social-psychological and political practices, is not to reinvoke privilege and stir up hope for a revived modernist project. It is, rather, an endeavor to both reconsider work and self under post-industrial conditions of production and to redress the current under-emphasis on work in critical theory.

MODERN DISCOURSES OF OCCUPATION AND SOLIDARITY

I wish, at this point, to draw attention to the importance of "what is said" as well as what is done. Work, like any other human activity, cannot be separated from the discursive fields of which it is an integral part. The primary premise of this study is that the material and discursive practices[3] of work fundamentally influence the construction of social life, and of individual life. My discursive approach is drawn from Foucault's (1972) understanding that discourse is a historically contingent body of regularized practices of language that are condoned by a society. These practices make possible certain statements and communicational practices while disallowing others. A discourse is made up of rules and procedures, the empirical and "discursive" object or idea, that construct and legitimate the way we see things and talk about them. Considering the "discursive practices" of work draws attention to the way communications (about work) are formulated, legitimated and accepted as "true" and "correct" within our present society. It draws attention to what is said, and not said, and the "body of anonymous, historical rules" (Foucault 1972: 117) that are socially constructed and that determine our particular historical period and place. It enables attention to be focused on both the material and the communicational practices of work which in Chapter 5 and 6 are addressed in their corporate organizational cultural dimension.

The discourses of work have a long history but in the modern era the theories of Marx, Durkheim, Weber, and others, although differing in important ways, fundamentally shaped the dominant modern discourse on work in capitalist societies. Their writings have decisively configured the discursive categories in which ideas about work and society have been developed and enunciated. The sociology and psychology of work in the academy retains significant traces of the orientations of the traditions bequeathed by the earlier theorists.[4] I will not review that extensive literature here. Chapter 2 explores practices of work and production more fully and the sociological and psychological literature on work is discussed there, but I do wish to review here our modern sociological understanding of occupation. Occupation has been regarded as a key element in the social organization of work and significant in shaping the individual's experiences of work and of life.

Occupation

Social thinkers and sociologists (LePlay 1858, Durkheim 1933, Weber 1908, 1919, Pareto 1935, Sorokin 1927, Parsons 1964, Mills 1956) have regarded occupation as a primary element in social organization and as an indicator of social status and role in modern western societies. Occupation has also been regarded as a primary locus of cohesion and a site of practical solidarity in the factories and cities of industrialism. In pre-industrial societies people identified each other not so much by what they did, but by their social relationships as wife, husband, son, servant, all of which carried considerable economic duties as well as relational ones. Recognizing people by what they do, and naming them accordingly (cooper, weaver, tailor, chandler and so forth), occurred well before the industrial revolution, and was particularly commonplace in medieval cities (Joyce 1987). But the social identification of persons primarily with their place in the economic sphere became more typically characteristic of modern industrial societies. The emphasis on occupation derives from the practice of the division of labor, and the notion of vocation emphasized by Calvin and later Protestant thinkers, both of which became institutionalized in industrial society in the organization of work.

The division of labor in society was recognized by the medieval thinker Thomas Aquinas but was more fully explored by Adam Smith some centuries later. Marx considered it to be a necessary process in the development of society and as underlying the class struggle for social progress. The division of labor played a pivotal role in Marx's analysis of the relationship between production and social organization in a class-stratified society. Similarly, Durkheim placed considerable emphasis on the division of labor and the effects of occupation in locating and identifying people. But he regarded the division of labor in society, by which he primarily meant occupational specialization, as central to the nature of solidarity. Industrialization produced a rapid and sophisticated expansion in the division of labor and a vastly more complex society. It fundamentally altered the way in which society achieved integration and cohesion. As occupational differentiation expanded a concomitant diversification in the norms, values and outlooks of people occurred. The source of social stability and cohesion could no longer be found in simple mechanical solidarity.[5] "Indeed, since mechanical solidarity is growing ever more weaker, social life must either diminish or another form of solidarity must emerge gradually to take the place of the one that is disappearing"

(Durkheim 1984:122). Durkheim proposed that social solidarity in the modern world is to be found in the inevitable interdependence of members of occupational groups among each other. "Organic solidarity" arises out of increased differences between people rather than from similarities among them. The greater the ability of the elements to operate independently of one another the more social harmony and cohesion are possible. The unity of the organism increases as the individuation of the parts is more marked, and the division of labor, therefore, spontaneously produces solidarity. Durkheim envisaged the "mature industrial order," in which a fully developed organic solidarity that is laterally differentiated rather than hierarchically differentiated, would characterize the modern industrial world.

Like Durkheim, Weber also theorized on the specialization of function and the status function of occupational groups. He recognized the importance of the division of labor in social organization and particularly emphasized the acute specialization of function and rationalization that typified bureaucracy. He was concerned with the prevalence of these elements, and foresaw their domination, in modern western society. Marx analyzed class interests in the formation of solidarity, and did not regard the condition of solidarity in monolithic terms. He saw the dynamics of conflict, struggle and control rather than social cohesion as the problems of modern capitalist society. But it was the foundational theories of Durkheim and Weber that underpinned those developed in the 1950s by Talcott Parsons, for whom specialization of function necessitates "the instrumental complex" in which "occupation, exchange and property . . . are all inextricably interdependent" (Parsons [1948] 1964: 326). For Parsons, "by far the most prominent structure of modern Western society is that organized around the work people do" (ibid.: 325). Parsons argued that the socioeconomic structure of society must be treated not as a single entity, but as composed of analytically distinct variables. For Parsons, and his followers in the modern academy, this shift of emphasis away from the Marxist problematic of class and the capitalist enterprise of profit and exploitation, directed attention to the structure of occupational stratifications and roles within the system of industrial society.

The above glimpse of these foundational thinkers on occupation is intended to indicate the assumptions bases of the subsequent elaborate fields of stratification theory and the sociology of work, of occupations and professions that have grown out of these early- and mid-twentieth-century ideas and approaches to social analysis. Analysis of work, occupations, professions, and organization through the 1980s and 1990s (Derber 1990, Eriksen and Vallas 1990, Kohn 1990, Pahl 1989 among the more recent[6]) continues to be formulated from such an orientation. The importance, and stability, of occupation and occupational groups in social structure and character continues to be assumed.

22

WORK, SELF AND SOCIETY

Generally within the broad tradition of the sociology of work there has been a reluctance to draw analyses of the relations between people's experiences of work and the effects of those experiences on self-psychological processes and broader social organization. Although an interest in the self in one form or another has long been present in sociological enquiry, the connections between self-processes of work practices and social organization has seldom been pursued. It appears that the rise of positivist social science in the twentieth century led to a preference for phenomena less ephemeral than the "self" as objects of analysis. The sociological interest in the self shifted to a focus on the individual: personality, behavior, attitudes, roles, motivation, feelings, and so forth (these themes are discussed in Chapter 3). As a result, work and self were generally studied in abstraction.[7]

In the 1990s, however, a revived interest in the self and identity (and not *personality*) is apparent. It seems that the current doubt in the meta-discourses of modernity including those of modern sociology of knowledge is encouraging a renewed interest in the processes of identity and subjectivity, in what it means to talk of the self, in contemporary post-modern conditions. Debate about the composition, social patterning and positioning of selves is now broad and vigorous. Some analysts, observing the current social and cultural changes occurring in advanced industrial capitalist societies, are theorizing the emergence of a "new self" (Gergen 1991, Turner 1976). The new self is described as diffuse, fragmented, multiple, discontinuous, momentary, impulsive. In some analyses (Deleuze and Guattari 1979, Kroker and Cook 1986, Gergen 1991), these characteristics are seen as a product of the postmodern turn in which the renunciation of the whole, the universal, and the essential allow for multiplicities of identity and selves.

My use of the concept "self" assumes that the self is a compilation of processes and constituent events, both conscious and unconscious. A sense of self provides an experience of agency, continuity and coherence over time. There is no "hard core" or unified, monad self (as once proposed by modern ego-psychologists) but there is a sense of identity and personness that is socially acquired and recognized. Deleuze expresses quaintly the view of many contemporary self theorists when he argues that the self is constituted by processes of the "outside" (*le dehors*) and the "inside" (*le dedans*). Deleuze privileges neither psychic nor social processes but he does uphold a distinction between them. It is with Deleuze's perspective that I approach the discursive constitution of self in contemporary practices of work. The social relations and the discourses of production of late modern capitalism are co-constitutive of the production and transformation of the self. The project of self-construction, as Foucault points out, is

23

constrained and made possible by those conditions and discourses (Foucault 1989).

The questions as to how selves are produced within and against the practices of corporate work lead into the second question that I explore in this book. Are there effects of the new institutional self processes (in work) on the formation of new forms of collective practice and social solidarity in the post-industrial era? Social theorists have long attempted to address this question. For Marx, "human essence is no abstraction inherent in each individual. In its reality it is the ensemble of social relations" (Marx 1846). Human character is an ideological construction that reflects the particular mode of production and social organization dominant in specific historical epochs. For Durkheim, the rise of industrial society had produced a new person, one who was progressively freed from the constraints of traditional society and whose interests were increasingly centered around the pursuit of a higher and moral self-interest. Industrialization and the dramatic expansion and sophistication of the division of labor produced the phenomenon of individualism, and fundamentally altered the forms of social solidarity and cohesion in society (Durkheim 1915, 1933). Modern society produced a modern self, and organic solidarity that depended on reciprocal relations and cooperation between individuals and groups of individuals replaced the mechanical solidarity of traditional society. Weber (1905) in turn analyzed the psychological conditions which made possible the developments of industrial capitalist society. He postulated a Protestant religious foundation of the character of the industrial capitalist self – a point I consider again in the final chapters of this book.

Several decades after Durkheim and Weber, the cultural critics of the 1940s through 1960s (Horkheimer and Adorno [1944] 1972, Horkheimer 1941, Marcuse 1964) disputed Durkheim's moral progressivism and liberal individualism. Later Foucault too argued that history has always been a patchwork of disjunctures and discontinuities, as excavations of human behaviors and institutional practices have revealed. For others (Bellah *et al.* 1985, Lasch 1984, Sennett 1977 – see Chapter 3), the present condition results from the collapse of the meta-discourses of the modern age, and the concomitant disruption in the modern production of the self in western industrialized societies. The decline in the "quality" of the self is seen to be the result of the "tyranny of inner compulsions and anxieties" that are socially produced. Libidinal desire is displaced in a narcissistic pursuit of consumer comforts and possessions (Lasch 1984) and community life gives way to its mass-mediated television substitute. These thinkers recognize the historical specificity of the self, linking its production and character to the capitalist mode of production in the modern industrial period. For Lasch the narcissistic self of contemporary capitalist society is produced by the "technological forces of the market place" (Lasch 1984). The social relations and discursive practices of production in post-industrial conditions again affect self constitution and character. The forms of social solidarity of the modern industrial era are now, similarly, under processes of transformation. Chapter 7 addresses these concerns further and considers possible new forms of social solidarity and what Durkheim called "sources of happiness."

CONCLUSION

The current rejection by most forms of critical theory of production and work in favor of cultural studies is premature. The transformation of both work and its traditional forms of social solidarity has not yet eliminated the central place that work holds in social organization in the current manifestation of the post-industrial era. Work at this juncture still remains a dominant activity in people's lives. Whether one is in or out of employment, preparing for it, or seeking it (cf. Gorz 1989), and certainly whether or not one likes one's job, work as it is conventionally organized significantly shapes everyday life experience for most people in industrial societies.

Productionism, the logic and project of modern industrialism, is still widely and routinely endorsed in social and political discourses as the basis of social life and citizenship across the western world. What people produce and consume, and the social relations engendered by that production, remain at the present time primary constituent elements in defining the social and cultural relations of post-industrial societies as we currently observe them. Although the post-industrial condition presents a disjuncture in the cultural meanings of work, formed in an earlier time, modern meanings of work remain operative for many people in the midst of changing practices of work. The crises that post-industrialism is presenting in work and social meaning production are accordingly affecting the patterns of self formation, and of social solidarity. Chapter 3 continues the discussion on self matters, but I wish now to elaborate more fully on the current transformation of work that is occurring in advanced industrial societies.

2

THE TRANSFORMATION OF WORK

INTRODUCTION: THE MODERN CONTEXT OF WORK

The social, economic and technological changes that have occurred in advanced industrialized societies in recent decades have, among other things, called into question the meanings of work bequeathed from an earlier time and firmly established in modern society. The modern values of work and production and their considerable importance in the organization of modern social life and the formation of selfhood are becoming increasingly problematic in a world in which work, as it is conventionally understood, may never again be so widely available and universally valued. At the present time, in addition to increasingly apparent ambivalence about the value and meaningfulness of work, there is a series of questions concerning the form and necessity of work itself, its nature, and its availability under conditions of technological and organizational transformation. It is these questions and the factors contributing to a transformation of work which are explored below. But first, a discussion of the context of contemporary work is in order.

Historical meanings of labor and work[1]

Human activity, labor and work have interested philosophers and religious thinkers for centuries. The distinction between work and labor, although the words are often used synonymously in modern English, lies in the connotations of labor with pain and trouble, and work with effort and product. For the ancient Greeks, who did not distinguish between labor and work, all work was considered the domain of slaves and women. It was viewed as painful drudgery that debased the mind and made man unfit for the practice of virtue. Those who performed such "labors of necessity" were marginalized from social life and denied the privileges of citizenship. In the early Judeo-Christian tradition, labor was regarded as a "blessing" or "joy" of life. Labor linked human beings to the fertility and productivity of nature, it was as integral to life as giving birth (Arendt 1959: 106). The

26

natural rhythms of exertion and gratification, production and consumption were a potential source of pleasure and happiness. Although the fall of man from paradise carried God's curse, it was not labor itself with which man was punished, but *harsh* labor and sorrowful birth. It was thus that later theologians equated labor with harsh work and borrowed from the Greeks their disparagement of work. Work came to be seen as punishment for sin but it should be pursued zealously as a "scourge for the pride of the flesh" (Augustine [1958]). The ambivalence about work as being both the source of life and as punishment for sin continued in thinking about work for many centuries, and indeed continues to be evident in contemporary human experience and thought.

The Protestant Reformation added some refinement to earlier ideas about work. Luther's idea was that work is natural to "fallen man" and to maintain oneself by work was a way of serving God. Work was elevated to the status of a "calling" and a religious pathway to salvation. The idea of work as the "base and key to life" (Tilgher 1930) began to become established in the modern mind. Similarly, Calvin taught that it is necessary to act in the world in a rational and methodical manner. Working hard and continuously enabled one to ease guilt and to lead a good and pious Christian life. Accommodation to the rhythms and demands of work required a discipline of the body that was also good for the soul.

With the rise of philosophy and political theory a distinction emerged between contemplation and activity, and a tradition of distinction between labors was instituted – the distinction between productive and unproductive labor, between skilled and unskilled work, and finally the division of all activities into manual and mental labor (Arendt 1959: 85). These distinctions were elaborated upon by Adam Smith and later by Karl Marx. Both thinkers regarded labor as the source of all property, wealth and value. The earlier distinction between labor as the exertion of the body for the maintenance of necessity, and work that produces an objective product, diminished. For Marx particularly, human labor possesses an inherent productivity of its own. For him, labor produces life, and therefore all laboring is productive. Productive labor is the human being's essential activity and the main source of human self-development and fulfillment.

There was some reaction to the utilitarian meaning of work during the Renaissance, in which man was viewed as a "tool user." For some Renaissance thinkers the idea of work as purposive, intrinsically meaningful human activity conflicted with the emerging capitalist form of the organization of work. For Ruskin and Tolstoy, and others, the ideal of work came from a pre-capitalist notion in which free artisans worked for necessity of livelihood and simultaneously the act of working created in the worker a state of inner calm and meaningfulness. The reasons for work are in work itself and not in any religious or ulterior realm. The technical processes in work and in its physical carrying out are in themselves gratifying to humans. Locke developed a notion that labor was the cornerstone of individual ownership and the fundamental source of economic value. Labor could be sold and bought and accumulated as capital. Adam Smith developed this perspective in *The Wealth of Nations* [1776], arguing that work and capital were the premises upon which the exchange market could be established.

The "labor theory of value" was later developed extensively by Marx. The Protestant bourgeois notions of work and of the moral status of the worker became the culturally dominant view of European capitalist societies. But the processes of rationalization were never smooth nor complete. Other subordinate work ethics continued to exist beneath the dominant discourse. Some elements of the Renaissance idea were retained in the humanistic conception of work and of labor developed subsequently by Marx. But for the most part, Weber showed that the convergence of the salvation "through works" theology of Protestantism, especially its Calvinist form, encouraged the development of the "industrial worker." This worker, who was "called" to do "good works" and to perform the duties of his work as religiously as those called to the monastic religious life of Catholicism, required regular, modestly profitable work. He became, for Weber, a type of man capable of ceaseless methodical labor. The religious man and the economic man coincided into the sober bourgeois citizen who lived through his work, and enabled the rise of industrial capitalism (Weber 1958). The Protestant work ethic produced the disciplined workers required for the expansion of rational, methodical capitalist processes.

Modern work

Work as we now typically understand it is a modern invention. It is a product of industrialization and it is governed by the rules of economic rationality (Appelbaum 1992, George and George 1968, Gorz 1989, Tilgher 1930, Weber 1930). The convergence of work and virtue (through methodical adherence to one's "calling") and the establishment of a dominant Protestant work ethic set in place a type of citizen-worker that would subsequently come to typify modern citizenship and undergird modern forms of social organization. In modern society people have defined themselves, and in turn have been socially defined, by the type of work that they do in the public sphere. Work that is socially determined and usually paid for in the form of a wage or salary (cf. Gorz 1989), has been a primary factor in socialization, in social cohesion and personal identity formation in modern societies. The predominance of production and of work in modern industrial society has defined and shaped the character of the public sphere in which paid work is carried out. At the same time the practices of work have been articulated with a process of differentiation of public from private spheres. The private sphere, in which unpaid and reproductive work is carried out, has been regarded as the domain of women. But the private sphere too has not withstood the encroachment of instrumental rationality. Feminists have long criticized this separation of public and private spheres, usually on the basis of women's exclusion from the former. Much effort has been spent on measuring or "counting" (Henderson 1978, Waring 1988, 1989) women's private-sphere contribution to the maintenance of the public sphere, and demanding a wage for housework. These efforts have inadvertently contributed to a dominant definition of industrial society that Gorz (1989) describes as a "society of workers" in which participation in paid work is a normative condition. Industrial society is thus distinguished from all earlier forms of society.

As the capitalist economic system developed it increasingly required that its economic rationality prevail over all other forms of rationality (as in pre-capitalist production), and human goals and interests. Hence, as Marx and Weber demonstrated, the rise of industrial capitalism and the creation of modern work intrinsically linked material production with cultural production. Work and workers were placed in a more clearly defined structural location in the advancing rationalization processes of industrial capitalism. It was not always this way – pre-industrial western societies held different views on the nature and meaning of work – but in the modern industrial era work and occupation came to prevail as primary elements in social organization. It may be that, once again, as a result of the transformations currently occurring in modern industrial society, different meanings and practices of work are instituted, a matter to which I return in chapters 6 and 7. I wish to turn now to a discussion of the changes in the material practices of work and production that have become evident in recent decades. Subsequent chapters elaborate on the discursive practices of contemporary work that, I argue, are increasingly important as we increase production of "discursive" or "symbolic" goods. The discursive practices of work, in addition to the material practices, are exerting formative influences on the self at work, and the culture of production- and consumption-driven western societies.

THE TRANSFORMATION OF WORK

In advanced industrial capitalist societies vast changes in production and work have occurred in the decades since World War II. These changes are associated with the deployment of advanced automation technologies and advanced electronic communication and information technologies (based on the micro-processor) that include CAD/CAM, CIM (Computer Aided Design, Computer Aided Manufacturing, Computer Integrated Manufacturing), electronic data processing and financial transfer,

29

integrated telecommunications, artificial intelligence (that include "smart" machines and "seeing" robots), and their derivatives, in industry and commerce, and in social life more broadly. These developments are part of a qualitative shift that is occurring in society that is both a manifestation of, and a generative force in building a post-industrial society. The arguments in the "new technology" debate, as we called it in the 1970s and 1980s, are reviewed briefly below but the main intent here is to describe the actual changes in work that are being brought about by the expansion of computerized production and advanced information technologies in the workplace, and our attempts to understand them.

The new technology debate

Since the 1950s social analysts, industrialists and labor unionists have been aware of the growing impact of new technology (Lumer 1962, United Steel Workers of America 1960, Walker 1957) especially of automation, on traditional industrial production. Coinciding with the advance of "new" technologies[2] into the workplace some analysts have argued that a shift from an industrial economy based on the production of material goods to one increasingly centered around the provision of services and information, is simultaneously occurring in advanced western societies.[3]

This shift in the productive sphere has generated considerable debate about the precise nature and impact of these changes. Some of the early observers (Bell 1973, Toffler 1971, 1980) believed that the problems generated by industrial capitalism would be "solved" by evolutionary transformations in technology and the economy. The shift from blue-collar, noisy, dirty and physically demanding work, into cleaner, quieter and allegedly more complex and desirable white-collar work, would resolve many of the problems associated with the organization of industrial work and related traditional sources of dissatisfaction and conflict. They, and other commentators of this period (Bahro 1978, Illich 1972, Roszak 1972, Schumacher 1974), although with important differences among them, viewed the coming post-industrial era optimistically. These early analysts of the 1970s argued for a low-technology, de-industrialized, "small is beautiful" alternative to the corporate state. They saw in the new service economy and in automation possibilities for freedom from the drudgery, oppression and gradual deskilling of industrial work. They argued for the possibilities of decentralized, cooperative, non-bureaucratic and "peaceful" economic and social alternatives, and placed emphasis on the growing educational opportunities and attainments of a growing majority of the population. They believed that for those workers remaining in the corporate sector white-collar jobs would become more interesting and rewarding as they correspondingly demanded more highly educated people to perform the tasks of "knowledge work" in the new economy.

Some theorists looked for the potential in post-industrial societies to liberate people from the need to work and for possibilities for "post-capitalist" social and political systems to emerge, and postmodern social movements for the pursuit of non-economic human goals (Bahro 1978, Frankel 1987, and again more recently Drucker 1993). In particular, Andre Gorz's 1980 book, bade "farewell to the working class," and celebrated the new era's departure from class and class-based politics, and the centrality of work in social organization. He advocated "freedom from work" (Gorz 1980, 1989) as the utopian promise of the post-industrial era.

Others (Aronowitz 1981, Beniger 1986, Braverman 1974, Gill 1985, Gouldner 1976, Silverman and Yanowitch 1974, Touraine 1981) viewed the changes in industrial production and the shift into post-industrial conditions with critical concern. They argued that, in the first instance, automation displaces millions of workers from factory and machine work, many into unemployment or into a growing class of low-paid and casualized service workers. They argued that a further deskilling of work is occurring as automation takes over the tasks formerly performed by people, and that a new polarization in skill and occupation (Aronowitz 1981, Gorz 1989, Harrison and Bluestone 1988) and consequently in social life, is evident. Moreover, some argued that post-industrial society is the "programmed society" (Touraine 1981) in which technocracy controls the production and data processing apparatus and the social organization of life (Touraine 1981: 6–7).

By the late 1980s and early 1990s technological transformations in office work were becoming evident (Baran 1988, Carter 1987, Garson 1988, Hartmann 1987, Rozen 1987, Wright 1987), although they were less dramatic than the late 1970s images of chimney stacks tumbling and iron works rusting following the demolition of hard-core industrial plants. The computer integrated, "informated" (Zuboff 1988) office, like computer integrated manufacturing, requires fewer workers to perform existing and expanded operating tasks. The results of empirical studies (Alic and Harris 1988, Ayres and Miller 1983, Gill 1985, Hunt and Hunt 1983, Leontief and Duchin 1986) indicate that a technologically advanced post-industrial capitalist economy no longer requires as much work, from as many workers, as industrial economies did. Manufacturing, formerly so important in industrial economies, is experiencing considerable increases in productivity capacities. In the United States manufacturing production from 1975 to 1990 was more that twice that of the previous decade (Drucker 1993). At the same time manufacturing employment fell by almost half in the 30 years from 1960 to 1990 (Drucker 1993: 69).

Across the industrialized world in the last years of the twentieth century societies are facing considerable social changes as the world of work is transformed. Some analysts point to the emergence of a new form of class polarization resulting from the current transformations taking place in the economy (Harrison and Bluestone 1988, Gorz 1989, Reich 1991). Others argue for "post-industrial possibilities" (Block 1990) and for the emergence of new political practices in "disorganized capitalism" (Lash and Urry 1987); again others talk of the emergence of a "post-capitalist" society (Drucker 1993) in which production and value is based on "knowledge work." In a few decades it is possible that most of those who remain in work will either be retained by corporations in relatively privileged echelons in highly specialized occupations (Drucker 1993, Gorz 1989, Handy 1989, Reich 1991), or be confined to insecure, sporadic service work or restricted to marginal occupations. While there are differences in the patterns and impact of post-industrial changes in different economies – especially between the United States and Europe (Lash and Urry 1987) particularly with regard to unemployment (Harrison and Bluestone 1988, Drucker 1993),[4] the similarities in the effects of advanced automation and the reorganization of work in post-industrializing societies are striking.

INDUSTRIAL WORK

The project of the industrial revolution was the elevation of rationality and production over human being and human doing. At the core was the vision (anonymous and "never-said" to appropriate Foucault's terms) of continuous motion and continuity in production. The realization of the vision of industrialism took many decades. It required technology and techniques that greatly expanded upon and surpassed simple manual technology and human skill, and it required the compliance of appropriately acculturated industrial workers (see Chapter 4). People invented machines to reproduce and extend the capacity of the human body as an instrument of work. Industrial machines that are precise and repetitive are able to be controlled according to a rational set of principles in ways that human bodies cannot be. The limitations on production formerly imposed by the limitations of the human body were surpassed by industrial technology, and society's ability to produce and consume things was vastly extended.

Industrialization embodies three fundamental processes: specialization of function (and elaborate division of labor) mechanization and standardization (cf. Hirschhorn 1984). Like Adam Smith and Emile Durkheim, the early industrialists believed that productivity increases with the division of labor. The division of labor and the specialization of work tasks that began to emerge in the preindustrial craftshops, and that were greatly expanded in the first factories, led to the development of specialized machines for performing particular functions of the production process. The first mechanical devices grew out of a simulation and extension of human action (the flying shuttle, the spinning jenny, the metal lathe). Powered by the invention of the steam engine that launched the industrial revolution in the mid-eighteenth century, these machines with specialist functions in weaving, spinning, pumping, pressing and other rapidly expanding functions took over, and surpassed, work formerly performed by craftsmen and their laborers. Gradually the systematic linkage of specialized machines enabled the mechanization of the entire production process. Further specialization of work tasks enabled large-scale production, and the elimination of customized craft work.

In the wider social sphere occupational specialization also effected dramatic social changes in the way people worked and in the ways they organized their lives. In the towns, the system of the craft guilds that craftsmen had established to maintain skills, knowledge and product standards and to set prices, was undermined by the system of mass production and a vastly expanded market. The social system and conditions of rural agricultural life similarly underwent a period of significant change. In the course of the societal shift from agricultural to industrial work, the problem of time and later of skill emerged. Time-keeping was one of the first new requirements of industrial work. No longer was the rule of the seasons and of the weather the standard for measuring the working day. The invention of gas lighting made possible a further extension of working hours. Greater numbers of women and children were employed because they were easier to discipline than men and more easily retained on lower wages. In addition to extended hours, the time factor generated a set of new skills that included dexterity, economy of motion and speed which became the new physical requirements of industrial workers. By the turn of the twentieth century and the invention of the assembly line these skills, combined with endurance and disciplined compliance to the rhythms of the machine, began to displace physical strength as the primary requirement of industrial work.

The production technology and labor organization of the assembly line represented the culmination of the industrial vision. Its achievement was epitomized by the Henry Ford system of production and style of management based on scientific management[5] in the manufacture of automobiles in the early decades of the twentieth century. Although assembly work represented only a portion of all industrial labor (that still required considerable labor in raw materials preparation as well as in handling and transportation), it typified the drive toward "mechanization and super-machines" (Hirschhorn 1984: 7–8) and the development of continuous and controlled movement, of both mechanical parts, and human labor. The assembly line embodies the core principles of industrial culture: rationality, mechanization, efficiency and standardization, order, constraint, and continuity, and the reduction of work to simple specialized labor. Its smooth, continuous operation is reliant on the standardization and precision of parts, and the continuous action of the workers. For workers on the assembly line, the inflexibility of the mechanical process imposes rigid constraints on physical and mental movements. As a result, the assembly line requires and achieves the subjugation of the human body to the power of the machine. The assembly line's highly routinized and controlled practices of work organization epitomize the character of work in industrial society.

The limitations on production formerly imposed by the limitations of the human body had been surpassed. Alongside the diminishing role of the worker's body in the production process, industrial technology and its management system also brought about a diminution in the value of the worker. The reduction in the amount of physical and mental skill required from workers as the productive process was mechanized and centrally controlled, enabled the thinking, planning and creative functions of workers on the floor to be taken over by management. The control of productive activity was forcibly wrested from the hands of the workers, as the old artisan and craftsman skills became redundant, and as Taylor (1911) envisaged and advocated, tasks of conception were increasingly divorced from tasks of execution. The removal of brainwork from the execution of tasks rendered the simple labor of the worker more readily expendable. The perceived expendability of the worker in the scientifically managed factory became a useful rhetorical strategy that was employed against workers attempting to organize in opposition to the fragmentation of their work and the restructuring of their workplaces.

The vision of scientific management completed the process of industrialism's vision of the "worker as machine" until the late twentieth century. The rise of bureaucratic administration and management systems, which embody and reflect the same logic of industrialism, enabled rationalized production and the reliable and predictable transfer of information and finances. The rationalization and bureaucratization of knowledge became the basis of control over production and workers. Scientific management, however, was never a complete nor smoothly implemented process, for alongside the triumph of the machine and the rationalization of work there remained a human element which defied complete rationalization. As factories became more and more systematically organized and productivity increased, workers, who had become increasingly disciplined by the inexorable rhythms of the machines imposed upon them, became increasingly alienated from their labor and their products. The workers' labor became devoid of inherent interest or value. Their psychological and physiological needs were taken into account by the owners and managers of industrial plants only to the extent that difficulties and pathologies affected the smooth operation of the industrial enterprise.

Evidence of alienation in modern industrial work, following Marx's early observations, has been well documented.[6] Alienation is usually measured in its more quantifiable form as rates of absenteeism, wild-cat strikes, and workers' disruption and sabotage of factory production or bureaucratic processes. By and large, worker alienation and its resultant "industrial conflict" has been regarded as an inevitable, but manageable, problem of industrial work. The theory and practice of industrial relations and of industrial and organizational psychology are devoted to its mitigation and management and numerous industrial reform projects have been attempted from time to time.[7] The effects of the experiences of industrial work on working selves are are addressed more fully in Chapter 4.

TECHNOLOGICAL CHANGE: A POST-INDUSTRIAL SHIFT

Following World War II there were signs that a major change in the direction of industrial technology had begun. The rapid development and expansion of electronic technology made possible the development of automated production systems. Early, relatively simple, forms of automation in the 1950s and 1960s were rapidly surpassed by highly automated computer integrated continuous-process technology, flexible manufacturing systems (FMS)[8] and computer integrated and informated offices. These developments did not immediately indicate a break with the project of industrialism and its drive for increased production and consumption. But there did emerge some important implications for, or disruptions to, the continuing march of industrial practices. Among the immediate implications, although by no means immediately recognized (as I argue in Chapter 5), of advanced automation and FMS was the reversal of the typical trend of industrial society toward an increasing division of labor and specialization of function. This appeared initially as changes in skill levels.

At first analysts observed changes in skill requirements as an effect of technological change in production and work organization (see Block 1990). Considerable early attention was given to the role of skill and the place of skilled workers in heavy industry and manufacturing.[9] Feminists, and others a little later, noticed similar trends and problems in office work (Aronowitz 1981, Carter 1987, Eriksen and Vallas 1990, Garson 1988, Frank Fox and Hesse-Biber 1984, Hartmann 1987, Wright 1987). The discussion below includes the traditional domains of work including blue-, pink- and white-collar work in manufacturing, offices and services (transport, hospitals, retail) by no means only traditional so-called "masculinist" blue-collar work,[10] and the rise of new forms of work in services and information.

Skill changes and decline in specialization

The decline in specialization of function was first apparent in the change in the place of the worker's piecemeal labor as simply a unit in the elaborately specialized production process. The simplest, most reductionist mechanical labor was immediately displaced by the automation of those tasks. The place of the worker in the overall process began to change. Consequently, workers who had performed those simple repetitive tasks now performed by automated machines were displaced from their jobs. For those workers still required in an automated plant, there began a process of "multi-skilling" and "up-skilling." Analysts and observers debated the shift in skill requirements, the degradation of work and the control of the labor process. Deskilling, more apparent under typical industrial conditions, it was argued, was now occurring among workers formerly regarded as highly skilled (Aronowitz 1981, Noble 1984). The low-skilled workers still retained by manufacturing companies were being retrained with a broader skills base than previously required (Ayres and Miller 1983, Blauner 1964, Gallie 1978, Hunt and Hunt 1983, Zuboff 1988).

The experience and structure of work is simultaneously changing with the restructuring generated, and enabled, by the technological developments, and the concurrent production of more and new information. Mechanized industrial work was divided up into its smallest parts, and organized by linear hierarchies of supervision and control. In the new automated and computer integrated workplace, "multi-activity" jobs combine the tasks previously carried out by workers with different skills, and even occupational designations. In the office multi-activity teams, whose members all possess computer skills and can access data storage and processing networks carry out the tasks previously performed by clerks, secretaries and lower-level administrative workers. Much of the unskilled, rote clerical work such as routine tasks in typing, filing, data processing, inventory, accounts, payroll, and the like, has been eliminated (Carter 1987, Eriksen and Vallas 1990, Pahl 1988, Wright 1987, Zuboff 1988). Similarly, advanced automation and flexible manufacturing technologies no longer restrict the worker to one highly specialized, routine task. The worker is both able to perform a wider range of tasks, and to take responsibility for the overall operation of a complex unit of production. At the very least, line workers know the tasks and procedures of other jobs on the line and can be redeployed readily as required. As a result, multi-skilled (yet not necessarily more highly-paid) workers can perform the tasks of formerly more specialist workers.

In both the factory and the office middle-managerial and supervisory staff are required in diminishing numbers (Harrison and Bluestone 1988, Strassman 1985, Garson 1988, Block 1990). Notwithstanding wide differences across industries and firms in the experiences of technological applications the literature points to a mixture of down-skilling, up-skilling and multi-skilling generally occurring. The reorganized open-plan office alters traditional status and job differentiation. Multi-activity teams operate with much higher degrees of flexibility and adaptability. Each member of the team can perform each of the range tasks of the team's work function. Some analysts argue that this renders the workers increasingly more "professional" and highly-trained than in the past (Hirschhorn 1984,

36

Zuboff 1988). There is a consequent collapse of old boundaries of work tasks and an altered hierarchy of supervision and control. Importantly, a halting or reversal of specialization of function and the division of labor characteristic of industrial work is becoming evident. (I illustrate this development in Chapters 4 and 5 and discuss its implications.) The management and organizational literature develops these themes under calls for restructured organizations with flatter hierarchies, blurred boundaries and more fluid structures (Drucker 1993, Handy 1989, 1990, Kanter 1989, 1992, Kilman and Covin 1988, Peters 1991, 1992).

In the factory another significant change accompanied the decline in specialization. The fundamental requirements of industrial work, bodily exertion, manual dexterity and endurance, have been increasingly displaced by the requirements for rapid perception, attentiveness and the ability to analyze problems and make decisions (Hirschhorn 1984, Zuboff 1988). The rudiments of industrial work have visibly shifted from physical effort to the manipulation of electronic symbols through keyboards and press buttons (see Garson 1988, Gill 1985, Gorz 1989, Hirschhorn 1984, Howard 1984, Zuboff 1989). Furthermore, the capacity for "flexibility" enabled by flexible manufacturing systems was extended as a skill requirement of the worker (Parker and Slaughter 1988). Workers must be willing and able to learn and perform new tasks, take on different roles and be easily redeployed in the flexible new workplace. Similar processes have occurred in office work. The former typically industrial characteristic (and ability) of mechanized constraint has given way to a post-industrial flexibility in skills acquisition and deployment.[11]

By the 1980s a number of occupations and former job categories such as welder, riveter, switchboard operator, salaries clerk, bookkeeper, typesetter (among many others) had disappeared. In the 1990s, ledger machinists, typists and insurance underwriters are a rare sight. These jobs have been either automated, integrated or informated away. The tasks are performed by robotic systems, data processing packages or their remnant operations undertaken by remaining multi-skilled workers.

Reduced labor costs, increased production, fewer workers

Among the first effects of automation in work practices observed by analysts in the 1970s was a shift in the place of labor costs in the production equation. In a cross-cultural study of French and British oil refineries (Gallie 1978) that were undergoing extensive automation in the 1960s and 1970s, Gallie observed that the cost of labor was dramatically reduced in proportion to the costs of introducing the highly expensive automated production technology. Labor costs were also reduced in real terms as the requirement for manual labor declined and workers were laid off. At the same time, labor costs became a much more stable component of total costs, a fixed rather than a variable cost (Gallie 1978: 8–9). Furthermore, continuous-process technology needed to be continually staffed irrespective of the level of production. Management, therefore, could no longer offset temporary recessions in the market by laying off labor. Consequently, in contrast to traditional mass-production industry, the new technological workers achieved a much higher level of job security. This elevation of technical workers into a position akin to career status previously reserved for white-collar workers, because of their new highly demanded skills and job security, has also been examined by Gorz (1980, 1989) Gouldner (1976, 1979) and Aronowitz (1973, 1981) as evidence of an emerging polarization and technicization of skilled workers.

By the 1980s a second and enduring effect of the deployment of advanced automation, CAD/CAM (Computer Aided Design and Computer Aided Manufacturing), and subsequently CIM (Computer Integrated Manufacturing) and ICMS (Integrated Customer Management Systems) (and their variations) was the displacement of labor. Studies in the 1980s showed that as manual work operations are taken over by automation operations, millions of workers are displaced from their jobs. One extensive empirical study in the United States (Leontief and Duchin 1986) argues that the "intensive use of automation will make it possible to achieve over the next 20 years significant economies in labor" (Leontief and Duchin 1986: 12). They claim that in 1990 over eleven million fewer workers [were] required and over twenty million fewer will be required in 2000. They predict that there will be a progressive increase in the proportion of professionals and a steep decline in the number and proportion of clerical workers. The increased demand for professionals is mainly for computer specialists and technologists. In the old, hard-core heavy industries of steel and fero-alloys there will be a further increase in their decline, not just because of robots displacing workers, but because of the rise of computer-controlled machine tools that require less heavy metals in their manufacture and use, and the miniaturization of circuits, computer mainframes and PCs. Similar findings are reported in Block (1990) and Kleindorfer (1985).

Furthermore, a study in the electronics industry in the United States (Alic and Harris 1988) shows that in the manufacture of televisions from 1971 to 1981 production output nearly doubled – from 5.4 million sets to 10.5 million. At the same time jobs for production workers dropped by half over the same period (Alic and Harris 1988: 670). Productivity on a unit output basis grew dramatically over the decade. During the same decade United States industries moved many of their manufacturing operations to low-wage developing countries. It is estimated by the United States Department of Labor that more jobs were created in those off-shore plants than were employed in domestic television manufacture. Similarly, in other industries it is estimated that American manufacturing companies have carried out 90 percent of all assembly work overseas.

The situation in Europe especially regarding growing unemployment is arguably even more visible and acute. In Germany, for example, unions and companies negotiate over delaying the introduction of increasingly sophisticated new technologies into workplaces that are already highly automated (see Gorz 1989, Lash and Urry 1987). Disputes are over the timing of the introduction of further advanced technology, not over the issue of its introduction *per se* – the latter issue is regarded as no longer realistically debatable as it was in the 1970s and 1980s. Rather, it is hoped that delaying deployment of increasingly advanced technologies and their carefully managed timing will enable the ensuing social disruption to be somewhat lessened, and the potential for political instability averted.

Labor control, labor structure

None the less, the issues of control, management and integration of the workers and the work process remain contentious (Heckscher 1988, Kochan 1986, Knights and Willmott 1990). There is substantive documentation of the increased exercise of control over workers' productive activity and their work habits in the period of mass assembly-line production (Braverman 1974, Burawoy 1979, Edwards 1979). Beniger's (1986) account of what he terms the "control revolution" comprehensively outlines the transition from preindustrial to industrial systems of control and organization. He argues that the shift into the "information age," or the post-industrial era, where production and exchange are controlled by computer technologies, is a continuation and acceleration of the control processes that began more than a century ago. "Microprocessor and computer technologies . . . are not new forces only recently unleashed upon an unprepared society, but merely the latest installment in the continuing development of the control revolution" (Beniger 1986: vii).

Similarly, Aronowitz (1981) while generally taking a deskilling view of industrial work, directs attention to the implications of the polarization and restructuring of the traditional class bases of work. He points to the dramatic rise of the professional middle class in the 1970s and 1980s and, following the introduction of automation technologies into the workplace, the increasing proportion of skilled to unskilled workers, seeing a simultaneous degradation of skill as a result. The new skills are not those which have traditionally been associated with the skilled workers of trade unions and socialist movements, and they correspond with the traditionally non-unionized professional middle class. The new "technical intelligentsia" has shown "little propensity to conduct struggles about class formation" (Aronowitz 1981: 83). Like Gallie (1978), Aronowitz observes that the new manual workers within industries that have adopted advanced automation technology – oil, chemical, electronics – are relatively highly paid, and separated from the traditional skills of prior generations. They in turn, in the United States at least, have become depoliticized because of the decline of labor traditions and the industrial migration to small-town, historically non-union areas, south of the border into Mexico and beyond. As a consequence, organized labor's political contestation of post-industrial trends is undeveloped.

Aronowitz argues that the "third industrial revolution" now underway in advanced economies implies a "transformation of the nature of the labor process" and also of the "character of labor" (1981). Following Marx's labor theory of value in which value is measured by quantities of labor time necessary for the production of commodities, Aronowitz argues that under the new technological changes, production becomes "more and more based upon technocratically-controlled systems of knowledge organization, rather than the control of labor" (Aronowitz 1981: 86). This does not mean that labor has disappeared as a central aspect of production, or that its "metaphoric/ symbolic significance as the key to production is no longer present." It remains the significant measure of value in abstract, and the "regulative principle" of most of the world's production. However, the "quantity of labor required for production can no longer be evaluated in terms of time frames, since *knowledge* has become the main productive force" (ibid.: 83). These themes are echoed later by Derber *et al.* (1990) and by Drucker (1993) and Reich (1991).

Furthermore, advanced information technologies enable new forms of surveillance and control over workers' activities to be built into the production process itself. Workers may be "observed" and monitored by the computers they work on (Baran 1988, Garson 1988, Webster and Robins 1986, Wright 1987). These matters have been raised by labor organizations, civil liberties groups and analysts concerned with privacy issues and the ownership and control of knowledge products.

Service sector

Alongside the emerging new knowledge work there is the development of a vastly expanded service sector. The management processes of industrialized manufacturing generated the rise of a service class of white-collar office workers, from clerical to management, and a sector of scientists, technical and health-care workers. The history and character of the service class has been well documented over the decades (Abercrombie and Urry 1983, Gershuny 1978, Giddens and Mackenzie 1982, Kanter 1977, Montgomery 1979, Nelson 1975). But in more recent years, the "old" service class has itself undergone post-industrial transformations, in composition, services provided and in work tasks. Significantly, a growing new division in the service sector has emerged. Many of the middle-management workers comprising a large sector of the service class are no longer required by automated offices and the "lean and mean" corporations of the 1990s and there are accordingly fewer manual workers to supervise. Some of these people are finding work in consulting businesses and contract services to multi-national corporations (MNCs). This emergent development awaits empirical measurement and analysis although Reich's (1991) projections on this matter are illuminating.

Most readily observable is the growth at the lower-paid end particularly in the sector of fast-food workers, custodial, domestic, and leisure industry workers. Furthermore, in keeping with the post-industrial trend of a halting of increased specialization of function, these new service workers, although low paid and quickly trained, are required to perform a wide range of responsibilities in dealing with customers and operate according to a company masterplan of standardized procedures and principles. Consequently, a process of up-skilling and lowering of wages is commonly practiced in the service sector. In manufacturing previously deskilled jobs are automated away or integrated (multi-skilling) into the jobs that remain. In white-collar work both skill enhancement and breadth of responsibility is required. The productive output and quality levels have also risen (Drucker 1993).

Another trend in the transformation of the service sector is "outsourcing" in which the service work is contracted out of the organization requiring the service (Drucker 1993). Outworking, in which workers (usually women) assembled piece work in manufacturing such as clothing, packaging, mailings, and some telework was common in industrial conditions. Such workers were employed by a company and although off-site were considered part of the organization. The practice of outsourcing does not involve the employment by the recipient organization of the persons providing the service. Maintenance, custodial, clerical and many telecommunication operations may readily be outsourced to individuals or service organizations. High-skilled work in drafting, design, mathematical analysis, and some legal work may be outsourced to "consulting" individuals or small organizations. Furthermore, another recent development is the "virtual corporation" that employs a minimum of staff and operates like the cast and support staff of a film set in which employees are contracted for specific productions for specific time periods. There is no "down time" in which workers are retained during periods of low productivity or recession. The expansion of the service sector is commonly regarded by business analysts and management theorists (Drucker 1993, Reich 1991, Handy 1989) as the source of future employment opportunities as primary production and manufacturing require fewer workers.

POST-INDUSTRIAL DISCUSSIONS

In the 1990s there is now little debate that work in advanced industrialized societies, whether performed in automated manufacturing production sites, in the informated office, or in the recently emerged new service and communication industries, has changed significantly. While many, however, still hope that the future will bring back the past, most analysts in the academy no longer argue for a return to full employment. Full employment is no longer regarded as possible even if, in the modernist view, it is still desirable.

Post-industrial work refers broadly to two levels. The first level contains the more readily observable and quantifiable changes, such as those effected by the widespread deployment of advanced automation and information technologies in the production of material goods and services. It involves an integration of skills and knowledge work in production tasks, centralized control of the information process: productivity, stock, markets, finance (which may be globally disseminated), and the reorganization of the workplace. The latter includes an alteration of traditional bureaucratic hierarchies of control and a more integrated role for the worker (now the employee). It is also typified by the displacement and dispersion of workers, occupational de-specialization, the growth of a polarized service sector and global markets. Moreover, the capacity of late-twentieth century, technologically advanced, societies to produce more with fewer workers is a significant post-industrial condition. The second level pertains to the changes brought about by advanced computer technologies in the nature of production, and in what is being produced and valued. Central among these changes is the commodification of knowledge and information as the "informated" workplace transforms production and product.

Enthusiasts for the expansion of new technologies in the workplace suggest that not only can production be increased, labor costs reduced, global markets established and financial operations electronically integrated, but the experience of work can be enhanced and enriched. Their typical argument, which I draw substantively from Hirschhorn (1984, 1988) and Zuboff 1988), runs as follows: in industrial society, the assembly-line semi-skilled worker of the factory is tied to his tasks and constrained by the rhythms of the machines. His mind is not utilized and his capacities for enjoyment and meaningfulness in work are greatly limited. His private self, therefore, is alienated from his labor which does not require his full mental attention. The worker's labor is experienced as only an extension of the machine.

In post-industrial conditions, however, the "new" worker in manufacturing operations is the prototypical control-room operator of a range of tasks and functions. She is required to bring her conscious awareness to the tasks at hand by coordinating and controlling both her own selective attention processes and behaviors, and the activities of the plant. The operator is required to be multi-skilled, aware and flexible. She must be able to understand the entire production process, so that she is ready to respond to unpredictable situations. Hirschhorn sums up this perspective in the view that, "the post-industrial worker . . . performs developmental tasks, operating at the boundary between old technical realities and the emergent ones" (Hirschhorn 1984: 79). The worker's ability to learn and adapt becomes more important than his past training. A worker's tacit understanding of a particular machine or set of processes is more important than his general education and knowledge. He retains a substantive self-concept as an agent in work. In the office, the computer-proficient clerical worker becomes an "office administrator" performing tasks formerly reserved for specialist accountants, record keepers or receptionists.

Zuboff (1988) argues that alterations in the material conditions of the workers' means of production,

> were manifested in transformations at intimate levels of experience –
> assumptions about knowledge and power, their beliefs about work and
> the meaning they derived from it, the content and rhythm of their social
> exchanges, and the ordinary mental and physical disciplines to which
> they accommodated their daily lives.
>
> (Zuboff 1988: xiii)

Zuboff suggests that these changes gave workers new opportunities for self-realization through work. Zuboff hopes that the advanced automation and information technologies now in place will enable the worker to gain a greater sense of control over the work process and will make work more meaningful. It may result in a humanizing restructuring of the workplace. Again, these views are popular in management and organization literature that emphasizes "empowered" and responsible employees (Handy 1990, Kanter 1989, 1992, Kilman and Covin 1988, Peters and Waterman 1984, Peters 1991, Ouchi 1981, Senge 1990).

This view of the possibilities enabled by advanced automation and information technologies suggests that the new technologies will provide workers with opportunities in which they can exercise new forms of skill and knowledge, especially critical judgment in managing the new machines. As work becomes more abstract, requiring flexibility and manipulability, workers experience new challenges and forms of mastery. In the workplace, the technological transformation engenders new approaches to organizational behavior, "in which relationships are more intricate, collaborative and bound by mutual responsibilities of colleagues" (Zuboff 1988: 6). The application of new technologies in workplaces can allow managers and employees to move beyond their narrow functional perspectives and to create new roles and opportunities. A "data-rich" environment requires new forms of work organization and new management practices that recognize and exploit the blurring of boundaries and de-specialization made possible by the new production technologies. As the range and quality of skills at each organizational level become similar, hierarchical distinctions become blurred. Authority becomes based upon appropriate fit between knowledge and responsibility rather than upon traditional organizational rank and status structures. The new flows of information between multiple users create opportunities for innovative methods of information sharing and exchange. Team work among broadly skilled and knowledgeable employees, less fettered by the constraints of traditional hierarchies and spheres of responsibility, engenders a heightened sense of empowerment, commitment and collective responsibility.

Moreover, this view believes that advanced automation and advanced management information systems (MIS) will lead to a high degree of social integration within the organization. The work conditions associated with more traditional technologies and industrial relations have been definitively altered by the de-differentiation capacities of advanced information technology. This has led to a reduction in the level of industrial conflict and to closer relations between management and the workforce. Consequently, the integration of employees into the company, and the social structure of advanced capitalist society, is achieved.

The other main cluster of viewpoints describes an opposing scenario, pointing to the persistence of traditional social relations of ownership and control and displaying a historical mistrust of management-initiated workplace re-organizations. Labor organizations, while rapidly eroding in this new era (Aronowitz 1981, Fantasia 1988, Feldman and Betzold 1990, Heckscher 1988, Kochan 1986), and other critical analysts raise questions over the effects of increasing deployment of advanced technologies on jobs, wages and working conditions, skills training, labor markets (Piore and Sable 1984, Harrison and Bluestone 1988). These commentators have focused largely on traditional work in blue- and white-collar sectors of manufacturing, office work, hospitals and other traditional services, but others are expressing critical concern about the effects of technological change on organizations and employees (Kunda 1992, Martin 1992, Smith 1990). This view is less enthusiastic about the possibilities for transformed workplaces and "empowered" workers (Parker and Slaughter 1988).

Some critics argue that computer technologies fundamentally reorganize the infrastructure of the material world and not just, although most immediately, of the workplace. They argue that the advanced new technologies (including Artificial Intelligence (AI) as well as IT and their derivatives) of the 1990s surpass even the elaborate automated technologies of the post-War decades. The new "smart" technologies equipped with expansive artificial intelligence capacities not only surpass human physical capacities, but perform the functions of human brainwork as well. Notwithstanding the routinization and deskilled labor of early automated production there remained some capacity for human critical judgment and for localized modification of work practices and habits. Such capacity, it is feared, is now given over to the new intelligent machines. Consequently, workers may become servants of the smart machines and become more docile and dependent in the workplace. Furthermore, while employees are not as bound by the rhythms of machines they are now more subtly monitored and controlled by the electronic eye of management surveillance (Beniger 1986, Garson 1988, Shaiken 1984, Webster and Robins 1986). This situation can cause workers to become more cynical, distrustful and distanced from one another. They perform their jobs routinely and perfunctorily and look for more ways to escape their jobs. Conflicts in the workplace increase. Social alienation and disaffection exacerbate already serious social and political decline and the resurgence of sectarian political influence.

The new surveillance techniques that enable constant monitoring of workers' every activity may ensure a greater level of conformity to the new work practices and elicit the manifestation of bonds of loyalty to the company. The ability to manage by remote control circumvents the traditional face-to-face encounter, and the negotiating process with workers. New information technologies can displace interpersonal contacts, and the technologies themselves can become a new site of tension and sublimated confrontation. Critics also point out that multi-skilling and up-skilling does not not necessarily led to increased pay and improved work conditions (Bamber and Landsbury 1989, Kassalow 1989, Stinchombe 1990). Increased productivity with fewer workers threatens the availability of jobs and the future of work. Employees can, once again, be controlled and disciplined under these conditions, despite "empowering" policies, job enrichment and "joint ownership" programs.

Theorizing the changes in work

Efforts to interpret and analyze the changes in work and economy include a range of approaches, some focusing on the organization of production and workplaces and others attempting to analyze these changes with respect to broader social implications. Analysts focusing on the level of production changes in the factory (Piore and Sabel 1984, Wood 1982, Webster and Robins 1986) describe a condition of "post-Fordism" or "neo-Fordism". This term is useful in describing changes in manufacturing production, including flexible manufacturing and flexible accumulation, and work organization in particular. It points to shifts away from the Fordism (and its predecessor scientific management) and its hallmark of assembly-line production in which fragmented, routinized labor and mechanistic rationality prevailed. The integration of work tasks, the introduction of team work, Just-in-Time (JIT) production systems and various "quality control" processes that require greater participation and understanding of workers in the production process are examples of post-Fordist practices. Although post-Fordism is popular among labor-relations analysts the term loses its usefulness in situations, and at levels of analysis, beyond the factory.

Bluestone and Harrison (1982), observing the 1970s trends in the United States economy, describe a pattern of "de-industrialization." This condition occurs when domestic (in the United States) industrial work is moved off-shore to Mexico, Puerto Rico or other neighboring developing countries. In the United States the industrial cities and regions declined into "rustbelts" with high unemployment, urban decay and economic recession. This process of deindustrialization, they argue, is not just restricted to the United States but is evident in western Europe and other developed regions in Asia and the Pacific. At the same time, the developing host countries are struggling to industrialize, and they welcome the job opportunities created by the home country's investments. None the less, the segmented labor market that is created – in which a few well-paid jobs are created in the home country among white-collar and highly skilled technological employees to assist the expansion, and production jobs are relocated to the host country – creates a dual economy. The displaced workers in the home country have diminished purchasing power and the low-paid production workers in the host economy can not afford to purchase the goods they now produce.

This trend continues the pattern of advanced industrial capitalism, but at the same time it contains serious implications for the continuity of the production–consumption couplet firmly established in advanced industrialism. It is a development that may also be seen as an indication of a wider shift occurring toward a post-industrial society in which the hard-core manufacturing industries of coal, iron, steel, shipping will never again exert the defining prevalence they did in industrialism. Deindustrialization is part of the qualitative shift in the sphere of production, and in social organization that results. It ensures that the traditional production of consumer goods is acquired at the cheapest possible source, while the knowledge work, information production and financial control of an enterprise's overall operation remains centralized.

Others describe the present condition as "disorganized capitalism" (Offe 1985, Lash and Urry 1987) in which older organized capitalist forms are breaking down and new social structures will emerge. The "end of organized capitalism," for Lash and Urry (following Lyotard 1984), converges with the postmodern turn in cultural and social life that is associated with advanced information technologies and a crisis in the legitimation of knowledge. For these thinkers, and a number of others (Baudrillard 1981, Frankel 1987, Harvey 1989, Smart 1992), the postmodern disjuncture is manifested not only at the cultural level of meaning and social organization, but at the level of material alteration in production. Lash and

Urry argue that there is a movement toward a "deconcentration of capital" within nation-states, "increasing contradiction between the state and capital" and an "increase in cultural fragmentation and pluralism" (Lash and Urry 1987) which they describe as a "disorganized capitalism". Harvey (1989) similarly recognizes these impulses but prefers the descriptive term "postmodern" as the interpretive category. Again, others employ the term "post-industrial" in their effort to understand these emergent conditions.

Post-industrialism was initially coined in the 1970s to refer to important discontinuities in production, economy and social development. Its focus encompasses a wide range of events and processes in technological, organizational and societal change. The term does not necessarily invoke one or other set of industrial ideologies – the right or the left – in its effort to describe and interpret, however provisionally, present and emergent conditions. As Block (1990) suggests, a reformulation of post-industrial theories can provide useful tools and categories for demonstrating the inadequacy of the old industrial ones. Aligned with insights from postmodern thought, these theories may assist a critical reading of the conditions and conventional categories and make possible a fruitful thinking through the conditions of this time. This of course discloses a political intent, for the social outcomes of post-industrial transformations remain politically contestable despite the strong technological and economic impulses fueling present developments.

GLOBALIZATION AND WORK

Observers in the 1990s have identified a process of "globalization," that is a pattern of events facilitated by technological changes and economic shifts. The rise of the multi-national (MNC) and transnational corporation (TNC) and the supranational organization in recent years has been greatly facilitated by the capabilities of advanced information and telecommunication technologies. Differing from internationalism in an important sense – the diminished role of the nation-state – globalization points to the rising importance of the MNCs and TNCs that now control a large percentage of the world's economy and exert considerable influence on global policy agenda-setting and legislation. The latest developments in the General Agreement on Tariffs and Trade (GATT) effective from 1995 may have been signed by leaders of sovereign nation-states, but the influence of transnational business operations and supranational associations such the European Union (EU) throughout the negotiations was considerable.

The implications of globalization are immense and the debates over the future of the nation-states (or some of them), the emergence of regional blocks and "global webs" (Reich 1991) are likely to continue for many years. The transformations occurring in work are co-constitutive of these developments – they are at once facilitating some of the global reconfigurations as they are an outcome of the technological, political and social decisions made in this arena. There are two major implications for work. At the level of the workplace as it is conventionally understood, information technologies in the first instance extend the process of mechanized and early automation technologies to displace human agency. They also, simultaneously, accomplish the production of information. The technological systems that make it possible to automate office work and financial transactions also possess the capacity to develop comprehensive central data systems that record all the organization's operations.

Employees across geographic locations, with access to centralized data bases, can access and coordinate many levels of data for a variety of purposes. Airlines, libraries, databanks, and informated organizations have global computer access to their own, and other contracted users', information twenty-four hours a day. These capabilities enable information processing work to be performed across the globe. Insurance companies in the United States have many of their routine accounts processing functions performed by educated women workers in Ireland who never need to see their employers or their customers. Likewise, translation services, copy-editing, multifarious document processing, even computer design and mathematical analysis are performed by contractors located in the South Pacific for global companies headquartered in North America, Europe or Asia.

Hence the second level of implications for work point to what I call an emerging "decentered workplace" in which knowledge workers or "symbolic analysts" (Reich 1991) and "outsourced" specialists with their laptop computers and cellphones can work anywhere they have access to a modem, fax or airport. Alongside the global knowledge workers with diminished attachments to home nations, corporate "families" and specialist occupations, are workers and non-workers experiencing dramatically altered conditions in existing workplaces and the effects of management practices designed to cope with the globally competitive marketplace. These workers' experiences of corporate work and organizational culture are explored in detail in chapters 5 and 6.

The course of the transition from industrial work to post-industrial work raises important questions about work, self and society. One of the outcomes of the changes in work is the problem of worker displacement from both the old forms of work and the new. Notwithstanding the displacement of workers from traditional work and their variable incorporation into new work, work remains significant in shaping the lives of individuals, in the character of the self, and in social organization. The productive bases of social life, and the institution of work, that became deeply entwined with the cultural sphere throughout modernity, remain fundamental in determining the structures and processes of social solidarity and cohesion – at least transitionally – in the emerging new era. The next two chapters discuss the self and what happens to the self at work, and the questions of solidarity and social life are addressed in the final chapters.

3

DISCOURSES OF THE SELF

THE PSYCHOLOGY OF SELF

Introduction

Postulations and hypotheses about the nature of the person, the soul, or the self have interested philosophers and religious thinkers for centuries, from Plato and Augustine, Maimonides and Aquinas, to Descartes and Locke. The historical and cultural specificity of the concept of the "self," evident in earlier notions, has bequeathed a modern notion in the West that holds distinctive new emphases. The moral philosopher Charles Taylor (1989) points out that any exploration of the self in modern thought must recognize the intertwinement of self with the notion of the good. In particular, modern moral philosophy has focused on "what it is right *to do* rather than on what it is good *to be*" (Taylor 1989: 3, emphasis added). Selfhood and morality have been coupled in modern thought with a significant emphasis on human doing over human being. This emphasis is in manifest congruence with industrialism's penchant for production. The silent legitimacy of productionism has generated dominant discourses on selfhood that both shape the character of the modern self throughout modern industrialism and delimit the context of our thinking on self that I explore in this chapter.

In the early decades of the twentieth century the study of the self, continuing earlier philosophical endeavor, was an important focus in the rising discipline of psychology. There followed some decades of relative inattention as empirical psychology rose in prominence, and then in recent years the study of the self has attracted renewed attention in sociology, as well as within social psychology. There is now a vast body of literature on the self, the person, and identity. I discuss in this chapter our modern sociological and psychological understandings of the self.

The dominant themes in the modern literature on the self emanate from the major schools of thought in social psychology: psychoanalytic thought, symbolic interactionism and modern empirical psychology. Modern

50

empirical psychology in all its many guises is currently the most popular in the academy. Its contemporary scholars have been influenced to some extent by the other traditions and they, by their own claim, aspire to advance the older traditions including the behavioral-cognitive school. In the second section of this chapter I discuss the views of the cultural critics and critical social theorists who address the historicity of the self and the social contexts of its production. This tradition of social criticism, which includes a feminist social psychology (Benjamin 1988, Wilkinson 1986), also includes criticisms of social psychology in general (Wexler 1983) as well as specifically its theories of the self (Lasch 1984, Wexler 1983). It encompasses those who have attempted, from varying viewpoints, to provide a grand analysis of the character of the self in late capitalist industrial society and to illuminate the conditions and trends of our time (Bellah *et al.* 1985, Ehrenreich 1989, Fromm 1955, Lasch 1978, 1984, 1991, Riesman 1950, Slater 1970). Social analysis of the self, in which it is assumed that the self is historically produced and culturally patterned, provides the theoretical orientation of the case study of working selves discussed in later chapters. This approach incorporates the post-structural view of the contingency of self and its multiple constituent elements.

In the middle decades of this century much psychological literature tended to employ the term "self" and "personality" somewhat interchangeably. By the 1970s following the influential works of Allport (1954), Rogers (1951), Smelser and Smelser (1963) the term "personality" was the preferred term. Although the reasons for this shift in preference were rarely made explicit, it seems that it occurred because social science theorists became reluctant to use the metaphysical term "self" that did not manifest itself as a visible material object and did not yield sufficiently to positivist scientific investigation. In 1963, Smelser and Smelser who consistently preferred "personality" defined the study of personality as the focus on "the individual as a system of needs, feelings, aptitudes, skills, defenses, etc." (Smelser and Smelser 1963). The use of the term "self" remained in the form of compound nouns, such as self-concept, self-esteem, self-image.

By the 1990s some scholars are tending again to prefer "self" or "identity" (Giddens 1991, Kondo 1990, Lash and Friedman 1992). And yet there remain of course, clear differences in understanding of the self among those who, simply put, prefer to see the self as a structured cognitive system with a core of "hard-wired" mechanisms, and those who regard it more as a process of historical, cultural and institutional constituent elements that are mediated through internal organismic processes. The term "self" is used throughout the following discussion and the differences in its implied definition by different schools of thought are elaborated. The discussion includes those social psychological theories in which the concept of personality means virtually the same as self.

51

In the twentieth century the major schools of thought in social psychology concerned with the self have been in the tradition of psychoanalysis following Sigmund Freud and the school of thought bequeathed by C.H. Cooley and G.H. Mead in the 1920s and 1930s known as symbolic interactionism. The other major branch in social psychology from about the 1940s onward emerged out of the influence of behaviorism (Skinner 1938, Watson 1930) and cognitive development psychology (Piaget 1952, Rotter 1954). This empirically oriented school, usefully labeled "psychological social psychology" (Boutlier, Roed and Svenson, 1980) to distinguish it from the allegedly more socially focused school of psychoanalysis and symbolic interactionism ("sociological social psychology") has, in addition to the work of B.F. Skinner, been influenced variously by Lewin, Festinger and Allport among others. All of these branches have sub-branches and disagreements among themselves and there are inevitable overlaps.

The study of the self divides generally into two approaches. There is some convergence of interest among some theorists (Dobert et al. 1987 for example) but most of the theoretical and empirical interest arises out of the conventional micro-level focus of psychology associated with human developmental psychology and cognitive psychology which is interested in the intrapsychic processes by means of which the individual "develops," the "stages" one goes through and the mechanisms of one's learnings and bondings. This approach is typified by experimental research methods. There is additionally some effort in social psychology to consider macro-level social processes and the relation of the individual to society. But the epistemology and focus of this branch has remained bound by the constraints of traditional positivist methods.

The other major approach to the study of self arises out of a "grand theory" orientation to the study of the individual and society. Within this tradition there is, as expected, a variety of interest in the issues of self and identity. But its focus is primarily on the self–society relation in which society is conceived more broadly than the "social context" typical of psychological orientations. This tradition, which includes historians and other cultural critics as well as sociologists, includes a group informed by a critical social theory focus on the self in relation to structural social conditions and cultural practices. It also has a branch stemming from an older tradition, from de Tocqueville on, which follows a liberal historical orientation to the study of the individual in society. In these traditions the development, or the production, of the self is linked to the specific historical conditions and social relations of a national culture (typically American), or of advanced corporate capitalism more broadly. The latter descends from the influence of the grand theorists, especially Durkheim and Marx, and the former assumes a more eclectic historical cultural criticism.

Psychoanalytic thought on the self

Freud's psychoanalytic theory, developed in the years around the turn of the twentieth century, advanced a concern with the self that had long been present in philosophical and religious thought. There was some compatibility between the notion of the self in Freudian theory and those who pursued an interest in the "soul" as the spirit or essence of the person. The early American philosopher William James thought that there were three categories of self-experience: the material self, the social self and the spiritual self. For James, the person's awareness of himself and the sense of mental activity "is often held to be a direct revelation of the living substance of our Soul" (James (1892) quoted in Gergen 1971: 7).

Freud's one-time colleague, Carl Jung, also retained a keen interest in the "soul of man." Freud developed a theory of human development around the central concepts of the "ego", the "id" and the "superego" (Freud [1915–17] 1966 Lecture XXII). The ego, conceived as being mostly conscious awareness, is rational, realistic and innately protective. It develops out of the id as the young child learns to repress instinctive drives and wishes. The id refers to the unconscious instinctual drives and other repressed elements of the psyche which vie non-rationally with the ego for gratification according to the "pleasure-principle." Unconscious elements come to the ego's consciousness under certain conditions, but generally the ego develops defense mechanisms to protect itself from the "demands" of the unconscious and to ensure that repressed elements remain so. The "superego", which tells the child what is right and wrong, good and bad, is the internalization of parental authority through the process of identification.

In Freudian theory, the self is shaped by the way in which an individual deals with instinctual drives ("libido": sexual or psychic energy) and with their associated anxieties that are produced from obstructed satisfaction of libidinal desires.[1] In Freudian theory, the pivotal event in the development of the ego is the Oedipus complex. The Oedipus complex[2] (Freud [1915–17] 1966 Lecture XXII) is the model of how individuals achieve autonomy. Surpassing the pre-Oedipal conflicts such as separation anxiety and bodily hungers (at the oral and anal stages of development) the Oedipus complex crystallizes the core conflicts of human development. The successful resolution of these conflicts contributes to the development of the psychic structure and enables maturation through life's "stages." The successful resolution of the crisis results in the child's superego performing the paternal function within his own psyche. Autonomy is gained at the price of sexual renunciation and former dependency. This process of differentiation within the psyche ensures the subsequent development of the superego through identification. Likewise the successful resolution of the Oedipal crisis ensures the transition from fear of external authority to self-regulation

– authority is replaced by independent conscience, prohibition by self-control, need for approval by autonomy (Benjamin 1987: 213). The process of identification also enables the individual to move away from infantile self-satisfaction toward a pleasure-giving relationship with another.

Classical psychoanalytic theory argues the necessity of an authority relationship between parent and child and the internalization of that authority as superego. Later followers of psychoanalytic theory have suggested that while the superego does consist of parental introjects, these internalized images of parental authority bear little resemblance to the actual figures of his parents (Lasch 1984: 175). In this view the superego cannot be understood as the representative of established morality. Rather, for Lasch, the "superego consists of the individual's own aggressive impulses directed initially against his parents or parental surrogates, projected onto them, internalized as aggressive and dominating images of authority and finally redirected in this form against the ego" (ibid.: 175). This view suggests that it is not the parents' actual prohibitions but the "unconscious rage of infancy" that arouses anxiety which has to be directed, not against the parents, but against the self. This view diminishes Freud's determining importance of the Oedipus complex, and regards the Oedipus complex as the culmination of earlier conflicts arising from separation anxiety (ibid.: 176). All of these conflicts, Oedipal and pre-Oedipal, seek to resolve the tension between desire for union and fear of separation. Emotional maturity is attained by the individual maintaining a creative tension between separation and union, individuation and dependence.

Within the broad tradition of psychoanalytic theory there were important departures from classical Freudian thought concerning the development of the self. The various works of Adler (1927, 1928), Horney (1942, 1950), Fromm (1947, 1955) and Jung argued that Freud exaggerated the influence of early instinctual factors in the development of the self, and instead gave more weight to the ego's role in shaping self-development through the processes of social learning. While there were in turn differences among the "neo-Freudians," they (except Jung) by and large rejected his "libido theory," and emphasized the role of social needs and the influence of cultural and interpersonal factors in the process of self-development. Jung (1921) retained the Freudian notion of libido as a general psychological life-force. Adler (1927) theorized a notion of will, and a striving for power or superiority.

For Jung, as for Freud, the individual passes through maturational stages in childhood, but these stages are accorded much less importance. Jung developed the notion, resembling the id, of the "dark" side of the personality or the "shadow" which consists of uncivilized wishes and feelings rejected from the conscious persona. He also postulated the existence at a deeper level of the unconscious of a counterpart to an individual's dominant sexual identity: the "anima" and the "animus." He developed four "functions" of personality: thought, feeling, intuition and sensation, which characterize a person's relations to the world (Jung [1921]1971; 1961). For Jung, the ultimate goal of personality development and individuation is the achievement of selfhood, which he conceived as the totality of psychic life.

A social psychology in the tradition of psychoanalytic thought in both theoretical and therapeutic domains continues to be practiced today. Following the influence of the Frankfurt School theorists, Horkheimer, Adorno and Marcuse, who integrated Freudian psychological theory and Marxist social theory, and the later French psychoanalytic theorist Jacques Lacan, psychoanalytic thought informs many current social and cultural critics. Within the tradition, feminists have criticized classical Freudian thought, and argued for a reformulation, although not rejection, of many of its key categories.

In an effort to redress the male bias in the Oedipus complex, Julliet Mitchell (1974) offered a revision of the thesis which interpreted the phallus as not identical with the actual penis, but as signifying the potency desired by both girls and boys. More critically, Nancy Chodorow (1979) argues that male identity, which is achieved through identification with the authority of the father in the resolution of the Oedipus complex, is characterized by a preoccupation with difference, separateness and distance in ways that female identity is not. The boy's identification with the father, and the acquisition of his masculinity, are both made at the expense of identification with the mother. Chodorow argues that because women are primarily responsible for the care of the very young, in the infant's mind, the mother is the first basis for identification. Boys, and not girls, must break with this primary identification in order to achieve their gendered individuation. Because the achievement of gender identity is more precarious for boys than for girls, it has lead to a repudiation of femininity.

For Jessica Benjamin (1987, 1988), the repudiation of identification with the mother leads to a "denial of her subjectivity." This denial therefore refutes the classical claim that the Oedipal resolution fosters relatedness with the other as an independent subject (Benjamin 1987: 220). In her view, the Oedipus complex, while attempting to explain gender identity and the development of individual selfhood, did so on the basis of collapsing individuality and masculinity.

> The oedipal father represented our peculiar form of individuality; his authority represented the only alternative to remaining undifferentiated, his freedom until now the only freedom. He taught us the lesson that she who nurtures us does not free us and that he who frees us does not nurture us but rather rules us.
>
> (Benjamin 1987: 221)

55

For Benjamin, the classical Oedipal resolution requires a polarity between two human needs, for nurturance and for freedom. This polarity is assigned gender. Under the "masculine" rule of the superego the individual fears regression to dependency and loss of the self. Benjamin's critique of classical psychoanalysis led to an attempt to offer a feminist reconfiguration. She questioned the process of identification being directed against opposing parents in the Oedipus complex, and the requirement that individuality consist of rejecting identification with the female parent. In her alternative view, the growth of the self is based on two fundamental directions: the striving for connection, attachment, closeness; and the striving toward assertion of self, for activity and for mastery (ibid.: 223). These two strivings are intertwined from the beginning of life and they cannot develop independently of one another. Both constitute the process of successful differentiation and successful attachment. Rejecting the conventional view in which dependence is understood as the opposite of independence – the former feared, the latter desired – Benjamin argues instead for thinking not in terms of dependency but in terms of attachment. Assuming such innate disposition, differentiation is achieved not by prohibition and injunction by authority, but by recognition by a loved other (ibid.: 224).

The psychoanalytic tradition, including the feminist contribution, continues to develop theories on the self, gender, power and interpretations of the human construction of the social world. Most of its categories have been rejected or disputed by other schools of thought in empirical self-psychology. But in cultural criticism its categories have continued to provide important insights into contemporary social life. These are further discussed below.

Symbolic interaction

The tradition of social psychological thought known as symbolic interaction arose at the University of Chicago under the influence of Charles Horton Cooley, George Herbert Mead and Herbert Blumer. It is a perspective which emphasizes the production of meaning in human life and action. Theorists in this school have recognized and emphasized the social construction of meaning and of the self, and the immediacy of social interactions. They stress the importance of cultural and social specificity of norms and of morality, and they emphasize the importance of subjective interpretations of social meanings.

For Cooley and Mead the self arises out of social interaction. For Cooley, the self is "that which is designated in common speech by the pronouns of the first person singular, 'I', 'me', 'my', 'mine' and 'myself'" (Cooley 1902: 36). He thought that it is only through subjective feelings that the self can be identified. This notion of the "subjective feeling state of having a self" was later taken as an underlying assumption of much psychological research. Cooley theorized that the subjective feeling state is produced by the belief that one has control over events, or by cognitive discrimination, such as noting that one's body is different from other people's bodies. He developed the notion of the "looking-glass self" which refers to an individual perceiving herself in ways that others perceive her. The individual tries to imagine what others think or feel about the individual's actions. She imagines that others make judgments of her actions and she reacts to these perceptions of others' judgments. The individual then feels an emotional reponse to his perception of others' evaluation (Cooley 1902). Therefore, the meanings of an act for an individual emerge in the contexts of interactions with other people.

Mead expanded upon Cooley's notion and postulated that the self-concept arises in social interaction as an outgrowth of the individual's concern about how others react to him. One learns to perceive the world as others do in order to know how to behave appropriately. The individual thus acquires from the "generalized other" a source of internal regulation that guides his behavior in the absence of external pressures. This requires that the individual be able to take the role of the other and to assume the attitudes and values of the community toward her own behaviors and linguistic acts. In this way, one becomes conscious of oneself "as an object or individual, and thus develops a self or personality" (Mead 1934). For Mead there are as many selves as there are social roles. Mead regarded the individual as the basic unit of analysis in symbolic interactionism. He emphasized the role of language and symbols in the creation of meanings, the latter being open-ended and subject to change in specific situations of human interaction. For Mead, when the meaning of a verbal or non-verbal communication is shared by both sender and receiver, then a significant symbol is involved. Sharing significant symbols or meanings with other members of a group is essential to the development of the self and the mind (Mead 1934). Social behavior is a necessary condition for the emergence of the self.

The later work of Erving Goffman rejuvenated thought in symbolic interactionism and its contribution to sociology and social psychology. Goffman's work was interested in the many ways individuals present themselves to others, and how they influence each other in face to face interaction. Goffman (1959), argued that interaction could be compared to drama. People perform an "act" to strengthen their impression of competence when they are performing a legitimate role such as teacher or doctor. There is an expressive and not just a functional dimension to one's performance. This approach directs attention to the construction of status and the illusory elements of social interaction. It suggests that the constitution of status by superficial and artificial elements does not diminish its importance. Goffman thought that the intention of the person to deceive is partly conscious, but the presentations may still be sincere as the "performer is fully taken in by his own act." Goffman devised a vocabulary of "dramaturgical principles" which included the metaphors of "performance," "routines," "props" and so forth. He stressed the role of other actors in setting up the stage for one's and others' performances. The presentation of the self in certain ways implicitly invites complementary performances from others and support for one's pretensions to one's role.

Goffman's work prompted other studies following his dramaturgical principles.[3] The concepts in "labeling theory" (Becker 1963) emerged out of this approach. Symbolic interactionism following Goffman's influence developed a view of social life that is somewhat amorphous and instantaneous. An important implication of the theatrical analogy of interaction is that people do not have any central reality or "self" beyond the performance they present for others. Even emotions are seen as a "ritual move" in a performance. People develop a certain style and multiple self-identifications. The self is a "process" rather than a system of mechanisms and needs. The wider social context of immediate inter-individual or group interactions was ignored by symbolic interactionism.

The symbolic interactionists were concerned with the problem of identity which they understood as a psycho-social process. The concept of identity was the sociological equivalent of the concept of the self (see Dobert, Habermas *et al.* 1987). The individual's integration into a particular social system is achieved by acquiring "symbolic universals" – signs and symbols that the group recognize as conveying the sent and received meaning. Further identification with increasingly more abstract groups and structures enables the individual to organize his interactions autonomously and in his own biographical context. Identity is a symbolic structure that enables a personality system to gain consistency and to ensure continuity under one's changing biographical conditions and in different positions and roles in the social communities in which one lives. Identity is something that an individual must claim for himself or herself in relation to others. The differentiation of self from others, self-identification, must be recognized by others as well as by the individual. In this view, the reflexive relationship of the individual that is self-identified depends on the intersubjective relationships that she has with those others by whom she is identified (Dolbert, Habermas *et al.* 1987: 226). As individuals acquire their identity they also acquire the intersubjectivity of understanding between themselves and others. There is thus a structural relationship between the forms of identity of individuals and the forms of social integration in the life context in which they interact with each other.

All three major schools of thought in social psychology have attempted to deal with identity, as well as with the notion of the self. There are conceptual continuities as well as differences among them. For each of these theoretical traditions, development is characterized by increasing autonomy with respect to particular environments. Both psychoanalysis and symbolic interactionism conceive of a transposition of interaction patterns into intrapsychic patterns of relations, which they call "internalization." Internalization is also connected with the principle of achieving independence from external objects, reference persons and one's own impulses. Independence is achieved by actively repeating what one has first passively experienced. For the cognitive psychologists (see below) the process termed "interiorization" by Piaget refers to the way in which one learns the rules for the manipulative mastery of objects. These rules are internally transposed into schemes of thinking and comprehension, and become the mechanisms by which an individual learns to develop – to become agentic and individuated in the world. The interest in individuated and agentic development, more than identity, was pursued by the empirical cognitive psychologists.

Modern empirical psychology and the self

Modern empirical psychology has attempted to deal with the development of the self from an assumption base in which the self is viewed as a set of cognitive mechanisms and structures, that there is at some nascent level in the human being, a fixed, "hard-wired" core of mechanisms, impulses and potentials that are irreducible and constitute the basis of all human beings (Deci and Ryan 1985, 1991). They have also been premised on a rejection of earlier psychoanalytic theories and categories. Even those psychological theories which have been concerned with the influence of social forces on the psychological processes of individuals have retained this primary cognitive orientation. The social, in this tradition, has been treated as a background variable in the procurement of cognitive development.

Psychological social psychology has a long heritage in behavioral and cognitive psychology that includes the seminal influence of Skinner and Watson, and of Piaget's cognitive developmental theories (1932). Later influences include Allport's (1937) theory of conscious personality development; the "field theory" of Kurt Lewin (1951) and Festinger's (1957) theory of "cognitive dissonance." Allport believed that there was some inner core of consistent self which he called the "proprium." The proprium has a number of "propriate functions" of personality which contribute to the sense of inward unity. Allport rejected the psychoanalytic emphasis on the unconscious and the belief in the genetic origins of instincts. He thought each individual has a unique personality that is composed of personal and common traits.

Lewin's "field theory" refers to a method of analyzing causal relationships that are assumed to be occurring in a "field" – as part of a totality of co-existing facts which are believed to be mutually interdependent. Any event is determined by its relations to a wider system of events of which it is a part. In this schema, the person or the self existed in the behavior of the individual in response to one's perception of his relations to the environment he perceives. The "environment" refers to the objective situation or stimulus which confronts the individual at any given moment (Lewin 1935). Festinger's "dissonance theory" essentially holds that inconsistent cognitions or thoughts are intolerable for human beings. A person will go to great lengths to eliminate inconsistencies in his thought, when he is cognizant of them. The objective is to establish and maintain a state of equilibrium. Dissonance theory, which in turn influenced other theories favoring a "self-consistency" model of the self (Gergen 1971), was opposed by theories postulating a "self-consistency" model of the self. In the latter view, the person has multiple concepts of the self that are specific to certain specific circumstances.

Learning theory, influenced by the behaviorist theories of Watson (1925) and Skinner (1938), holds that a person can acquire varying conceptions of self in different situations. These manifestations of the self were motivated by external or internal stimuli. Later, Seligman developed his theory of "learned helplessness" (1975) to account for individuals manifesting defeat behavior from having learned an attitude of inability to control their life situations through repeated experiences of loss of control. An effort at resolving these two opposing viewpoints on the self gave rise to a theory that argued that there is no genetic basis for the tendency to reduce dissonance. Rather, a person learns to dislike inconsistency in the same way she learns to reason inductively and deductively (Gergen 1971: 22). Similarly, "attribution theory" (Heider 1958) postulated that people have ways of summarizing, describing and explaining behavior – their own and others – that attribute specific behaviors to generalized disposition in the actors. While behavior might be quite situation-specific, people tend to construe each other and themselves as though they were highly consistent. They tend to construct consistent selves and perceive unity even in the face of relatively inconsistent behavioral actions (Mischel 1977: 55). Mischel (1968) argued that this cognitive construction of continuity is not arbitrary, but is often only tenuously related to the events construed.

Skinner (1971, 1974) and other radical behaviorists tended to avoid invoking the person or the self as the causal agent in events. Instead they attributed the cause of behaviors to the individual's immediate environment and genetic history. Arguing for the "contingencies of reinforcement" as determinants of human behavior Skinner claimed that "Whatever we do, and hence however we perceive it, the fact remains that it is the environment which acts upon the perceiving person, not the perceiving person who acts on the environment" (Skinner 1971: 198). The person is subsumed under the agency of the environment. This view was criticized as "situationism in psychology" (Bowers 1973) which tended "to ignore organismic factors or to regard them as . . . subsidiary to the primary impact of the external stimulus" (Harre and Secord 1972: 27). Subsequently, the debates in psychological social psychology moved into questions concerning the "locus of control," perceived variously as within the person or the environment, later formulated as "internal" and "external" locus of control (Rotter 1966). Motivation theory developed these themes and ideas further. The contemporary work of Deci, Ryan and Connell (Deci and Ryan 1985, 1991, Connell 1991, Ryan and Lynch 1989) attempts to advance this orientation by postulating the existence of three primary psychological needs: autonomy, competence and relatedness. Their theory attempts to integrate aspects of the individual and the social environment (see below).

The cognitive developmentalists, following Piaget, refer to "schemes of action" as the rules by which one acquires manipulative mastery over the external world of objects. Piaget elaborated the concept of developmental logic, in which he believed that the individual passes through a formative process of sequential and irreversible, increasingly complex stages of development. It is a hierarchical process and no stage can be skipped over. Later elaborations of the stage theory of development (Ericksen 1958, Kohlberg 1958, 1963) have maintained its paradigmatic influence over the field of psychological development. Influenced by Piaget, and also by others including Murray (1938), Maslow (1943), Shipley and Veroff (1952), White (1959), the contemporary self-psychology theorists attempt to further explain and advance upon Piaget's schema, and to account for the driving force of developmental stages.

For Deci and Ryan (1991), the self "goes deeper than cognition." The self is not just a set of cognitive mechanisms and structures but rather it is a set of "motivational processes." They claim that the importance of their conception of self is that it provides a framework for distinguishing theoretically and empirically "those internally motivated, intentional actions that represent human agency and self-determination from those that do not" (Deci and Ryan 1991: 3). They offer their work as an advance on more conventional cognitive self-psychology, and they claim a greater degree of appreciation of the "social" than their forebears.

For Deci and Ryan, and for most in the empirical tradition from which they have come, human beings, from birth, are engaged in a developmental process that is characterized by an orientation toward the active exercise of their capacities and interests. They seek out and master new challenges and they integrate new experiences (Deci and Ryan 1991: 4). This tendency toward elaborated organization is central to the definition and development of self. Deci and Ryan believe that there is an inherent rudimentary self – a set of innate interests and processes (e.g. exploratory tendencies, innate preferences, and the motivation to relate and assimilate) – that develops as the person interacts with its environment and with "unintegrated aspects of itself." They believe that this interaction is a dialectical process.

The development of self occurs by a process of integration of new experiences and regulatory processes with one's intrinsic self. Upon full integration the behaviors that are consequently regulated are said to be self-determined. When material from the social world is not fully integrated, it later provides the "scripts" for non-self-determined behavior (ibid.: 6). Self-determined behaviors are described as those that are either intrinsically motivated or that arise from well-integrated personal values and regulatory processes. Behaviors that arise from non-integrated processes such as internal pressures and socially acquired introjects are not self-determined (ibid.: 3). In this approach, which the authors describe as "organismic and dialectic" (ibid.: 68), the central feature of human nature is an active agency and a synthetic tendency that is ascribed to the self. In this view, the key concepts are intrinsic motivation and organismic integration. Intrinsically motivated behaviors are those that a person undertakes for the "sake of the activity itself" or out of "personal interest." The authors do not concern themselves with accounting for the sources of "personal interest."

This group of self-psychologists has also attempted to synthesize the work on intrinsic needs and motivations by suggesting that there are three primary psychological needs – competence, autonomy and relatedness. Competence refers to the individual's striving to experience control over outcomes and to understand and master the "instrumentalities" that such desired outcomes require. The need for autonomy, or self-determination, refers to the individual's effort to be agentic, to have a voice or to exercise some control over one's own behavior. It is the desire to experience one's actions as emanating from the self. Thirdly, the need for relatedness encompasses a person's efforts to relate to and care for others, and to be in reciprocal relation to those others. It also refers to a feeling of satisfying and coherent involvement with the social world more generally. In this view, these three "innate psychological needs" are exhaustive and account for a substantial variation in human behavior and experience (Deci and Ryan 1991: 11).

The theorists claim that the most basic strivings of the self can be considered at two levels of analysis – first is the tendency toward unity in one's self, toward coherence in one's regulatory activity and experience. The second is a tendency toward interacting in a coherent and meaningful way with others. They argue that this is a dual-level process of seeking integration and cohesion within oneself and with others (Deci and Ryan 1991: 12). It is the essence of the "agentic self" in development. They also believe that the dialectic process of development involves the integrative tendency of the self as it interacts with or contacts the forces and events of external circumstances. The environment is thus acted on and changed in the process of the person's contact.

Deci, Ryan and Connell recognize that some forces cannot be integrated

– specifically those that are inconsistent with the three basic needs of human nature. Instead, these processes lead to conflict, internal fragmentation and anomie (ibid.: 14), processes they shy away from attempting to explain. For these exemplary social psychologists, the sense of the "social" encompasses the individual's relations with other persons around it and the degree to which such a social context supports or obstructs "effective behavior," and consequently facilitates the person's development of inner resources required for "adaptive self-regulation."

Alongside the work of the contemporary self-psychologists is the recent appearance of ideas associated with postmodern and post-structural thought. Postmodern ideas are exerting some influence on ideas about the self in social psychology. Gergen and Gergen (1988) and Gergen (1991) have elaborated a narrative of the self in which it is conceived as "relationship." They propose that the traditional concept of individual selves is fundamentally problematic. What have traditionally been understood as individual traits, mental processes or personal characteristics Gergen and Gergen view as "relational forms." The form of these relationships is that of a narrative sequence (Gergen and Gergen 1988: 18). In their view, the narratives of the self are not fundamentally possessions of the individual, rather they are products of social interchange. For Gergen, in the postmodern world, "selves may become the manifestations of relationship, thus placing relationship in the central position occupied by the individual self for the last several hundred years of Western history" (Gergen 1991: 147). Individuals make sense of life events by constructing a self-narrative. These narratives are not simply "psychological structures" but are fluid, on-going constructions that are "properties of social accounts or discourse" (Gergen and Gergen 1988: 19). They are social constructions undergoing continuous alteration as interaction progresses. Self-narratives are symbolic systems used for social purposes.

In a similar effort to develop diachronic and relational theory in social psychology, Barclay (1990) and Barclay and Smith (1993) suggest that selves are composed through processes of "autobiographical remembering." Cognitive, emotional, social and cultural activities work together to create "remembered selves" (Barclay 1990). Selves "emerge" through productive remembering and productive interacting in everyday life (Barclay and Smith 1993). One's "remembered self" at any particular moment is "a gestalt composed and objectified in constructed and reconstructed 'personal' and generic memories" (Barclay 1990: 2). According to this view, remembered selves are formed in language and thought, both of which, Barclay acknowledges, are shaped by cultural practices.

It is interesting to note here that these writers have not been directly influenced (or do not say so) by post-structuralism in cultural theory. Yet their effort to depart from their predecessors in modern psychology to conceive of a fixed and firm "proprium" of self, and to theorize fluid positionings in relationship, is, I think, a postmodernizing of symbolic interactionism. The "narrative-self" displaces the "looking-glass self" and is conceived as a process occurring over time, and in relation, rather than momentarily as for Cooley and Goffman. Other recent work including Shotter (1990) and Neisser (1990) shares similar perspectives to those of Gergen and Barclay. The admission of the cultural world into the process of self-construction is a welcome development in contemporary self psychology. But they retain a narrow concept of culture and avoid an analysis of social context that goes beyond the post-structural recognition of linguistic practices and multiple positionings.

My comments here lead into the second part of this chapter in which the critical voice in social psychology discourse is recorded. From there, the chapter moves into a discussion of what I call the cultural analyses of self and society that are not so much concerned with micro-level understandings of self-developmental structures and processes, but rather attempt to analyze the macro-level processes of society and their effects on the self.

THE CRITIQUE OF SOCIAL PSYCHOLOGY

The critique of conventional social psychology includes some internal critiques over research methods and conceptual preferences (Gergen 1971, Harre and Secord 1972) and a variety of feminist critiques and refinements of gendered categories and biases (Benjamin 1988, Buck-Morss 1987, Walkerdine 1986). There has also been some effort to discredit the stage theories in human development psychology (Baltes 1979, Elder 1979, Lerner 1983) that assume the individual is a self-contained entity, and to direct attention to "social reality production/ reproduction" and "social allocation" processes (Dannefer and Perlmutter 1990). Still others have attempted to argue for the inclusion of historical awareness (Gergen 1971) and to expand the notion of the social by including the individual's family and school experiences as the "social context" (Connell and Ryan 1984). While each of these critical efforts offers some challenge to the tradition they criticize, they fall short of dealing with macro-structural social phenomena and the social relations of their production, and the role of social psychology in the cultural ideological apparatus. A much more serious critique of academic social psychology was launched by a group that Wexler (1983) has labeled the "dissenting critique," and subsequently by Wexler's effort at theorizing a "critical social psychology," both of which anticipate and incorporate the latest developments in academic social psychology.

At its best, conventional social psychology of self recognizes the influence of social interactions with the family and immediate social group on the formation of the self. But it fails to analyze and recognize a self–society relation as an aspect of broader social relations. The basis of the radical critiques of social psychology is its neglect of the broader social dimension and its tendency to make the individual the only important reality and the sole unit of analysis. The social has been included only in an abstract and general way. Social psychology has failed to examine its ideological role in containing the social and cultural contradictions of modern capitalist society. Social psychology performs this ideological role by assuming and reifying as natural and universal phenomena that are socially and historically specific. For the Marxists (see Armistead's 1974 collection), social psychology has ignored the social relations of production and their impact on the individual psyche. In this view, all human relations in capitalism are an outcome of the forces of production and exchange. Bourgeois social psychology produces and reproduces the structures and processes of cultural domination. In its place, the Marxist effort at a social psychology was to promote phenomenological, interpretive research and a social analysis that exposed the system's coercive interactions and socially patterned inequalities (Wexler 1983: 21).

Wexler's critique of social psychology and his effort to establish the theoretical basis for a critical social psychology went beyond the more traditional mechanistic Marxist dissenting voices. Wexler argues that social psychology has isolated intra-individual processes from collective social tendencies and, at the same time, reified dynamic social relations as individual attributes or fixed role requirements (Wexler 1983: 16). It has ignored the "socio-historical formation of capitalism" as central to the definition and constitution of social psychological processes. Phenomena which are held and abstracted as general psychological processes are integral aspects of the specific dynamics of capitalism. Especially important is the "denial and the elimination of the structure of social relations from social psychological theory" (ibid.: 4).

Wexler argues that the questions of academic social psychology are aspects of the production and reproduction of social relations. This is revealed most clearly in the traditions in psychology that have viewed the self as a fixed set of cognitive schemata, or as a "mirror" of social evaluations (viz. Cooley 1902; Mead 1934). Like the symbolic interactionists and empirical self-psychologists, the psychoanalytic self-psychologists have denied the deeper social relations in the production of self. For Wexler, the abstraction of the self from social production characterizes the cultural denial of production. "The abstraction and destructuring of the socially specific into an 'organic whole' is a way that the social is simultaneously admitted and denied" (Wexler 1983: 42).

Following the Frankfurt School, especially Horkheimer and Adorno and Marcuse, Wexler's knowledge critique of social psychology hinges on a critique of positivism[4] that has paradigmatically contained conventional social psychology. Expanding upon this critique, Wexler demonstrated that social psychology had created a discourse on the self that was historically specific and culturally patterned. It had effectively obscured and denied its own ideological interest. It had unwittingly served the process of cultural domination while ostensibly seeking to understand the self, and reduce human suffering. Likewise, Freud's classical psychoanalysis was criticized for its confinement to a description and cataloging of the bourgeois self in abstraction from the "private costs of capital accumulation" (Wexler 1983).

Adorno had earlier criticized Freud's neglect of the concrete social dimension and his apparent obliviousness of it (Adorno 1968). The Freudian "healthy" internalization by the superego of the prevailing cultural rules through paternal authority delimits the possibility for fundamental social change. Marcuse similarly criticized Freud's ahistorical social psychology and his concept of "necessary repression" – understood as "additional controls arising from the specific institutions of domination" (Marcuse 1962: 54). This notion underpins Marcuse's and Wexler's conception of cultural domination conceived as "self-limitation" that occurs through sublimation, repetitive repression and instrumental routinization (Wexler 1983: 26, 46–50). Other critical theorists (Reich 1966, Jacoby 1975) attempted to create a subversive method of psychoanalytic theorizing and to develop categories for social and cultural analysis of the self.

Cultural analyses of the self and society

The other tradition of thought on the self has consistently viewed the self as historically produced and socially structured. For Durkheim (1933), the modern person was produced by the processes of industrialization and the transformed social order that resulted. Changes in society yielded changes in the self. The self was a product of collective moral beliefs and behaviors. In his analysis, the idea of the individual person that is separable from family and community began to take root during the Renaissance and became popular during the Enlightenment. The idea was to become pivotal in later thought as industrialization expanded. These social changes included the disruption of traditional community life, and made self and community identity based on institutional definition problematic. Likewise, for Marx, the self was a social product, "the human essence is no abstraction inherent in each individual. In its reality it is the ensemble of social relations" (Marx [1888] 1983: 145).

Social theorists, influenced by the traditions of grand theory, have in recent decades elaborated on the ways in which contemporary social configurations have produced a particular type of self or character. In the last few decades many thinkers interested in the relationship between self and society have focused their attention on gaining a deeper understanding of the social and cultural world. While adding to discourses on the self, they have also criticized ideological theories of the self that have been produced by psychology and that abound as commonly held beliefs in, particularly, American society. In elaborating a theory of the modern self many of the social critics directed attention to American society in part because it was a nation of immigrants who brought with them many characteristics of traditional society and the character of an agrarian self-sufficient community. Following Durkheim, they believed that as industrialization advanced it was clear that a transformation of the self was simultaneously occurring.

The discourse about the self in American cultural criticism has followed a pattern of contradiction and ambivalence, usually manifested in a dichotomy of optimism and pessimism, that pervades modern society. This dichotomy of pessimism and optimism is not, I think, a peculiarly American condition. But American society epitomizes the culture of modernity at its latest stages of development. The typically modern conflicts between *gemeinschaft* and *gesellschaft* appear most acute and more readily observable in American society. Trends in the emergence of postmodern culture and post-industrial capitalism, although shared by Western societies more generally, are also most discernible in the United States of America. The following discussion therefore attends selectively to primarily American social critics.

American cultural criticism manifests a characteristic pattern of optimism and pessimism. Hewitt's (1989) study of the American self makes much of this dichotomy. His thesis is that American culture is divided along an individual/community axis of variation. People are pulled toward both autonomy and community. The tension between these axes produces a character that is torn between conformity and rebellion, dependence and independence (Hewitt 1989: 17–18). Personal and social identity, the former rooted in community, the latter in society, are in a constant state of tension in modern society. In Hewitt's view, society has not replaced community, despite the pull of modernity toward that. Rather, both community and society as contrasting modes of social life continue to exist in a state of "natural" tension. Individualism has its counterpoint in communitarianism, which for Hewitt continues to be as important in the American psyche and rhetoric as the proclivity toward individualism. This is evidenced for him in the persistence of local and ethnic identities and the endurance of images of community as a place of warmth and support, despite its alleged disappearance. Hewitt's thesis also offers a model of understanding American culture in the similar axial relationship of pessimism and optimism. The axes of optimism/pessimism are closely linked with the more fundamental bifurcation of individualism and communitarianism.

The optimism/pessimism dichotomy is a popular one among American commentators, and although somewhat superficial and subjective, it can usefully provide a vantage point from which to view the theories of self anchored in social criticism. The important contributions in the so-called "pessimistic" discourse include Riesman *et al.* (1950), Wheelis (1958), Slater (1970), Trilling (1972), Lasch (1978 and 1984) and Bellah *et al* (1985). The core of the arguments of these social critics of American culture is the issue of modernity and the conditions of modern life. Implicitly, the theory of modernity adhered to by these critics often hearkens back to the idea that there was once a "golden age" of a more stable social order founded on traditional values and community bonds. In pre-modern times the social order produced individuals whose identities were secure and whose sense of self was shaped by institutional, primarily family, involvements and commitments. People knew their place in society and had little experience of "identity crises." Their lives were circum-scribed by the social roles and stratification of the society and individuals found comfort and security in conforming to established social custom. People lived with little self-consciousness in a network of family, class and interpersonal relationships. The psychic security of the individual was acquired at the expense of individuality.

Riesman, Denny and Glazer's (1950) thesis in *The Lonely Crowd* focused on what they called "social character" that included both a psychoanalytic meaning as "the more or less permanent socially and historically conditioned organization of an individual's drives and satisfac-tions" (Riesman *et al.* 1950: 4), and a sociological idea of conformity to social and cultural dictates. The authors were especially interested in how society manages to induce its members to do what society wants them to do. They developed a typology of character types based on differences in the way societies have historically ensured conformity to their demands. Basically, they argued that in traditional society the social character of the individual was "tradition-directed." It is one in which the individual is adapted to society, and there is very little possibility or desire for change to occur.

Following the Renaissance there emerged an "inner-directed" character, in which the source of direction for one's life is found inside oneself, having been implanted there early in life by the elders and bearers of traditional values and customs. The society in which this character type occurs is a modernizing one, and the individual needs an inner direction to maintain an equilibrium between the demands of society and one's own needs. As society continues to develop and production to expand and the division of labor to become more complex, there emerges a third character type, the "other-directed" individual. The other-directed person is sensitive to the needs of others and to what their actions imply for one's own behavior. *The Lonely Crowd* pointed to the role of conformity in shaping the American character and to ambivalence about that conformity.

By the 1960s, interest had shifted somewhat from the issue of character to one of "identity," to questions of meaning and relationship in one's life. While addressing similar questions to those of Riesman *et al.*, Allen Wheelis's *The Quest for Identity* (1958) introduced into the discourse an articulation of the problems of identity in the modern world. In his view the change in character involved the ascendancy of the group over the individual. The traditional family life of the nineteenth century and its stable value system ensured the authority of the family over the developing individual. It created a strong superego. In the mid-twentieth century values are no longer stable and the world is changing too fast. As a consequence, the superego has declined and the ego has expanded. Hence, the social character of the present age, for Wheelis, is one adapted to fit a "culture of change." Accordingly, people feel a diminished sense of direction, and weakened sense of purpose. They follow the crowd rather than their own inner compasses which have become weakened by the decline of the role of the superego.

The cultural critics (including Slater 1970, Sennett 1977, and Trilling 1972) lament the decline of community and public life. They argue that the socialization of the individual in modern society, the rejection of traditional institutional authorities and the quest for privacy has led to the depletion of the self. The erosion and weakening of the self and its increasing fragmentation is relative to the time and place in which, they believe, the self was whole and centered, in which it existed in a state of unity, integration and relative harmony.

In an effort to adopt a more neutral social scientific perspective Ralph Turner's (1976) essay attempted to describe the features of an historically "new" self. His thesis was that cultural changes in the modern world have led to a transformation of the self. The basis of experience of one's "real self" had shifted from a historically "institutional" one, to a new "impulsive" basis. In his view, the self was transformed from being spontaneously experienced in everyday life to one that was increasingly self-defined. In the institutional mode of self-experience, "The true self is recognized in acts of volition, in the pursuit of institutionalized goals, and not in the satisfaction of impulses outside institutional frameworks" (Turner 1976: 991). Conversely, in the impulsive mode, "The real self consists of deep, unsocialized, inner impulses. Mad desire and errant fancy are exquisite expressions of the self" (ibid.: 992). Institutional selves believe the self is created through effort. They place emphasis on self-control and volitional acts, and they value commitments to others and to institutionally valued social roles. Impulsive selves, on the other hand, wish to do things spontaneously, regardless of the social value or prohibition of the act. One rejects institutional ties that restrict the expression of the true, impulsive self.

In Turner's view, there has been an observable societal shift away from the institutional self toward the impulsive self. People are seeking to anchor their conceptions of reality in themselves and not within social institutions as repositories of values and acceptable behaviors. Although Turner does historicize the self, he does not locate it in concrete historical social relations, particularly in relation to the social structure of production, and he does not describe the nature of the social transformations that are producing the "new self."

The cultural critic Christopher Lasch (1978, 1984) provides a social analysis of the new self that directs attention to capitalist social relations in contemporary historical conditions. He is concerned with the absorption of the individual by the state and the corporation. Lasch uses the psychoanalytic theory of narcissism to describe the character of the person in the corporate world. In part echoing the concerns and analyses of Wheelis, Lasch regards the person as no longer under the guidance of parental authority, and as manifesting a new selfishness that cares neither for the past, future nor for others. People have a "live for the moment" attitude and have lost a sense of self and of social belongingness.

At the heart of this decline in the self is the rise of the state and corporate bureaucracies that have disempowered ordinary people and undermined their historical sense of cultural competence. People have become dependent, not on themselves and traditional communities and a sense of inner judgment, but on the authority of bureaucracies: the corporation, schools, helping professions, mass entertainment media and so forth, have captured control of culture. The ways of thinking, feeling and being in the world, previously the domain of local and generational production and reproduction, have been lost to the corporate state. Individuals, lacking any sense of commitment to a common life and the inner resources that might compensate for such isolation, become bereft of skills and confidence. They become dependent on the bureaucratic apparatus and its culture of experts. Narcissism is the psychological result of this dependence.

The narcissist lacks a strong sense of self, but is preoccupied with his or her self. The narcissist suffers from a pathological anxiety that comes from not having much of a self. He is characterized not by love of self, but by loss of self. For Lasch, this loss of self is largely due to the decline in institutionalized authority. Parental authority figures and the strength of tradition have lost their power. This has not resulted in the decline of the superego as such, but has produced a harsh and punitive superego, derived increasingly from the child's primitive fantasies about his parents, "rather than from internalized ego ideals formed by later experience with loved and respected models of social conduct" (Lasch 1978).

Narcissism, for Lasch, is the pathological condition of the modern age. With the decline of tradition and authority and no models of the ideal self, the individual becomes a victim, not just of a punitive superego, but of a culture in which everyone has lost a sense of everyday competence and is dependent on experts. Rampant consumerism, in an effort to ward off inner emptiness, substitutes satiation for satisfaction. One develops only a "minimal self," a defensive, strategic self, emotionally disengaged from others and cut off from the past and future, dependent on corporate bureaucracy and mass culture to know what, at least, to do (Lasch 1984).

The "optimistic" view

Lasch's view of the corporatization of culture and of the self is not shared by a group of so-called "optimistic" cultural analysts. The "optimistic" discourse about the self celebrates American individualism and the potential of the individual to achieve whatever it wishes in triumph over society's domination of it. This view emanates from the American tradition of the pioneering spirit, the quest for success and the belief in "rugged individualism" and self-reliance. Underlying the optimistic view of the self is a view of the person as creator of society rather than its product. Provided that the repressive forces of society can be controlled, the potential for the individual to seek and achieve success and personal happiness and fulfillment is available. The "positive thinking" genre of humanistic psychology believed that by acting in "self-actualizing" ways (Rogers 1951) individuals can contribute to the building of a better society that will be even more supportive of the individual, and that will generate the "greening of America" (Reich 1970).

Rather than being critical of modernity as undermining the self and community life, the optimistic view regards the modern transformation of the world as beneficial to individuals. The processes of modernity are seen as enabling the liberation of the person from the past and its repressive mores. This general theory of individualism varies according to different authors. One form, that of the critique of contemporary American culture by Bellah et al. (1985) which attempts to straddle the optimism/pessimism polarity, stresses the pursuit of individual economic ends, which the authors label "utilitarian individualism." In this view, the self is defined by its accomplishments, and the maximization of opportunity to succeed in life. Bellah et al. also describe the term "expressive individualism," which stresses the pursuit of individual ends, but not just in economic terms. It stresses the pursuit of happiness, the expression of individual talents and the need for individuals to live according to their own natures rather than the constraints imposed upon them by society.

The underlying optimism of both utilitarian and expressive individualism accords to the individual the capacity to overcome obstacles and social constraints, whether they are economic or repressive social forms which interfere with the pursuit of happiness and individual advancement. Optimistic views of the self are generally found in the liberal humanistic psychology tradition that was discussed in the first section of this chapter.

They represent the typically "asocial" view of self formation, failing to recognize or explain the forces of macro-social structures and concrete historical social relations.

THE SOCIAL ANALYSIS OF THE SELF

All of the cultural critics discussed above attempt to describe the character of the self in modern cultural conditions. Turner's formulation of a "new self" recognizes a historical cultural shift although it does not provide an analysis of any depth to account for the social structural dynamics of this shift. Lasch makes a linkage between the character of the self and the nature of the social conditions of modern society, particularly advanced capitalist America. He takes us, importantly, to the site of corporate bureaucracy as the source of the new self – or the contemporary character of the self. At the same time he points to the decline of the superego and the waning of family authority that surrenders the self to formation by the abstracted authority of experts and managers of corporate culture. The forces of the unconscious and their inadequate management by a frail superego are, for Lasch, the crux of the matter. He believes that the surrender of the self to corporate culture could be resisted if a renewed (old) self was asserted against it. Lasch's recognition of the forces of corporate culture is important and revelatory.

A social analysis of the self–society relation transcends the cultural interest in optimism and pessimism. More importantly, for Foucault and Wexler, a cultural analysis must go deeper into the materiality of the social. For Foucault, it is the body that is the primary site of the operation of power and knowledge, and that is a priori to the formation of the self. For Wexler, it is the materiality of social production, from which all human relations are produced. Each author attempts to describe the dynamics of the relational processes of capitalist culture and specifically their effects on the self. For Foucault, the primary materiality is the body. It is the site at which the self is constituted by the operation of power/knowledge schema that are historically specific and culturally mediated. The discipline and subjugation of the body mediates the subjugation of the conscious and unconscious spheres of the self. The "technologies of the self" (Foucault 1988) effect the processes of cultural domination. Others following Foucault, especially Deleuze and Guattari (1979), explore the psycho-physical effects of capitalism on the psyche and the body, and describe the schizoid personality of late capitalism.

For Wexler, the self must be understood in terms of the structure of production and therefore of class. The self is the "subjective moment of class conflict" (Wexler 1983: 121). He argues that the new self, or the bourgeois self in dissolution, is part of a changing set of production relations. In his view, following Marx (1867) and Lukacs (1923), commodification, as a general aspect of the social relations of capital, is the central structural problem of capitalist society. It is a social form in which the product of human labor is separated from its producers and standardized to such an extent that the product becomes confused with the social process in which it is produced (Marx 1867). People fail to recognize human labor in the things they exchange, and they ascribe causation to those products rather than to themselves. Social relations become commodified as all human activities assume a social form in which the product, or its abstract representation, becomes more important than the humans who made it (Wexler 1983: 121). In the workplace separation of product from process occurs in the organization of all types of work. In post-industrial work, characterized by changing production processes and relations, reification is increasingly complex and advanced. Commodification of human social relations necessarily affects the dynamics of the self.

Cultural critics have provided important analyses of the processes of self formation, and Lasch's attention to the family as a primary site of self formation is, of course, necessary and accurate. (Lasch 1991, furthermore, does include reference to the institutional practices of work.) But the general lack of attention to social production, specifically to work – to the lived everyday practices of production – has occluded attention to another primary site of self formation, and therefore neglected a primary route into understanding the nature of both corporate culture and the character of self it is forming. This other route into understanding the nature of corporate culture and the character of the new self is taken in my examination of the effects of corporate culture in the workplace. The next chapter discusses the self at work in typical industrial, and emergent, conditions. It is followed by an elaboration of an empirical investigation of the discursive practices of corporate work and their effect on self formation.

4

THE WORKING SELF: SOCIALIZATION AND LEARNING AT WORK

The technological and organizational changes currently occurring in work are co-constitutive of new discourses of production that affect the discursive formation of individual selves and the character of the generalized self in the post-industrial interregnum. In this chapter I explore discursive processes of work and their shaping of industrial selves. Work is an educational site in which pedagogical and learning practices have always taken place. Sociologists of education recognized in the 1960s and 1970s that education practices contain both manifest and hidden curricula. The discursive practices of work, like other educational practices, similarly contain manifest and hidden curricula that are practiced simultaneously with the material practices of work. The discussion in this chapter is particularly concerned with what I call the "hidden curriculum" of work, by which I am referring to multi-level communicational practices – overt and covert, formal and informal, conscious and unconscious – which shape the everyday contexts and experiences of work, and the self at work.

Material practices of work and the manifest curriculum visibly affect a person's experiences of work but the hidden curriculum contributes to self-constituent processes in less visible ways. The concept of the hidden curriculum is a useful device for beginning to probe the effects of discursive practices of work on self formation. The primary focus of the humanistic psychologists discussed in the previous chapter was the individual person and their ontogenetic development. For the cultural theorists, seeking to look beyond the specificity and privacy of the monad self, attention was directed to macro-level social structures and cultural processes that affect the character of the generalized self at any historical moment. This latter orientation underlies the approach taken in this discussion of the self at work. Discourses on industrial work have long held an implicit, common-sense view that people learn in the course of being at work. We already know a great deal about alienation in industrial work and the effects of the material conditions of work and occupational tasks on the person of the worker. We know less about the effects on the self of

74

discursive institutional practices, and their current configuration in post-industrial conditions. An exploration of socialization and learning at work provides a vantage point from which to examine the relationships between post-industrial work and self formation.

SOCIALIZATION AND LEARNING IN MODERN INDUSTRIAL WORK

Theorists and commentators have expressed views about what people learn at work since at least the industrial revolution. Adam Smith succinctly expressed the view of the industrial age about "men and work:"

> the understandings of the greater part of men are necessarily formed by their ordinary employments. The man whose whole life is spent in performing a few simple operations, of which the effects too are, perhaps, always the same, or very nearly the same, has no occasion to exert his understanding, or to exercise his invention in finding out expedients for removing difficulties which never occur. He naturally loses, therefore, the habit of such exertion, and generally becomes stupid and ignorant as it is possible for a human creature to become.
>
> (Smith [1776] 1974)

A century or so later Marx indirectly theorized about what people learn at work. He postulated that one learns to submit to externally imposed controls, including the rhythms and demands of industrial work operations themselves; to internalize the power relations of the capitalist economic and social system and to learn one's place under these relations. The individual, and class, internalization of the capitalist relations of power and industrial control, he argued, were manifested in the worker through compliance, cynicism, docility and ultimately in alienation and stupification. For Marx, the capitalist mode of production affects the worker exposed to it by "mortifying his body and ruining his mind." In Marx's analysis alienation is a psychological and social process in which one becomes estranged by and from the processes and products of one's own labor, and ultimately from one's self and one's companions. The creative, generative, essentially human nature of work, in which humans might potentially become most fully themselves, is contradicted and destroyed by the process of industrial labor under capitalism. The processes of capitalist ideology obstruct the ability of the worker to see through these power relations, and to take appropriate class action (Marx [1844] 1978, [1867] 1978). The humanistic Marxists tried to identify ways in which the actual laboring activities of particular classes and communities influenced the formation of class cultures and the class character of the self. They argued (Hoggart 1957, Williams 1961, Thompson 1963) that specific values and beliefs, individual and collective dispositions, and behavior

75

patterns and norms of the social formation are circumscribed by the particular work activities around which these classes are organized. Their views were shared by the labor movement in which the implicit assumption that people learn things through the practice of, and by being at, work was widely held. In the late nineteenth century the rising labor movement in industrializing countries sought to build its strength by politicizing workers' awareness around the indirect and less visible things that workers were learning at work. The recognition of the power relations of production and in the workplace enabled labor leaders to build workers' organizations around workers' awareness of exploitation and of the potential for political strength in solidarity and collective action. Business leaders and managers also knew that workers learned many things at work: the rudimentary lessons of discipline, respect, time-keeping and economy of motion, as well as specific skills and habits necessary for carrying out their work tasks. The project of Taylorism sought to manipulate workers' attitudes, learning and behavior in the workplace to increase their productivity. The workplace was generally regarded as a site of training workers for specific job tasks, and of managing their tendency to unruliness and laziness.

Industrial work required a major shift from the habits and routines of agricultural work. The traditional rhythm of the seasons and of the day's labor and recreation belonged to a different world from that of industrial production. Agricultural workers performed only as much work as was necessary for their own and their family's sustenance. The idea of working for some intrinsic value or to accumulate a surplus beyond seasonal needs was foreign to agricultural and early factory workers. As the industrial revolution progressed and the demands of increased productivity heightened, the forging of the "industrial worker" with new habits and skills was required. Supervision of workers was introduced which further distanced this new breed of workers from both the skilled, semi-autonomous craftworkers and agricultural laborers of pre-industrial times. The new industrial workers did not learn their new habits quickly or easily, or without resistance. Early factory workers continued their habits of regular drinking rounds and play activities in the course of the industrial "working day" (see Gutman 1976, Joyce 1987, Pollard 1965). Absenteeism was the norm and haphazard attention and performance were expected. The wish to work only as much as was needed for sustenance, or as much as one wanted to exert one's physical energy, was carried over into early factory work.

As Weber (1930) demonstrated later, the habits of the sober bourgeois citizen were forced upon the new industrial worker, whose spontaneous and instinctually gratifying behaviors had to be suppressed and the energy redirected into industrial production. Expansion of industrial capitalism, and increasing specialization of function, required the production of an individual self who would live in an increasingly differentiated and privatized world. The worker internalized the social discipline required of

capitalist production as self-regulation, and as the ideal self. The everyday
rules and forms of social interaction which occur in production are
abstracted and reified as moral values to be extended into all other spheres
of social and private life.

THE MANIFEST CURRICULUM OF WORK

The business world has long recognized the link between education and
production. For many decades business leaders have demanded from the
formal schooling system young workers educated to have the skills and
attributes that companies need to compete successfully in an expanding
international marketplace. Large companies now employ their own staff
educators, curriculum officers and development consultants to plan and
conduct training programs for employees on site and on company time.
Many provide paid leave and tuition fees for their employees to gain
qualifications in formal educational institutions or to attend corporate
conferences and training programs. Similarly, continuing adult education
in the form of formal staff training programs and credentials, instruction
manuals, procedural designs of work styles and work behaviors according
to the company's business philosophy and rules are commonplace in
corporate industries. These deliberate educational activities in the workplace are designed to produce company workers formed in the "spirit" of
the company as well as to maximize productivity and promote the visibility
of the firm in the marketplace. The spinoff effects are personal benefits to
the workers accrued by gaining additional educational qualifications under
company sponsorship that provide higher status and reward and increased
opportunity for advancement.

Various university and college adult education programs emerged in
response to the demands of the business world for further education for
adult employees. The need for the re-training of displaced industrial
workers is generating a further expansion of traditional professional
education. These days many institutional providers of worker and professional education are forming partnerships with large corporations in
which re-training and skills upgrading are provided by means of a
mixture of on-the-new-job training and off-site education. There is a
growing demand for "trainers" and consultants in staff training and
development in the corporate sector.

Labor educators similarly stress the importance of education in the
workplace. They appeal to employers or state authorities for the quality
of the workplace to be evaluated in terms of its provision of educational
opportunities and learning environments for workers (Leymann and
Kornbluh 1989, Pipan 1989). Looking beyond skills training programs,
worker educators advocate the practices of worker participation, more
democratic decision-making structures and opportunities for individual

staff development of personal qualities and social skills in the workplace. Some of these calls are echoed in the new management literature (see Chapter 5) which claims to develop professionally and personally empowered and multi-skilled employees through participation in the new management practices.

All of the deliberate and overt educational activities that take place at work, or for work, comprise the *manifest curriculum* of work: the collection of deliberate learning activities that the company or company-approved educators provide and in which workers participate knowingly for the perceived advantage of both themselves and the company. Accompanying the manifest curriculum of work is the *hidden curriculum* of work that socializes and shapes adult workers. Work is a communicational or discursive practice. Its products are not only commodities for the market place but "acculturated" employees. These discursive practices, and not just the materiality of what one does at work, affect the self.

THE HIDDEN CURRICULUM OF WORK

Sociologists of education from about the 1960s focused attention on the class-based power relations and on persistent inequalities in society and its major institutions, particularly schooling. They[1] identified the hidden curriculum in schooling whereby dominant or official knowledge (ideology) integrates youth into the economic system. The hidden curriculum in the formal education system accompanied, often (although not necessarily) contradictorily, the operation of the manifest curriculum. This hidden curriculum contained a vast range of spoken and unspoken social and cultural messages, rules, codes and symbols that young people learn to ensure their selective appropriation of the formal school curriculum and their individual participation in the reproduction of social class divisions and dominant power relations in society (Bernstein 1975, Bourdieu and Passeron 1977, Bowles and Gintis 1976). For the critical sociologists of education, revealing and analyzing the content of the hidden curriculum enables a better understanding of the processes of school education and its role in the reproduction of social structures and cultural institutions.

Earlier, the concept "socialization"[2] was coined to describe the processes by which the young are formed as members of society.[3] According to the functionalist viewpoint, every society needs to have its young members learn the general values, knowledges and skills needed for functioning as an orderly and contributing member of society. In order to be functional and stable society requires that each of its members acquire the competencies and allegiances to social and economic roles and functions that will maintain and reproduce the integrity of the society. By and large, the socialization literature from the 1940s through 1970s identified and focused on the operations of deliberate and overt socialization processes

78

and agents. The family, race, religion, neighborhood, peer groups and the formal institutions of education and state authorities (legal, health and civic) were identified as the sites of primary socialization. Most attention was accorded to the formal system's role in the socialization processes of the young.

More recently, some attention has focused on processes of adult socialization through such processes as "life stages" and crises (Levinson 1978, Neugarten 1968, Rosow 1974). These studies have emphasized the socialization processes in adult life that surround "stage events" such as marriage, parenthood, retirement and death, and promoted the individual's successful mastery of stages and crises as evidence of effective socialization and normalization. Although the notion of "life stages" has been subsequently criticized (Dannefer 1984) it points to self-formative events and learning experiences in individual lives that occur outside formal institutional socialization and learning.

However, what the studies of socialization, and of life stages, did not address in their early studies, and likewise, the sociology of education more recently, was the way in which work also functions as a site of primary socialization, and consequently, the ways in which it affects the person of the worker. Industrial psychology, particularly the work of Hughes and of Becker *et al.*, did recognize the psychological effects of work on the person. But much of that effort became directed at discovering ways to increase the worker's motivation, efficiency and productivity and to eliminate conflicts, dysfunctions and disincentives. Industrial and organizational psychologists were, by and large, interested, as are their successors in management psychology, in what people learn or feel at work to the extent that the results of that learning and feeling lead to increased productivity and manageability.

Early research into the psychology of work undertaken in the 1950s stressed communication processes and individual adjustment needs and worker motivation. Following Maslow's hierarchy of needs schema (1954, 1956) researchers tried to find ways in which workers' higher needs, for self-esteem and self-actualization, could be met at work. Working conditions that allowed for autonomy, dignity, respect, getting praise and rewards for one's accomplishments, and by taking on and succeeding in challenges (Maslow 1954, 1956) motivated and retained workers.[4] On the other hand, alienation leads to an instrumental attitude to one's work, and a low degree of work satisfaction. Research using Seligman's "learned helplessness" theory (1975) and Rotter's "locus of control" (1954 and 1966) described a relationship between an individual's "attitudes" to actions and control locus, and their health and well-being. The perception of locus of control affects a person's psycho-social functioning.[5] Kohn and colleagues' work in the 1970s showed that workers in occupations that allow for greater control and autonomy at work experience higher degrees of satisfaction and well-being than those in jobs that are externally controlled (Kohn 1973, 1983).

A branch of industrial psychology from the 1950s through to the 1970s promoted a social psychology of industry that emphasized elements from physiological science. There were subsequent undertakings to improve the physical environment of the worker in the hope that improved design and organization of workplaces would diminish the number of industrial accidents, and more favorable psychological conditions would enable workers to increase their rates of production. More recently there have been studies focusing directly on the combined effects of psychological elements and social conditions of workers in the workplace (LaBier 1988, Lennerloff 1986, Hirschhorn 1988). These studies advocate that working conditions must be suited to both the physical and psychological characteristics of the individual worker. They argue that workers learn through their workplace experiences, and that their loyalty and levels of productivity are directly affected by these hidden learning experiences. Similarly, others interested in the effects of work and unemployment (Bellin and Miller 1990, O'Brien 1986, Skocpol 1990), and the effects of specific occupations on workers' personalities (Kohn and Schooler 1983, Miller, Kohn and Schooler 1986) have shown that alienation and ambivalence toward work affects workers' well-being and productivity. Workers *learn* productivity, not just the skills and competencies that are necessary to perform their job tasks.

Furthermore, LaBier's (1986) studies of the psychological effects of high-status, high-stress corporate work on the emotional lives of company executives and their employees (LaBier 1986) emphasizes the informal learning experiences of employees that affect all aspects of their working lives and their emotional lives. Again, this awareness of informal learning at work is typical of contemporary management literature that emphasizes team building and "family" style participatory structures to acculturate employees into the company. I return to these themes in chapters 5 and 6.

WORK AND SELF

Historical studies of industrial society and industrial workers have often focused on the effects on society of the transition from agricultural labor to factory labor. These broad analyses of societal transition through industrialization rarely considered the impact of institutional practices on the individual person. In the middle decades of this century the conventional assumption in most sociological and psychological literature was that the personality of workers was determined by their early socialization experiences. The interactions of the social processes of the family, the neighborhood, the religious and cultural environment, the school and the peer group were regarded as functioning as the primary sites of socialization. By the time one reached the age for participation in the paid industrial workforce, the necessary habits and dispositions toward authority and routine work activities, had already been well inculcated in the worker. All that was generally required was a little refinement and discipline of the young worker in his or her early months in the industrial workplace to ensure the transition from school to work was typically smooth and functional. Any disjuncture in this transition was viewed as deviant behavior of the individual.

But Weber and Sorokin had in the early decades of the century recognized the reciprocal relation between work, occupation and personality. Weber's early study of occupational careers and mobility patterns (Weber 1908) argued that the practices of work and the stratification structures of industrial society are inextricably linked. Similarly, Sorokin thought that,

> All psychological processes of any member of an occupation undergo modification, especially when one stays for a long time in the same occupation. The process of perception and sensation, attention, imaginative reproduction, and association bear the marks of a corresponding occupation. . . . Still greater is the occupational influence on the processes and on the character of one's evaluations, beliefs, practical judgments, opinions, ethics and whole ideology.
>
> (Sorokin 1927: 321)

Recalling Weber's and Sorokin's early work some contemporary empirical psychological and sociological studies of work and industry provide evidence that personality changes during adulthood are affected by the types of work people do. Industrial psychologists had typically assumed that people choose, or may be "fitted" to occupations according to personality characteristics and preferences. But the contemporary studies show that experience in so central a domain of life as work affects orientations to behavior in other domains as well. People become what they do. If job experiences restrict opportunities for personal control, skill-use and intimacy, workers tend to have diminished capabilities for self-direction, competence and interpersonal relationships – in their work and in other spheres of their lives (Kohn and Schooler 1983, Kohn 1990, O'Brien 1986, Vallas 1988). The level of personal development of workers as well as their job performance is diminished.

Kohn and Schooler's study of work and personality explores the relationship between position in the structure of society and individual psychological functioning. They argue that "social structure is significant for psychological functioning because it *embodies systematically differentiated conditions of life that profoundly affect people's views of social reality.*" (Kohn and Schooler 1983: 1, emphasis added). Their findings show that the relationships of stratification to values and orientations result mainly from the opportunity to be self-directed in one's work that comes with higher educational levels and occupational position. The use of initiative, thought and independent judgment in work is greatly facilitated by some job conditions and impaired by others. Kohn and Schooler argue that adult personality is affected by job conditions mainly through a direct process of learning from the job and generalizing what has been learned into other realms of life.[6] The "lessons" of work are directly carried over to non-occupational realms. What people do in their work directly affects their cognitive functioning, their values, their conceptions of self, and their orientations to the world around them. Kohn (1990) finds that the relationship between work and personality is not unidirectional, as occupational psychologists had long assumed: it is a reciprocal relation.[7]

Previous studies of work have usually looked at specific occupations such as teachers, steel workers, clerical workers and so forth. These studies have been useful in documenting the multidimensionality of occupations. But they have not enabled an examination of the psychological impact of any particular dimension of work apart from all the other aspects of work in which it is interconnected. Similarly, another approach popular among sociologists or economists has been to collapse the multidimensionality of occupations to a single dimension, ignoring all others. For instance, as Kohn (1990) points out, sociologists have often shown interest in jobs only in terms of the status they confer, and economists have concentrated attention on income levels and differentials within and between occupations. Kohn argues that occupational status serves mainly as a gross indicator of a job's location in the hierarchy of the economic and social system and it does not reveal much about the impact of that status on the personality of the job holder. The status of the job is closely linked to structural conditions of work, such as how closely supervised and complex it is, and what sort of pressure is involved. Kohn concludes that it is these structural realities rather than the status itself that affect personality (Kohn 1990: 37).

Kohn's work focuses on modern industrial work and its hierarchical organization. His principal proposition is that the *conditions* of work are the source of the effects work has on personality. He maintains the category of occupation as a principal structure of work and in the experience of work. Citing his own and others' longitudinal studies, Kohn advances the proposition that the conditions of work of gainfully employed men and women affect their values, self-conceptions, orientations to social reality and cognitive functioning. These effects can be considerable. A key example is that the "substantive complexity of work" has an effect on the "intellectual flexibility of adult men one-fourth as great as that of their own prior levels of intellectual flexibility, measured ten years earlier" (Kohn 1990: 40). Kohn claims that the results show a consistent, and reciprocal, relationship between conditions of work and one or other aspect of personality (Kohn 1990: 41). In particular, job conditions may also be affected by personality. Kohn claims that over time personality has important consequences for the individual's place in the job structure.

THE SELF AT WORK

Personality is the set of personal character traits, dispositions and propensities developed by the individual. The self, while usually manifested through personality traits, role preferences or disposition, also connotes to modern westerns something deeper. The self implies the amalgam of constituent processes and events. It is the sense of "personness" where emotion as well as reason is experienced. The study of the self at work elaborated in the following chapters attempts to go somewhat further than Kohn's effort in analyzing the work/personality relationship. Kohn's work, importantly, showed that job conditions affect a person's propensity toward favorable or unfavorable evaluations of self, and their general disposition toward their work. His project was to empirically explore many of the arguments made in a number of studies of alienation at work such as Blauner (1964), Seeman (1972, 1975), and Vallas (1988).

From a somewhat different angle, but sharing a similar interest in what happens to the person at work, Douglas LaBier's (1986) study set out to examine how people's emotional lives and mental health are affected by the culture of work. LaBier looked at the new breed of corporate workers, at middle-class professionals who presumably had, in the past, suffered less from the afflictions of alienation at work than had traditional industrial workers. His analyses of corporate, high-status work also cast many of Kohn's concepts and findings, such as "occupational self-direction," and the high self-evaluations of those who perform highly complex work, in a different light. LaBier identifies some unexpected pathological tendencies in certain types of apparently attractive, highly rewarded corporate work.

LaBier's psychoanalytically oriented work, which was influenced by Fromm and Maccoby out of the Frankfurt School, studied why certain people developed neurotic symptoms on the job and how these neuroses related to their particular workplaces. He looked at the emotional consequences of the character traits and attitudes that organizations do – or do not – support among the men and women who work within them. In short, LaBier's study shows how people working in highly competitive and finely-structured corporations facing onerous daily demands to adapt to corporate culture can literally be driven crazy. Among his conclusions, LaBier suggests that career conflicts are really part of a "larger malaise related to how we envision and practice adulthood in our society" (LaBier 1986: xiii). LaBier writes of "modern madness," the hidden link between work and emotional conflict. Its symptoms range from mild distress and pervasive sadness, to feelings of self-betrayal, stress and burnout, to acute psychiatric disorders and irrationality. These symptoms are generated by work and career within today's large corporations (ibid.: 3). They reveal a pervasive malady that affects increasing numbers of workers, particularly the new breed of careerist: achievement- and success-oriented men and women from the mid-twenties to mid-fifties.

LaBier's approach views the workplace organization as a "psycho-structure" which selects and shapes in the worker certain kinds of orientations that achieve a congruent fit between the requirements of work and the character of those who do it (LaBier 1986: 49). The person's values, attitudes and general orientation must mesh with organizational needs, and the result is that specific traits and attitudes that are useful to work are stimulated and reinforced. Those that are unnecessary or impede work are suppressed, thwarted and gradually weakened. Success-oriented individuals, in their upward movement in the organization, are more effectively molded by the needs and structures of the organization. Often, the values and attitudes required by the organization conflict with those of the individual. It is also possible for the psychostructure of the organization to stimulate, support, and make adaptive disturbed attitudes or tendencies (ibid.: 49).

While most individuals deal with conflicts, compromises and trade-offs in their work, the consequences can be quite different for different people. Some attempt to adapt ever more successfully and work harder. Others rebel either consciously or unconsciously. Still others suffer visibly or invisibly. LaBier's studies show that many careerists often display a surface sanity while they are disguising neurotic or psychotic symptoms in their inner lives. They function well on the job because their work environment and organization supports and rewards their sickness. The attitudes of toughness, aggressiveness and competitiveness, the abilities to create a flurry of activity – meetings, memos and fire-fighting – and to intimidate and humiliate others and to "get" one's enemies, are valued attributes in many organizations. Work environments in highly complex, fast paced and market-driven corporations, emphasize and reward the excessive pursuit of power and grandiosity – and also submission and masochistic enslavement. These pursuits are disguised as the standard of normalcy and commonly accepted as simply part of the job. The meaning of sanity and mental health in the workplace is thereby perverted. A person who is adaptive to a disturbed work environment tends to be maladaptive in other healthier organizational cultures.

The implications of corporate workers suffering from "modern madness" in their places of work are considerable – not just for the personal lives of such people, but for the mental health and well-being of their subordinates, the shaping of the culture of their workplaces, and the wider cultural character. The psychostructure of the organization both affects and is affected by the mental health of those who work in it. LaBier's extensive interviews of corporate workers suffering from corporate malaise reveals that the effect of their work upon their inner selves is destructive and pathological.

The organizational theorist and psychoanalyst Larry Hirschhorn (1984, 1988) similarly recognizes many of the problems that LaBier more systematically explores. But he does not consider the wider systemic and structural conditions and practices of the organization as significantly contributing to workplace malaise and individual illness that passes in everyday life as normalcy and appropriate adjustment to the demands of the post-industrial workplace. His effort is to develop new ways to manage workplace and intra-individual conflicts by attending to the psychodynamics of workplace interactions.

If LaBier were describing pathological conditions in the emotional lives of traditional industrial workers, whose habits have been inculcated through generations of authoritarian discipline and control, there would be no surprise. Many studies variously exploring similar questions on the character and form of alienation at work have been conducted among industrial workers. The working classes, their trade unions and other cultural institutions have always known the emotional as well as physical cost of disciplined, oppressive industrial work. But awareness of this has most often been repressed. Fearing industrial discipline, hunger and poverty workers were forced into compliance and collusion with the forces of industrial culture. As Weber demonstrated, the spirit of Protestantism successfully established an ideology of self that was useful for the forces of exploitative production. The hidden curriculum of schooling continued the cultural work of training workers in dependability, predictability, conformity and self-discipline.

But we have, generally, expected the picture in contemporary high-status white-collar work to be different. LaBier's study shows otherwise. Independently of Deleuze and Guattari's (1979) theoretical postulation derived from their work in a psychiatric hospital of the schizoid personality as the "normal" condition of the late modern age, LaBier returns to the site of everyday productive practices in the corporate workplace to trace the sources of the makings of modern madness, and of the new corporate self.

THE DISCURSIVE PRACTICES OF POST-INDUSTRIAL WORK

The technological, organizational and socioeconomic changes occurring in the world of work affect the everyday experiences of work, the character of the workplace, and the worker. Increasingly, work occurs in ever-larger and more complex organizations. Bureaucracy has expanded even beyond Weber's vision. Today it connotes multiple layers of organization, vastness and an even greater degree of impersonality in working life, precisely because of the substitution of human interaction with electronic and networked machine communication, and electronic surveillance of workers. Computerized bureaucracy has considerable potential to discursively control and more subtly exploit than industrial bureaucracy. Post-industrial work and contemporary corporate culture are producing new work, new work conditions and a new workplace. The discursive practices of work in post-industrial workplaces encompass many of the practices of industrial work.

But the new work is affecting the worker in many ways that are qualitatively different from industrial patterns. In early industrial work, and in modern industrial work, the primary impact of work was on the body. The physicality of work demanded bodily exertion and created bodily fatigue. However, the normal human rhythms of exertion, rest and recreation, traditionally in games and drinking, were regulated by the increasing impositions of bourgeois norms and values modeled as ideal citizenship. The psychological effects were less readily observable and understood, although they have since been studied among modern industrial workers.

Post-industrial work affects the worker in a number of ways that differ from industrial work. First of all, the primary impact is no longer upon the body, and the primary requirement is no longer physical prowess and endurance. The bodily presence of the worker at a production site other than a computer terminal is not always required, and even when it is, increasingly, the primary requirement is the quick, attentive, trained mind. Corporate employees are increasingly expected to have their minds and hearts "on duty" even outside of regular working hours. The use of cellular telephones, personal lap computers, modems, fax machines, and airplane telephones are extending the available hours of work into leisure and private time, making it possible for the "knowledge worker" to conduct business not only on the golf course, but from her home or car. Not only is the productive enterprise itself increasingly discursive, so is the labor required of the worker. In contemporary manufacturing, technological workers are often simply required to attend, to wait and to observe the smart machines controlling production. The worker's task is to problem-solve, trouble-shoot and manage. Yet even human expertise must now on occasion defer to or hand over to advanced technical systems, such as laser tools, which are more precise, stable and equipped with microscopic vision, tasks beyond human skill and capacity. Similar requirements are found in the new service and information work. Even at the low-paid, lower-skilled end of the service sector polarity that still requires some physicality (in for example fast-food preparation and portering), additional skills of "personality," congeniality, good humor and interactive skills are now required. The discursive or communicational practices of work not only socialize "normal" adaptive workers into work tasks and habits, they fundamentally affect one's emotional and psychic processes, sense of well-being and identity.

86

In the new workplace of contemporary corporate culture, the new forms of self-discipline are mediated through the rhetoric of self-actualization, flexibility and hyper-adaptability. Some analysts (Drucker 1993, Hirschhorn 1984, Zuboff 1988) claim that the new workplaces are "places of learning" in which the worker is required to diagnose and solve complex problems generated by electronic machine systems. But claims for increased self-actualization and autonomous decision-making and for generalizable learning need to be tested. The rhetorical devices of the "learning organization" and "learner-employees" may act as new forms of discursive domination through the technicization of learning and creative impulses, electronic surveillance and new forms of discipline and control. Chapters 5 and 6 examine this issue more fully.

Kohn's work on the work/personality relation has contributed considerably to the task of working out the effects of occupational tasks on "apparently normal" people, and the relation between occupation and social stratification. LaBier's work provides important insights into discovering and analyzing pathological conditions in the workplace. The approach I develop in the following study of the self at work is influenced by both Kohn's and LaBier's approaches and methods. Like LaBier I emphasize the self, and like Kohn I explore the multiple dimensions of work, as well as the character of its management relations, that affect the person of the worker. Kohn's work, however, defined a number of structured variables of personality and dimensions of the job, and employed a quantitative methodology. An attempt to study the effects of work on the *self*, rather than on personality, requires that a method other than linear analysis of structured variables be employed. The self does not yield well to positivist methods of investigation. It is not so readily broken down into components and variables as is personality into traits and disposition. The self, as much of the historical and contemporary debate about its existence and its nature attests, remains a metaphysical construct. It needs to be explored in ways that accommodate its variable constituent processes and forms.

Other analysts who are similarly attempting to understand the new work practices and their social implications have variously described those who work in the new work, specifically technological professionals and middle- to upper-level managers. Ehrenreich and Ehrenreich (1979) describe these new technological workers as the "professional managerial class" (PMC). For Gouldner (1979), they represent the "New Class" and for others including Derber *et al.* (1990) professional technological employees represent an emergent "New Mandarin Order" who legitimate their class power with claims to special knowledge. The approach with which I embarked on a field study of corporate employees, to which I now turn, was to regard them primarily as representative of the new technological and knowledge employees of the corporation. I suspended definitive positioning of their class configuration. LaBier's observations among the corporate careerists remind us of Gorz's (1989) prediction of the increasing bifurcation in the post-industrial workforce. Kohn's recognition of the persistence of many forms of industrial work practices even in organizations moving into post-industrial economic and organizational activities recall the persistence of forms of industrial class relations. We do not know yet the emergent class character of post-industrial work. My second intention below is to consider what patterns of social solidarity and social organization may emerge in society after industrialism. The following chapters describe and interpret an empirical investigation designed to explore questions of work and self in new conditions and practices of work.

5

DISCOURSES OF PRODUCTION

The classical theories of industrial capitalism held that the social relations of production – ownership and control of the means and forces of production (labor and technology) – brought about a distinct social division of labor and opposing social classes of people. The social relations of production determined class and social character, as well as the everyday life of industrial workplaces. Marx and his descendants considered ways in which the material social relations were supported and facilitated at the workplace by ideologies which were so firmly embedded in the technologies of industry that, while not always invisible, they were generally taken for granted. The classical Marxist effort usually focused on criticizing these ideologies and discerning their various political manifestations in the reproduction and legitimation of capitalist social relations in society. While ideology was, and remains, important among the discursive practices of production, there are other and new discourses that require excavation and analysis. These discourses are emerging in the wake of the decline of industrialism and its classical ideologies.

Over the past decade there has been growing interest among sociologists in institutional and organizational change, including a particular attention to culture and development in corporate organizations.[1] In organizational and management studies much of this interest is concerned with the relationship between cultural practices, organizational goals and strategies, and with managing corporate change. There is also an emerging critical interest in organizational analysis.[2] Still other social analysts exploring problems of technology, society, knowledge and culture consider corporate and institutional change as part of broader processes in technological and societal change.[3]

Notwithstanding the critical interest within organizational analysis the orientation of the field study of corporate work discussed here was influenced somewhat more significantly by the broader genre of critical social theory. My questions sought to probe the relationships between institutional practices and self processes. In particular, I wanted to explore the effects of post-industrial changes in the institution of work on the self. Like

Durkheim, I wondered if a post-industrial condition might be producing a new generalized self, and like Marx and the critical theorists, I hoped for signs that "new" selves would effect a social formation free from domination and exploitation in the emergent post-industrial society. At once burdened and enlightened by such a gaze I undertook an extensive field study of a large multi-national corporation in the 1991–2 academic year. I wanted to explore broad questions in the self–society relationship by returning to modern industrialism's base in the sites of production. For the sake of the narrative I will introduce the company and the field study briefly at this point. A full discussion of the study, the research methods and processes, and the style of interpretive analysis is found in the Appendix.

The company, which I call Hephaestus Corporation,[4] is a world leader in the development and manufacture of advanced technological machines and systems. Hephaestus Corporation ranks highly among the Fortune 500 companies for its development and pioneering of many of the new practices of work and organizational culture that include teamwork and "Total Quality Managment," and dedicated employees, currently much debated in business and industry circles. The company has operations throughout the world and employs more than a hundred thousand people. I conducted my research in the largest Hephaestus Corporation plant in the United States located in the city of Rusty River (a pseudonym) in the north east.

Most of the research was carried out within a large product development division, called the "Iris Product Team," which comprised several hundred employees most of whom were located in one vast building. The product team comprised scientists, engineers and technologists of various formerly specialist backgrounds, designers, computer systems professionals, financial and technical analysts, managers, and manufacturing workers. The company allowed me generous access to people, buildings and everyday operations. I observed a wide range of activities in the Iris product development – from the research and design groups through testing, manufacturing, marketing, sales, servicing and customer support. After a few months of observing operations and spending time with Iris Team members every day I conducted in-depth interviews with 60 employees chosen from among the larger team.

This chapter describes and analyzes the principle elements in the "new" corporate culture and work organization practices that Hephaestus Corporation has deliberately designed and implemented. The next chapter analyses the effects of these practices on the self and develops a critical social psychology of corporate work. More general theoretical propositions about the social meanings of the new corporate work, culture and solidarity are developed in the final chapter. My approach to corporate work, organization and culture departs from an emphasis on traditional corporate organizational structure, the distribution of power and control over corporate employees and their various accommodations to the chances of success and failure (Whyte 1956, Kanter 1977, Smith 1990). My emphasis is on the "new corporate culture" that, as I shall describe, is being deliberately designed. The new designed culture is profoundly affected by the capabilities of advanced automation and information technologies as well as the organizational changes such technologies have precipitated.

I proceed in this chapter from an important claim: that post-industrial technologies have brought about the end of the labor process as it is traditionally understood (that is, as described particularly by Braverman 1974 and conventionally held in the sociology of work). Advanced information technologies and automated manufacturing technologies have precipitated and facilitated the end of fragmentation, specialization and rigid bureaucratic structures of authority and control typical of industrial organization. To recall the descriptions in Chapter 2, in the first instance automation technologies eliminate acutely specialized functions and low-skilled jobs, rendering the remaining jobs more integrated, more skilled and more responsible. Fewer supervisors are required and employees carry out many of the functions formerly reserved for management or professional staff. Moreover, advanced information technologies have the capacity to integrate formerly separate work functions and knowledges. Networked and integrated production and office systems, which facilitate global communications simultaneously with local communications, enable production and exchange to be generated and implemented with little constraint by physical conditions and national boundaries.

In the workplace significant changes to the organization and management of work are being enabled by such advanced technologies. The new technologies have influenced a reorganization of the workplace under a new culture that recognizes and exploits the end of the Fordist tradition of the labor process. As a result post-industrial corporations are now able to design their own organizational culture more explicitly and carefully than industrial culture was ever planned. Of course, the deliberate design and orchestration of culture is never complete and interactions between employees in everyday practice make the everyday culture of an organization. None the less, the pedagogical devices of the new designed cultures are significantly altering the old industrial work culture and shaping post-industrial employees.

Few analysts have recognized or analysed in contemporary discussions of corporations and work the effects of what I suggest is the end of industrialism's intricate division of labor and specialization of function, and its elaborate culture of solidarity, on work and social organization more broadly. As I interpret the data discussed below, the industrial category of occupation is diminishing. The end of occupation has implications beyond creative flexibility and enhanced dispensibility in the workplace. It is not simply a matter of multi-skilling and job redesign. Rather,

91

what I call "post-occupational" work has significant implications for cohesion and social solidarity in the workplace and in society after industrialism. This view is a departure from the typical modern industrial view, and from much contemporary analysis such as Derber (1990) and Kohn (1990).

Furthermore, these events have seldom been explored in relation to the social production of the self, although the works of Maccoby (1981 and 1988) and Howard (1985) do explore the question of the corporate leader and the corporate self, and LaBier (1986) and Baum (1987) examine the psychological effects of work in large organizations on the employee. In this chapter I describe the culture of work in Hephaestus Corporation with an effort to explore the effects of designed culture on employee selves. The effects and relationships arising from the impetus of the new technologies to integrate previously specialized and fragmented functions are an important constituent of the corporate drive to implement the new culture program. My approach in this chapter is concerned not so much with the new technological materialities (hard and soft wares) themselves as it is with the event and development of the "social technologies" that advanced industrial and information technologies have brought about. I refer to these new social technologies as discursive practices that include the deliberately designed organizational culture and the new work and production structures in the corporation.

During the preparation for the field study I was aware that I was expecting to see and to hear reports from employees about the effects of working with new production and information technologies as Zuboff (1988) had found. Instead, I soon discovered upon commencing the study that familiarity with advanced technologies had quickly been integrated into the employee's working life. Rather than elevating these effects, it was the social effects that these technologies had on the organization of work that mattered most to people; that is, the advent of the new corporate culture of "Total Quality Management" and its new language practices which include the redesigned concepts of "team," "family," and "customer." These organizational constructs and cultural practices, at once made possible and required by advanced technology, represented the most significant shift in organizational life and exerted considerable influence on employees. For many technologists working with laser physics and similar advanced micro-electronic technologies had become as commonplace as using the telephone. Familiarity with the new cultural artifacts generated some unexpected adaptation problems to the new culture, usually expected from exposure to the new material technologies.[5]

The "new" discourses of production are *increasingly* crucial to production. Discourses of production do not include the materiality of production such as the physical plant and production technologies, and the physical conditions of labor, although ultimately the materiality of economic

92

relations of labor, capital, ownership and control, is also mediated discursively. They are held distinct from the discursive practices under study here. Discursive, or communicational and symbolic elements in production and work organization, include the corporate workplace culture, the myths, beliefs, history, norms, rituals and customs; the practices of "team," "family" and "customer;" and the character values of leadership, excellence, dedication and so forth, that are elaborated below. Discursive practices also include, as part of corporate design, the cubicled "panopticon" layout of the white-collar workplace, even though that appears, at first glance, to be a material condition of the workplace environment. The ability to observe, and the experience of being observed, is a non-verbal communicational practice. It serves an immediate and constant disciplinary function that remains unspoken and implicit. The new technologies, both material and discursive, are now, along with labor and capital, essential elements in the new production apparatus of corporate organizations.

DESCRIPTIVE THEMES AND ANALYTICAL CONSTRUCTS

For analytical purposes I have distinguished and drawn together clusters of major themes that emerged from the data I gathered. These themes constitute the framework of the description and the basis of the accompanying and subsequent analyses. The themes allow analytical drawing apart of a number of discursive practices in the patterns of culture and production at Hephaestus Corporation. There are complex interdependencies and overlapping features within the network of discursive practices. The first and underlying theme to be explored is the corporate culture. The culture of Hephaestus Corporation carries its own myths, beliefs and customary practices. It has its own distinct historical elements based in the time, place and personalities of its founders and their products. It also has a new face: a deliberately designed new culture that is shaping the way things are done at Hephaestus Corporation, its image in the world and the character of its employees. The second theme is the problem of "knowledge" and the work of "image." Knowledge is a discursive social relation of production. It is also a commodity that is bought and sold, and it is also an important element in the new organizational structure of the Hephaestus workplace. The image, or symbolic economy of the corporation trades in the currency of team, family, of excellence in customer satisfaction and in technological and organizational leadership.

The third analytical theme is the operation of the social structures and cultural processes of team and family; the role and meaning of the meetings; the disciplinary practices, and the efforts at forms of counter-culture practices. The fourth theme is discourse on the Hephaestus character. The culture designers, in their specification of "the customer requirements" have described the ideal features of the archetypal Hephaestus Corporation person. The primary desired characteristics are those of dedication, diligence and the cooperative-competitiveness of the team-player. My intention is to analyze and interpret these new cultural events and to discern their effects on employee selves.

PATTERNS OF HEPHAESTUS CULTURE

Founding myths

The culture of Hephaestus Corporation is underpinned by its foundational myth. This myth and its makers comprise the primary narrative of cohesion and organizational distinction, creating an ethos and guiding story that embody the "spirit" of Hephaestus and its principles that establish the rudiments of identification with the company. The continuity of the myth of Hephaestus is the foundation of the new culture. The myth is a complex narrative embodying the scientific inventive genius of the founding technologist Tom Sol and the charismatic business leadership of the legendary Jack Nicias, the first president of Hephaestus Corporation. Even Hephaestus employees who do not know the detail of the corporation's history – and there are many who do – are aware of the leaders, the prominent personalities and the triumphant experiences of the foundational years. The achievements of the founders and the team of people they built up around their technological inventions in the early decades have now become congealed, and reified, as the myth of the company's fortitude, inventiveness and style. This larger-than-life, apocryphal narrative has rendered the company, in the eyes of those who work for it (and those of many who do not in the city of Rusty River), much more than a large-scale technological and manufacturing operation. It is the giant in their lives. Hephaestus evokes for them images of heroic strength, resilience and innovation tempered by paternalistic care and responsibility.

Many employees can remember from their own experience a period in which the company, after decades of considerable success and rapid world-wide expansion and spendthrift management practices, suffered a sudden, and what was feared to be long-term, downward trend in the market. By a process of radical restructuring and the deliberate introduction of a "new culture," Hephaestus Corporation has managed a remarkable market recovery and is continuing to regain lost market shares against its Japanese and European competitors. These events have been documented in at least two books written by different witnesses astonished at the success of the corporation's recovery against wider marketplace trends of similar American corporations. These books, like an earlier one about the story of the company and a recent one written by a former Chief Executive Officer (CEO), continue to construct and celebrate the myth in its re-telling. A discursive bond-object is created.

94

The employees are participants in a corporate culture that while being deliberately created and recreated continues to be steeped in the Hephaestus myth of inventive genius, business acumen, courageous leadership, extraordinary productivity and hardworking team employees. The founding president, Jack Nicias, was also known for his civic involvements in the city of Rusty River. His exemplary citizenship has also become embedded in the Hephaestus myth. Many of the older men and women employed at Hephaestus, or who have retired, speak fondly, even reverently of the great Jack Nicias. For those who do not remember the man himself, he is now incarnated in the myth that is believed to be the modern Hephaestus.

Jim: I met Jack Nicias once. What a great man he was . . . Have you heard about Jack Nicias?

Catherine: Yes.

Jim: He was a great man; a beautiful man.

Catherine: Why do you say that?

Jim: Well, he was just great. He used to come in here, oh, that was years ago, and he'd go around the place, and he'd talk to us all. It didn't matter who you were or what your job was, you were always important to Jack Nicias. He always made you feel important, and people really loved him.

Mel: We all worked very hard in those days . . . not that . . . well . . . people [still] work hard here, but nobody complained then. It was like, we were all working for Jack Nicias and for the company, and we knew that the company would look after us . . . I never heard one bad word against him, you know? Everyone loved Jack Nicias. We've never had anyone else like him. Never. He used to know everyone by name, you know? There wasn't so many people here then, Jack Nicias would get to know everyone's name, and he'd remember you and where you worked, and that.

Gina: Oh, yeah, he (Jack Nicias) knew all of us by name, and he'd come up and down the hall and say "hello" to all of us every day.

Andrew: I got to meet Jack Nicias, who was Chairman of the Board of Trustees at the University of Rusty River and also head of Hephaestus at the time. I got to know him because he came out to these major fundraising events in California, that I was working on. And I said, gee, if that company is acting like that man, it has to be a great place to work. He was great . . . So I came to work for Hephaestus.

Many of the older employees talked about the early technological developments that Hephaestus had pursued. One of them remembers it at as time of extraordinary creativity:

Tom: I don't know if . . . we've had some great inventions . . . really great. Hephaestus has been known for brilliant science – you know, we invented the XXX (PC technology) but we didn't develop it, and then the Japanese did. I think we didn't know what we were on to then, and that's happened here a lot. We have great ideas . . . great inventions.

This new YYY Technology is something we've really worked on. You know, we started working on that about 20 years ago . . . that was way before Safron and Novocorp did.

David: . . . it is the control of electronic processes, the heart of the machine . . . and it's the excitement of Tom Sol – can you imagine, in the 1930s he was able, with just this kind of very primitive technology, to make the first Hephaestus machine and he spent the next 20 years trying to sell that patent to companies and nobody wanted it. And then Hephaestus bought it . . . and now it's all around the world.

On the recovery in the early 1980s:

Bob: You should have seen what happened. I guess we couldn't really believe it ourselves. Everybody was saying, and I mean outside of Hephaestus, the business papers . . . that we were done – nobody comes back after they've lost their market hold to the Japanese. But Hephaestus did.

The Hephaestus myth continues to be evoked. Toward the end of my field work at Hephaestus, the corporation underwent a major re-structuring. Although re-structurings had occurred periodically before, the present one was promoted, and perceived, to be particularly significant, with long-term implications for the company. I was present at the team meetings in which the reorganization outcomes were officially announced. For the Iris Team, the reorganization meant the loss, through promotion and relocation, of their Chief. For many weeks after the announcements the Chief, Sam Steele, tried hard to assure his team that his departure was not his doing, that he was following directions from above, and he reassured his inner team of managers that his loss would be quickly recovered from and that the new Chief was a fine person and excellent manager. The reorganization caused many ripples of consternation. The corporation, anticipating the concerns of its employees (and implicitly recognizing the breach in the cohesion and stability of the Team) and the possible disruption to morale and productivity such worries and fears produce, issued an internal communique in the form of a letter from the CEO, Tim Alott. Mr Alott's letter, in this time of (corporate-induced) crisis, invoked the name of the founder, Jack Nicias, to assure Hephaestus employees that the corporate changes taking place "will preserve and strengthen our corporate values" as laid down in "our earliest roots" under Jack Nicias.

Everyday culture: the "new culture"

Like a number of other large American companies Hephaestus Corporation introduced in the 1980s an extensive "new culture program" with the intention of ensuring the company's survival in a globally competitive market. Hephaestus Corporation had experienced serious market decline in the 1970s and following the planned introduction of its new culture program has now regained its market position. There had been other, lesser, efforts at workplace reorganization in the previous decade, but nothing as extensive and elaborate as the the "new culture program." The company continues in the 1990s to expend considerable sums of money and resources in creating and sustaining its new culture.

Hephaestus designed its new organizational culture and structural reforms following the recommendations of a commissioned report from the management consultants McKinsey and Company. The McKinsey consultants advised the new CEO, Callum Connor, that the company's vast bureaucracy and over-staffed operation was scrambling communication, crippling inventiveness and productivity and that decisions at the top were too frequently of a political rather than a business nature. The Hephaestus leadership subsequently developed a series of corporate reform packages (under various names) that used "benchmarking" and "employee involvement" as the two major strategies to "improve productivity and increase customer satisfaction." They also sought to develop a new culture, (echoing McKinsey and Co. and the management literature influenced by Deal and Kennedy 1982, Ouchi 1981, Peters and Waterman 1984, and others) in which employees would believe that their self-development, their source of self-fulfillment and identity are found in working for the corporation, and in the pursuit of company-defined "excellence".[6]

The strategies designed to implement the goals were two-fold. First, the effort to flatten hierarchies and encourage more participative decision-making structures included the introduction of the new form of "team" and "family" and the provision for employees to have their ideas and contributions valued and utilized by their managers, and their sense of identity with the company promoted. Second, the cultural values encouraged were the pursuit of excellence, leadership, customer satisfaction and a team-family atmosphere of caring involvement and commitment. The new culture carried new language forms and sought to design a "new employee" with a new set of attitudes toward the company, toward each other and toward the customer. Toward this end, the company introduced extensive training programs for all its employees that emphasized the skills of group and team building, of problem-solving processes, of inter-personal communication, of facilitation of meetings and the building of diverse and creative workplace cultures. The corporate aim was to develop a workforce that was not only more productive but reduced in size from its 1970s figures. (The 1992 re-organization continued to pursue this goal.) It was also intended that the "new Hephaestus employee" would be genuinely committed to the company's goals of excellence and customer satisfaction.[7] As the new culture took hold, assisted by various supplementary programs and continuing training courses available for managers, employees manifested the cultural values at least in their language forms and in their immediate inter-personal interactions.

Team and family are promoted as the forms of social organization that will achieve the company's goals of greater levels of employee involvement and attitudinal change in the pursuit of excellence and dedication to total customer satisfaction. While associated with a particular product, team and family become forms in which people identify their place within the corporation, increasingly displacing the former locus of occupational identification. Descriptions are by job title such as: Systems Test Manager, Marketing Module Manager, Customer Test Interface Manager, Worldwide Quality Launch Manager, Subsystems Design Engineer for the Iris Product Team, and therefore by team location, rather than as engineer, physicist, computer scientist and so forth.

Employees report how the new culture changed their working lives at Hephaestus:

Tim: In retrospect, I don't know, it wasn't fair . . . I would come up with ideas, obviously better ways of doing things . . . I would tell management that is the way things should be done. From my point of view their job was to put things in a better direction. But they would do nothing, because for the most part they were do-nothing people, and so my ideas were acknowledged as good, but they weren't, like they were too conservative.

Catherine: So the ideas weren't followed through?

Tim: No, particularly in our department. I would say that our department would nurture the conservative type management that was reactive rather than proactive. They didn't want any more ideas because they didn't want any more work . . . Now there is another part that is very important. Business started to change. The culture of business started to change, and I suppose mostly to cope with these Japanese management techniques and quality circles. Business started to talk about becoming more egalitarian and democratic . . . and I saw the opportunity and I was very frustrated.

Catherine: But you saw it coming in, this PQ program?

Tim: Not so much seeing it happen, I was frustrated that it is not happening, people were not accepting the new culture. I thought it was a great opportunity. Now I understood my managers not accepting it because they would have to give up some of their power, but I couldn't understand why workers weren't accepting it.

Another employee remembers it differently:

Ken: I am . . . I have always tried to believe in what the company says.
Catherine: Tried to believe it?
Ken: Yeah. You know, sometimes for a few years we would come up with a new slogan or something every couple of years. It just seems like, no point in being a cynic. I like to believe in our management. But some of the ideas are crazy, so I don't . . . Like using the problem-solving process on each and every problem. Well, I think we are coming around from that, but so far as the idea of being more customer focused and getting the common language (of PQ, the new culture) that really was helpful.
Sam: Yeah, I would say that PQ I think had a big impact on me . . . I feel good about it, I think it really did change Hephaestus. I think what it did is it provided a common language for everybody. Whether you go to Europe or you are here in Rusty River or the West Coast – everybody had at least some core language that they used, that was assigned, and you could have an argument about whether you were the customer or the supplier and what the requirements were . . . For the most part, it really changed us.

The organizational and social-psychological forms of team and family enable the tapping of employee knowledge resources and encourage group commitment to productivity that transcend occupational demarcations and exclusiveness. Team and family also enable a "culture of quality and customer service." The company insists that its dedication to excellence and to total customer satisfaction be shared, and manifested, by the employees. Hephaestus constantly compares itself to other companies in the same technological business and seeks to produce higher-quality goods at better prices. Benchmarking is implemented within the company by the encouragement of groups and teams to compare and compete with other teams within the overall Hephaestus Team. Competition within Hephaestus remains an important element of everyday workplace culture. Winning teams are rewarded with bonus payments, and high-achieving individuals also receive bonus payments or special weekend vacations in New York City. The culture promotes apparently more egalitarian participation, but retains internal competition.

Opal: I'm competitive, especially with my peers around me, who have started at the company with me. If they're a grade or two above me, then I always want to understand why I'm not there. Or if someone may be on the high potential list and I'm not, why is it working for them and not for me?

99

An elaborate corporate vocabulary has been developed to structure and communicate these corporate values and strategies. A key concept is that of the "customer" and the "customer requirements." The notion of customer has been expanded to include not just the buyer of Hephaestus products in the marketplace, but Hephaestus employees themselves. Employees regard each other and themselves as customers. Their interactions with each other, both between and within teams, are based on the view that they are buyers or suppliers and they have certain needs – "customer requirements" – that they and others must meet. In the marketplace and within Hephaestus interactions with customers are referred to as "interfacings," and a customer or customer agent is termed an "interface." The marketplace language of customer is promoted alongside the filial language of team and family.

An employee reports: "I am doing this job for Jeff. He's my customer for this set of requirements and so it has to be quality . . . He's my customer and that means that the customer requirements have to be met whether he's just down the hall or in some company in Pittsburgh or wherever."

Formerly, in typical industrial conditions, workers were regarded as producers. They served the production end of the market equation. Now, they are regarded, and must regard themselves, simultaneously as customers and as producers. The disintegration of the former differentiation in this equation furthers the erosion of occupational solidarities and opens up further channels for the company's incursion into the processes of self-formation that occur in the experiences of work. The employee is simultaneously in filial relation to her teammate-siblings and in commercial relation to them as buyer and deliverer.

Many employees reflected on the language and behavior associated with the team-family, but few appeared to consider the new concept of the employee-customer. Those who did regarded it as an effective concept in shaping employees' approaches to each other and in carrying out their work.

David: Well, there are certain guidelines and a philosophy in this PQ business, and it may be kind of trite, but in fact it works. It works because there is a cookbook of how to formulate a problem and how to address a problem. It, shall we say, demystifies the job and organizes the idea of problem-solving into logical steps and I think that most people here are logical otherwise they wouldn't be working for Hephaestus. So it takes a concept and puts it into bite-sized pieces for them and maybe that is the reason it works. So therefore people like "customer satisfaction" and "customer requirements" and "supplier specifications" – it channels your mind into thinking the right way.

David's comment that the language of the customer "channels your mind into thinking the right way" aptly describes the purpose of the new language. The new language not only blurs the differentiation between

100

producer and customer and enables the corporation to advance its formative influence upon employees, it enables the employees to perceive themselves as something they like to be outside of the workplace. The customer, in contemporary American market culture, is "always right" and is entitled to demand satisfaction in the purchase of the commodity and in the vendor's service. The commercial exchange is elaborated by cultural rituals that include some indulgence of and deference to the customer to enhance the pleasure of purchase. The corporate language of employee-customer indirectly serves employees' consumer compulsions and gratifications, affirming and cultivating those impulses into the production relation of the immediate workplace.

Accompanying the new corporate vocabulary is a recent emphasis on "valuing diversity," which encourages managers to hire new employees from minority ethnic groups. Like the expanded concept of customer, the notion of "valuing" diversity serves latent as well as official purposes. Officially, managers and team leaders are encouraged to recognize and develop the potential contributions from minorities and women employees. The valuing of diversity and minority employee involvement programs are promoted as examples that confirm Hephaestus' reputation for being a progressive, innovative corporation in the implementation of affirmative action and equal opportunity programs. At the same time, the company rhetoric simultaneously promotes the expediency of tapping human resources previously blocked through racial prejudice and discrimination against women. Valuing diversity serves a useful public relations function as well as a management function that now seeks to appropriate a broader range of skills and expertise among its employees as they are drawn beyond occupational specificity and become team-style generalists.

Opal: The one thing I'm beginning to deal with – and this one's kind of tough – is being a black female in an organization like this. When things happen to you, you don't know whether it's because people may be prejudiced because you're black, or prejudiced because you're female, or they just treat everybody like that. I finally got to the point where I don't think people see me as black or female, they just see me as another person.

Kelly: But you'll still get people saying to you that you've only got that assignment because you're a woman, and Hephaestus is really trying to promote women now. But I don't think it's true, and I still find that I get treated like I'm a girl and they just assume that I can't do some parts of the job – well not exactly that I can't do them, but like I won't for some reason, because I'm a woman . . . And there's this one guy, he does it all the time, and it's so obvious I don't know why he thinks he can get away with it. Like he will make jokes, just sort of jokes that aren't funny, about me, or some of the other women . . . And like if I'm not smiling or

101

easy going all the time he will make comments that, have I had a fight with my boyfriend, and like that, all the time . . . And I think you get left out of things, because they don't even notice, and they just go on together.

I think because I'm young and a woman that I don't get what the guys get, and they always look at you when you go into a meeting room, like, are you supposed to be there?

I go to the Women's Caucus [Hephaestus Corporation Women's Caucus], and Hephaestus is really good like that, they will send some of us, delegates, to Washington for the conference. And I went last year . . . We discuss the progress for women in Hephaestus, and make recommendations to Corporate [Headquarters]. And sometimes we take up grievances. I think it's good, but I think we've got a long ways to go.

Training courses teach employees, especially managers, how to practice the valuing of diversity, how to tap team resources and to behave constructively in meetings. Gone now are the smoke-filled rooms and the habits of door-slamming and overtly aggressive shouting matches between individuals that were typical, and legitimate, behavior of a previous generation of corporate managers. At both the training seminars and through the voluminous new culture manuals employees learn problem-solving techniques and group skills: how to facilitate the generation and flow of creative ideas, how to elicit participation from the junior or lower-paid members and the traditionally excluded members of the group. Above all, employees learn to be "team-players" and to be part of the Hephaestus "family." Inter-personal interactions are usually on first-name terms (except in disciplinary situations) with an emphasis on careful listening and congeniality.

This new culture is reinforced by plentiful references to the old foundational cultural values. The continuity of the Hephaestus myth is ensured in its retelling in various ways in the training seminars and in other written materials, and periodically at team meetings. It remains an important cornerstone of the new culture. Other everyday sources of reinforcement of the new values and desired practices are the liberal displays of posters, pictures and slogans on the walls in corridors, cafeterias, meeting rooms, and in individual cubicles. These displays constantly remind of the new culture and repeat the approved language and styles of employee interaction. All of these practices teach the beliefs, values and desired bahavior of the company's planned culture. They manifest the operation of an effective pedagogical function. The paper cups that are used by the million in the coffee vending machines carry slogans about the company's production strategies. Likewise, the shipping-container-sized trucks display the words "Team Hephaestus" across their sides, and some of the outer walls of the buildings, visible from the air, display similar injunctions to Teamwork and Quality.

Everyday culture: what employees believe

The "official" culture that Hephaestus Corporation has deliberately constructed and actively promotes also contains sets of latent values, beliefs and practices. Employees report beliefs and values that are shaped by the effects of the official culture. Many of these beliefs and values are not actually officially stated in the manuals or in company slogans but they are congruent with the values and functions of the new culture, especially the forms of team and family. Most employees report a high degree of loyalty to the company, and a belief in the company's loyalty toward them. They believe that Hephaestus will "look after" them, that if they do a good job then Hephaestus will reward them well, and they will not be laid off or displaced in re-structurings.

Chris: Oh, we'd never be let go. Good people never lose their jobs in Hephaestus. I think that if something bad really happened, like if Novocorp got their (product) ahead of ours, I still think Hephaestus wouldn't lay people off. They don't do that. We'd be looked after.

Si: There's always a place for good people. I've never worried that Hephaestus would let me go . . . I guess I've never really thought about it. It didn't happen to me during the restructurings about 1982 or 83, when thousands of people went, some people I knew well . . . They've always looked after me, they do.

Vinny: I feel real proud to be part of Hephaestus. I'm happy to give 110 percent to this company. You know Rusty River wouldn't exist without Hephaestus and Safron. We've made this town, and we're proud of it. I believe that people know that about Hephaestus.

They also believe that Hephaestus is a "good corporate citizen" as the company proclaims itself to be, and they believe that they are fortunate to work for such a company. They report a high level of derived status in the wider community by virtue of their working for Hephaestus.

Colin: Everyone in this town knows that Hephaestus is a good company to work for. You know, you just tell people you work for Hephaestus and they already think you must be someone.

Catherine: Why is that, do you think?

Colin: Oh, well, I guess . . . it's because Hephaestus is just known for being a great company, and everybody knows that. It pays well, and it's a good citizen, it's responsible . . . And you just have high status when you tell someone you work for Hephaestus.

Still others:

Joel: Ever since the days of Jack Nicias, Hephaestus has prided itself on being a good corporate citizen. Hephaestus is very fair. It has a very good name in Rusty River.

Maggie: It's nice to be known as someone who works for Hephaestus. There's a real good feeling when someone asks you at a party or something who you work for and you say Hephaestus. You don't even have to say what you do there. It's enough just to say that you work for Hephaestus, and people just respect that somehow, so they respect you too. It's nice.

Jenny: It sure does give you a socially acceptable identity and there is a status in the eyes of other people when you say you work for Hephaestus.

Only one person mentioned some of the legal cases Hephaestus Corporation has been involved in concerning the hazards and legacy of toxic-waste dumping in the ground, in the River and in the air over the last couple of decades. These cases are quite public, they are just not remembered or mentioned by Hephaestus people.

The employees also hold their own meaning construct for the phenomenon of Hephaestus Corporation.

Andrew: Hephaestus has always been known as a great place to work. When I joined in 1965 it was a real star company. I said to myself, gee, I really want to work for that company.

Drew: When I think of Hephaestus, I think of Imperial Hephaestus. When you think of what this company has done, and where it has come from, it's very imperial, conquering.

Vinny: Hephaestus is like a very moralistic, righteous parent. It's the kind of parent everyone should be lucky enough to have . . . It's a very moral company. It does the right thing.

Terry: Hephaestus has this aura about it, like I can't really explain, but it's there and I feel it. Everytime I go somewhere I notice if they have Hephaestus machines or not.

There are differences in beliefs among the older group, the over-45s, and the younger group, the under-35s. The middle group is a small numerical minority reflecting the hiring patterns of the 1970s downturn. As individuals they waver most in their allegiances and sentiments toward the company. It appeared that many of them wished to speak as favorably as their older colleagues, but were drawn to the instrumentalism of the younger group, especially the men. The older group, and the retirees, tend toward a more complete process of rationalization about their work and the company, and reify its qualities.

Gordon: Hephaestus has been everything . . . I mean, I don't know what my life would have been without it. I have two sons still working for Hephaestus, and my wife used to work there too. We've lived in this house for nearly 40 years . . . it's why we live out here . . . You know, it was Hephaestus who got the 401 (highway) extended out here.

We bought some stock, in the 60s, and we've done well. I mean, you couldn't have asked for a better company to work for. It's like, well, it's a great company . . . Hephaestus has always done the right thing.

Merv: Hephaestus has given me everything. I had the time of my life. We worked very hard, I don't think there was ever a period when I worked a forty-hour week. I always worked much more. We never had any arguments or anything, it was great. I don't remember ever getting angry at work. I never got angry at work in 35 years . . . I had a great boss for years. They were the best years then, for Hephaestus. Plenty of money around then, too. It was a great company. . . it *is* a great company.

KNOWLEDGE, IMAGE WORK AND OCCUPATION

Another important new discourse of production in the post-occupational corporation is knowledge. The role of knowledge in the work of Hephaestus has expanded with the expansion of advanced technologies and the reorganization of corporate workplaces. Specialist occupational knowledge used to be a central element in the organization of work, and in social organization. In the workplace knowledge and skill, which were occupationally categorized, determined access to technological and management functions. These traditional hierarchies of power and exclusion are undergoing important changes. The new production and information technologies are networked in ways that "informate" (Zuboff 1988) the workplace and enable the democratization and dispersion of certain knowledge functions. It is now possible (and desirable for both management and employees) for employees to know much more about the elements of production than they previously did. An integration of knowledge work, that was previously separated, is now being practiced in the post-industrial culture of Hephaestus Corporation. The former boundaries of occupational specialities are breaking down.

Gordon: When I'm at a party, or if I meet new people someplace, I usually just tell them I work for Hephaestus. It's easier if I say that . . . everybody's heard of Hephaestus and they have an idea of what you do because of Hephaestus products. But how are they going to know what my job really is? . . . I could say I'm an engineer, and I have a college degree . . . but I'm not exactly an engineer anymore. I work on the software of the XXX component of the Iris. And I do financial planning and reports . . . It just happens that you move and you get into things, and I've got involved in the launch . . . into marketing and the more I see of that I know I could do that . . . We just do it all on my team.

Another employee reports that his jobs seem to change often, and not always because he is seeking new opportunities.

Catherine: Tell me about your job . . . and the job title.

Hal: My job? Well, it just changed. Yesterday, I think. Principal Information Systems Consultant is what it changed to. And I used to be Manager Assistant Projects, I think it was called.

I match new technologies to productivity gains that could be had by the company. And once I match a technology with a set of productivity gains it's my responsibility to investigate, make sure that it's something good and that it is going to give the organization some benefits. I do all the financials and all the other stuff. Cost qualities analyses and that kind of thing . . . And another part of my job is to help transfer that technology to the rest of the organization and not just let it drop . . . And I go to pilot, I also take a look at where the support is going to be needed for that technology, and I work with those people too. I line them up and set up those partnerships with all the different groups and teams . . . a good part of it is marketing too . . . I would normally take those activities myself, and do all those negotiations . . . So I would understand the background of the technology, and know the support requirements, hardware and software, and what they need, and the finances.

Catherine: Marketing within the organization?

Hal: Yeah. But not always . . . I like to negotiate and I like to build proposals. I like to look at their side of it. I like to build strategies for getting people to sign up for things. I also like the idea of putting in a change, a new change, especially now within the organization which is really different from what I did before. Before it was isolated to a small pocket of people . . . and kind of now it's like we're across the whole organization. You have to know a lot and I like to know. I think it's the right thing to do. I like the challenge of it.

Computer aided design and manufacturing technologies (CAD/CAM) and computer integrated manufacturing (CIM) not only displace the need for individualized worker units, that is people possessing specific knowledge and expertise and restricted to certain tasks, they act to generalize and integrate certain knowledge functions previously held by expert professionals or highly skilled technologists. As a consequence, private expertise and contribution, which was usually occupationally and professionally bound and protected, is lessening. More and more employees, particularly technologists and managers, are able to possess previously specialist knowledge and perform wider functions in the corporate workplace than their predecessors. Employees with specialist degrees and formerly specialist skills now participate in functions, and acquire the knowledges, formerly reserved for other specialists. Many Hephaestus technological employees now gain an MBA degree.

David: I was a person who was one of a small number of experts in a very narrow field, I was a specialist in 1974. I came to Hephaestus because

106

they wanted something from me. I was a Ph.D. commodity. I was bought, I was given the golden handshake to come here, and I took it. And after being here two or three years and thinking it is great, I knew that I couldn't sustain it, being an expert, because Hephaestus was no longer interested in that field, so that meant that I had two options – that I either had to move into academia and continue my research, or stop being an expert and learn the business.

Well, I'm physicist, and I went from being the world's expert in a very narrow field to a person who was learning and understanding all aspects of Hephaestus because I felt that was the way to go.

I had been publishing two papers a year since my academic years . . . I was part of an elite clique of scientists, that went from one conference to another all over the world. So you would feed off each other, and you would get ideas and you would do more research, and in Hephaestus I was kind of limited and so by 1978 I had to give it up . . . I guess it was part of my life that had to end. I couldn't afford to go back to academia, Hephaestus was paying me too much, and the retirement benefits were such, and my life wasn't that bad, but I had to make a conscious decision to end my research development and become a "Hephaestus-oid."

David's knowledge was required to be deployed and directed in certain ways by Hephaestus through the team in which he works. Although still a scientist with specialized knowledge, David is no longer specifically a physicist, he is a "systems troubleshooter" with broad and detailed knowledge of the Hephaestus technologies. Yet David is not a member of the inner Iris team. He had wanted to be a research scientist in Hephaestus, as was intended when he was originally employed. He also was assured that there was a dual-ladder system for advancement, through which he would advance as a principal scientist to positions comparable to those on the conventional path of management. He now believes he has been misled. The company, he believes, values managerial skill over scientific and technological knowledge.

At the lower end, manufacturing workers[8] similarly organized in teams, must gain the skills and knowledges of their teammates and be able to perform multiple functions.

Doreen: Well, we have to know what's going on up ahead of us and just behind us on the line. Because if somebody's out you have to be able to move in and do her job just like you can do your own . . . See if Betty is out or if she has to go cover for somebody else, I might have to do her station so we don't get a build-up on that white line.

Betty: Yeah, and that's how we all do it here now. Sometimes you might know all the jobs on this line, and on this line you can, because it's a pilot line so we're close to the engineers who come out here and fix their problems while we stand here. And there's not that many stations on this

line, but if you go over to Building 909 you can't know all the stations
. . . This is a much better line . . . And we're all seniors here, so we
usually know most of the others [jobs] and we know how to work it. But
we know more than the boys inside [the engineers] how to make this line
work. If we did it their way we'd be on a just-wait-a-time line!

Doreen: But they never ask us, they don't think we know, so when they
come around we change what we're doing back to doing it their way, and
then go and have a coffee . . . They think they know their business.

The new technologies, and the new culture, have departed from specialization of knowledge and function, characteristic of industrialism (and
Fordism specifically), to a multiplicity of knowledges and roles. Specialization and demarcation are giving way to generalization and flexibility.
When, occasionally, this transformation is recognized by employees of
company "new culture" trainers, it is welcomed as essential to the desired
flattening out of traditional hierarchies through sharing responsibilites,
extending accountability, and empowering employees. Relinquishing
specialization and demarcation enables an expansion and increase in
work skills and creates a workplace that is apparently more open and
congenial. It also diminishes the occupational power and privileges of
expert professionals.

However, there are limits to this apparent democratization of knowledge.
A pattern of polarization is emerging within the Hephaestus workplace in
which the dispersion of knowledge is controlled by a new demarcation
between an upper level of technologists and managers and a lower level of
manufacturing workers. But at both polar ends occupational boundaries are
disappearing. In industrial society occupational designations traditionally
referred to a relationship to the material means of production. With the
increasing importance of discursive (including knowledge) means of production *occupational distinctiveness, in a large corporate workplace, no
longer matters*. Occupational designation still points to a body of skills and
knowledges, but even professional occupational groups (as individual
professions) can no longer guarantee an exclusive claim to an expert
body of knowledge[9]. They can, however, do this as a class[10] and this
importantly will shape the composition of the bipolar social structure
that is emerging in advanced capitalist society (compare Gorz 1989 and
Reich 1991).

Replacing occupation as a primary locus of class and self identification
in the corporate workplace is team and knowledge. The breaking down of
traditional occupational and professional boundaries effects the dissolution
of the bonds of social cohesion that their statuses and collegiality provided.
For the corporation it enables the dispersion of certain (not all) knowledge
and expertise among many people, and the capacity to tap the resources of
its employees more deeply. Ostensibly, it appears that this enables the

natural creation of teams in which people share knowledge, skills and resources and work cooperatively in the manufacture of their products. However, such sociality in *post-occupational* corporate teamwork is not natural within the over-riding corporate structure in which control of the apparent democratization of knowledge is retained under a newly polarized power structure. To be effective, the team requires the deliberate creation of a substitute, discursive social cohesion that is necessary for production to occur. A social cohesion without the primary element of occupation is provided by the corporation's simulated family. Relationship to a product, to team-family members and to the company displaces identification with occupation and its historic respository of skills, knowledges and allegiances.

Image production

In addition to the currency of knowledge the place of "image work" is a newly important discourse of production. Image work is a multifarious discourse that includes the symbol of the Hephaestus products carried by evocations of its name and myth. Hephaestus creates and promotes an image that embodies its name, products and employees. The corporation's new culture creates a carefully designed set of images of its products and of its employees. Not only does the company's marketing material extol the quality of Hephaestus smart machines, it extols the quality of its employees: their knowledge, skills and dedication to excellence are commodified and marketed. Central to the new Total Quality Management image (the Hephaestus version being labeled "PQ") is the pursuit of "total customer satisfaction." The image presented, and the one at the core of the marketing philosophy, is one in which achieving excellence in customer service is as important as excellence in the machine products themselves. To this end, Hephaestus Corporation describes itself as the "learning company" in which employees and management alike are totally committed to a path of on-going learning in the pursuit of an ever-better product and customer service. The "learning company" continues the process of reification that the foundation myth first established.

Sam: Hephaestus has really tried to learn from its mistakes. You know, what was going on here before the 80s just couldn't have continued. The rest of the world, prior to PQ . . . looked at us as non-responsive to customers – very arrogant in the marketplace. And, just, that it was the company that grew and became a lion and knew better than the customers. And I sat in a customer's office in Boston, and basically he said the same thing, and that in the last four years he has seen a real change in Hephaestus. A real change. This company learned from the 1970s.
Frank: When I was taking classes for my MBA at the University of Rusty

River about half the class was from Hephaestus. It was like we wanted everyone to know we (Hephaestus Corporation) were really into learning and studying . . . It was a big thing too, a real status thing . . . But it's not just about getting degrees, it's about learning here. There are many courses you can do.

In this way, the employees' knowledge becomes a new avenue for identification with the company. No longer private and occupationally bound, a general corporate knowledge that is protected by an oath of security becomes the collective embodiment of individual knowledges. The company's advanced technological products are the sum of individual contributions. Through the process of identification with their knowledge products employees identify with the company at a deeper level. As highly skilled generalists, and no longer product specialists, individuals are unable to lay claim to distinct products. They therefore claim their contribution through the team's products and through the company's image.

The notion of customer satisfaction is promoted as the driving force in Hephaestus' design and manufacture of its products. Trading in image work – in the symbol of the Hephaestus product – is now as important as the capabilities of the new technologies embedded in the Hephaestus machines. Employees are instructed that selling the image of the company occurs simultaneously with selling their products. The control of that image is as important as the quality of the technological products themselves. None the less, the discourse of customer service is also controlled by the corporation. Customer satisfaction was a recurrent problem discussed at Iris Team meetings. On occasion the Chief, Sam Steele, would remind his team members that "we can make customer problems go away, by "turning the customer off." He elaborated: "Making the customers believe that what they perceive to be a problem, isn't one." Beneath the rhetoric of total customer satisfaction, and the semblance of that being paramount, there remains a long-established process of manipulation and control. But this is rarely recognized by Hephaestus employees. They believe the image, and the myth, of Hephaestus.

Opal: If you take the engineering view of why a product works, or the application doesn't work, and then you see the marketing view that says, "well, but you're working on it, right?" and we say, "well, yeah, we're working on it." So there's the potential, the outside potential. So the marketing people don't tell the customer that it doesn't work . . . But you take two different perspectives. You can see it from the marketing perspective because the bottom line is profit for the corporation. They may not be telling the whole truth, but they're not really lying.

Employees are bearers of the Hephaestus image at multiple sites. For instance, employees are carefully groomed in their styles of personal interaction and appearance. Technical representatives who repair machines on the customer's premises must follow a dress code. An incident occurred at a team meeting in which a manager reported òn a disciplinary case against one of his team members. The employee had been travelling out of state to promote and demonstrate a new Hephaestus machine at a trade show. The employee was also responsible for the installation of machines on clients' premises. After completing a long shift on the job at the trade show the employee changed from his business clothes into casual attire. He received a telephone call while driving that instructed him to return to a client's premises to attend to a problem with the new machine. The employee went to the job wearing his casual clothes and was subsequently reported. The employee faced a disciplinary review for breaching company etiquette. He had failed to represent Hephaestus in the proper way as a smartly dressed professional who represents the high quality of the company and its products.

The company's promotion of itself as exemplary corporate citizen includes publicly visible displays of community involvement through financial sponsorship and through employee participation in programs for city youth. Hephaestus public-relations staff developed a "minority excellence" program in which Hephaestus employees volunteer time after-hours to assist disadvantaged urban youth in educational and developmental activities. The company gains photograph opportunities that promote its image as a good and caring citizen that is involved in the community and in the education of disadvantaged Americans.

THE DISCURSIVE SOCIAL STRUCTURES AND PROCESSES OF HEPHAESTUS CORPORATION

Team and family

The new organizational structures of team and family are discursive social practices. Hephaestus Corporation promotes these concepts as cultural artifacts and processes, and that is the sense in which they were first mentioned above. But team and family are deliberately designed social structures and processes. These processes act as the discursive mediation of the social structures of Hephaestus Corporation. This means that team and family are more than convenient cultural formations that promote certain desired sensibilities among employees to encourage greater involvement and productivity. The sense of organic agency, of human volition, in making culture is actually eliminated by the corporation's deliberate design and orchestrated control of these artifacts as structures – structures that are experienced through communications – that constrain the possible forms of cultural expression and shape the desired Hephaestus employee. Team and family in Hephaestus exist only as discourses – they are not organically, spontaneously created by groups of workers wishing to create community with each other, and they do not exist outside the Hephaestus workplace. In fact, spontaneous social life among employees has actually declined since the designer culture was introduced.

Maggie: We used to socialize with each other back then . . . I think that it started to fall away when the company decided that they would do all of these things, and they would give us picnics and stuff, and sports teams . . . and when they started arranging these company things, I don't know, but I think that it was the structures, where you knew that you were going to party on Wednesday the 19th, whereas before you would have all worked together, maybe ten-hour days, and accomplished a whole lot, and you felt on a Thursday night like having a few beers, then you would do it together, and there was no structure to it, and say, hey, that was a really bad day, let's go have a beer, and that stopped.

Jimmy: We don't socialize as much as we used to. I remember when we used to . . . go bowling together . . . and you know it's not just because we've all gotten older, it's just so organized now, I don't know.

Gina: It was a fun company. But we worked real hard, but we played hard too, and we would always have parties and get-togethers constantly.

The official discourse on team and family claims that these new de-hierarchicalized structures and processes enable greater levels of employee participation and involvement in the operation and productivity of the company. The team and family flatten out decision-making authority and accountability and broaden participation in management functions. No longer are employees expected to be engaged only in the tasks of execution of management-designed processes of production and work organization as they were under traditional, industrial Fordist conditions. Their knowledge, skills and experiential expertise are now valued in the wider processes of running the productive enterprise. Knowledgeable and skilled employees are now invited, and required, to have a substantive role in the design and management of production. The rewards to the employees for participating in this new function are feelings of greater involvement and a sense of "empowerment" in a partnership with a caring and committed employer, and a close-knit team of colleagues who share a passion for excellence and customer satisfaction. Hephaestus promotes the team concept as the way for employees to perform to their utmost, to feel valued and to have their resources of knowledge and skill more deeply tapped and utilized.

The extent to which team and family are promoted as essential (and not optional) new cultural forms reveals the architectural design of corporate culture and management structures that neutralizes employee-initiated practices, other than minor intiatives, that were tolerated under industrialism. The corporate designers of the new organizational structures know (as

112

Ouchi (1981) and Peters and Waterman (1984) informed them) that these new structures will not succeed without the creation of a culture of feelings, attitudes, beliefs, habits and behavior that correspond with the forms of organization embodied in the new structures. The new culture seeks to retain the integration forms of industrial culture. Hephaestus wants a corporate culture that has the solidarity and cohesion of industrial culture but eliminates the visibility and knowledge of structural conflicts inherent in traditional industrial culture. It seeks also to eliminate the allegiances of employees to external solidarity forms in the remnants of class and union formations. A corporate culture in which employees "feel good about themselves" enables their locus of identity to shift toward the source of that good feeling. The *effect* of participation and "empowerment" disguises their absence.

The "family" concept is promoted among the manufacturing workers and other non-exempt workers within the greater team. (Hephaestus itself often portrays itself as the great "Hephaestus Team.") The family metaphor actively evokes pre-industrial romantic images of human bonding and shared struggles against adversity. The family is also hierarchical, paternalistic and deferential to higher external authorities. It is the metaphor that accesses processes, as Ouchi (1981) called them, of "clan control." Employees assume family-like roles with one another and are managed by family rules and processes. Direct bureaucratic supervisory control is no longer necessary. The culture moves, *just in time*, to eliminate the need and role of hierarchical supervision as the technology eliminates, through automation and information technologies, its function.

Si: It's like a family here. We all get on well, and we're looked after. Sure, we argue sometimes, if someone hasn't done their job right, or something, but you never really get mad . . . We're a family, you know . . . and we stick together.

Bob: Hephaestus has looked after me . . . I've grown up here. It's been like a family. We're a family here.

Drew: I remember when they used to encourage us as managers to be like fathers to the younger ones coming on, and that's the way it was for me . . . And that's the way I am with some of my people.

Todd: I didn't have a father when I was a kid, and there were no real male role models for me. When I joined Hephaestus there were plenty of male role models, and one or two in particular become real father-figures for me . . . I still think of them like that.

The team is promoted among the professional groups. It evokes references to individual performance while sharing commitments to group styles of working and goals. Like the sports team, it has "star" players, coaches and owners. People are told what to do, but the quality of their performance is ensured by their skills and abilities, and measured by its contribution to the overall goals of the team. The metaphor also evokes images of deep loyalty and dedication for the life of the team. When the team's project is completed and the team disbands, the player-performers must join another team. While in the company's view, the team is not a family, and players cannot assume to be looked after when they are no longer productive or no longer required, this view is not necessarily shared by the employees who are often confused about what they can expect. They especially believe that they will be "looked after" by Hephaestus (as reported above) no matter what happens. Even when reports of some people losing their jobs, including very senior people, are circulated, employees find rationalizations for such events and deny to themselves even the remote possibility of it happening to them.

Len: No, I'm not worried about job security; I've never worried about it. I'd never get laid off. I'm a good worker. We all know that Hephaestus doesn't let good people go.

I asked Len about an anecdotal comment I had heard at an Iris Team meeting in which some senior Hephaestus executives in New York city had been fired while they were out at lunch. They had to vacate their offices immediately. Len responded with disbelief, "What?" he replied, "well, I don't know about that . . . I wouldn't make anything of that."

The two metaphors, team and family, are used deliberately among the different pan-occupational groups. At the same time it is common for both metaphors to be used interchangeably, especially when the desirable sentiments of one are particularly preferable. But the way in which the metaphors are understood by individuals varies considerably. The result for the employees and the company is that the desired sentiments and allegiances are formed among the employees and confusion about their relationship to one another and to the corporation is obscured, avoided and maintained. The outcome is that the rhetoric and practices of both organizational and cultural forms are widely used, believed in and acclaimed and their contradictions denied. As one senior manager in his mid-40s reflecting on the team concept describes it:

Donal: I think it's great. I think it is how you get through the day, and when you really have something that you have to deliver, and I mean, there are deliverables and there are deliverables and you are in the line. We have to deliver 350 machines a month . . . and I have been to about 10 of those accounts (customers) personally, and I jokingly call it dog-fighting, it is a real battle. You have people that are very vocal and in your face, and, well it is just the way they are, and I try to instill a sense of commitment to those customers; that we will satisfy them. You are not going to do it but by hard work and knowing what their demands are and meeting their needs and that takes a team, no one person can do that. So we have the team, I depend on the team.

And another:

Luke: We are very open. I am very close to my managers, we fight and yell at each other. We throw each other out of the room. We are very high-strung people. But we are a team.

Donal: I was in this building ten years ago and there was a lot of internal bickering, and today it is the Product Delivery Team. It's a team now. I think that I have made decisions, and (the other senior managers) have too – they are for the team. And so it is a mentality, and I can put a finger on it, it's like a religion almost, and it works.

Hephaestus Corporation, like other corporations, relies upon and encourages the bonds of loyalty, dedication and commitment to the company among its employees and expends considerable financial and human resources in establishing and maintaining these bonds. Under traditional industrial conditions with strong demarcations between production-line workers, bureaucratic and professional employees, companies could more readily rely on these bonds operating among its white-collar employees. Although impersonal bureaucratic structures can impede loyalty and dedication bonds, an elaborate career and reward structure and the expectation of lifelong employment (none of which now remain in place) assisted white-collar bonding (cf. Whyte 1956, Drucker 1960, Kanter 1977). At the same time, the solidarity (formerly) provided by professional occupational identification assisted company loyalties. For the manufacturing and other non-exempt workers the bond-object was their occupational status and the trade union (when not appropriated by the company in actively de-unionized plants) or its class remnant.

In Hephaestus Corporation these bonds are now steadily weakening – except among the manufacturing workers. The manufacturing workers still have their union, but have increasingly bonded with Hephaestus. They commonly express gratitude toward the company for allowing the union to continue to be present. The union which represents only the manufacturing workers has become an intermediary body, no longer representing a contest to company loyalty. But among the white-collar, technological employees Hephaestus is now engaged in a vigorous campaign to promote the sentiments and manifestation of loyalty, commitment and hardworking dedication to the company and its products. Most visible in this effort is the promulgation of new language forms and practices among its employees in the workplace. These practices are continually being updated and intensified. Only among the older group (over 45) – which is still substantive and in the leadership positions – can the company more reliably count on the effectiveness of the old social bonds of loyalty, dedicated hard work and belief in the company's "goodness." They are the real believers. But there are some disturbing signs, for Hephaestus, among some of them too. The older group reports sustained belief in what Hephaestus has done for them and for the country. But many of them also report that they cannot encourage the younger ones to believe as sincerely as they do, or once did.

Sandy: This is a good company to work for, but there's changes somehow . . . it's not like it used to be. You know they're cutting health insurance and retirement . . . it's tougher . . . I don't know what it'll be like for, like the ones who are young now . . . I don't want my son to work for Hephaestus anymore, I used to want him too, but I don't anymore.

Stan: It's not as good as it used to be here. PQ was supposed to focus on the customer, and encourage teamwork. But it hasn't done the really important thing of feeling in control over our lives . . . or our products . . . I felt more empowered in 1964 . . . It's like there's all these contradictions . . . between the talk of empowerment and . . . they have more hoops and controls since the 1970s . . . I'm not really part of the team.

Stan had, at one time, been on the fast track to be a chief engineer which did not eventuate. He had suffered a severe heart attack a few years earlier and was now looking forward to his forthcoming retirement. He often took naps in the Iris team meetings and was known for speaking his mind when he wished to. He had, at one time, been the manager of the current chief engineer and his dissenting voice was tolerated in meetings. Many of the younger team members admired his ability to speak up, which they regarded as unusual and probably as a result of his dissociation from the promotion ladder.

The members of the younger group (under 35) have lost their faith (but not the capacity to believe). This dissolution of belief began, I think, before their experience in Hephaestus (in high school culture (see Wexler 1992), as children of the Reagan years) and has been accelerated during their time here. They report a much higher degree of instrumental reasons for working for Hephaestus – the high pay, the convenience of the location, the advantages of tenure and health insurance. They rarely report the other sources of allegiance that the older group do. But they do go along with the team concept as a structure, and some actively believe in it for its ability to shape and encourage relationships that are collegial and open. For many, there is a willingness to believe, but belief seems to be harder for them than it was for the older group. Their bond to the company is tenuous and fragile.

Curiosity about the company, particularly its market success, its stocks and shares, its public image, is rarely expressed among the younger groups. Their interest in the company is focused on the terms of their own salaries and career advancement. Some of them are interested in the stock market in general, in how well similar companies are doing and in which companies are considered the best to work for. The loyalty to Hephaestus Corporation does not run deep. It is the older ones whose lives have been more overtly shaped by Hephaestus, who continue to express a familial interest in the company. That group will often know in detail aspects of Hephaestus' fortunes on the stock market and its market status compared with its Japanese and other American competitors.

The age differential in these expressions and forms of allegiance might simply be attributable to perceptions that each group holds about its likely future. The older ones rarely consider or imagine the possibility of not working for Hephaestus. Some of the younger ones do. But fewer people actually leave after they have been with the company for more than ten years. The under-35 group is therefore the primary target of Hephaestus' campaign for team, family, loyalty and excellence. These features were an expected part of industrial cultural socialization more broadly. Hephaestus simply had to appropriate loyalty and dedication from other objects and attach them to Hephaestus. This appropriation is actively worked at, and the daily repetition of language and interpersonal interaction styles of the new culture are important processes in this appropriation and re-shaping.

At the same time that it promotes family and team so vigorously, Hephaestus also recognizes the increasing trend toward privatization and individualism and the risk of a dissolution of social bonds. Hephaestus includes in its new culture strategy apparently counter-team promises of high individual reward for high individual performance. Similarly, small teams within larger teams also compete against each other for team excellence awards and earn bonus payments and other rewards. These apparent contradictions in the corporate rhetoric are rarely noticed by employees. They are obscured and compensated for in habitual use of the new language in which they regard each other as "customer," "inter-face" and "teammate." And they produce their "deliverables" (one's particular job responsibilities) as one would serve a customer in the marketplace.

Jerry is a fast-tracking engineer manager in his thirties with an outstanding record of achievement in the company. He suffered a heart attack a few years ago and has strongly ambivalent feelings toward Hephaestus.

Jerry: Hephaestus is very me-oriented, or it is now. Everyone is out for themselves. You know teamwork isn't all it's cracked up to be. I'd rather work for myself . . . But I guess they had to do something, or we would have lost it to Novocorp completely.

The differences in loyalties and allegiance to the company expressed by the under-35s and over-40s broadly are not just a matter of tenure. (There are examples of the converse in each group, notably among young ethnic-minority employees who identify with the team and in the older group by men who have been unexpectedly passed over for promotion and "let down" by their previously benevolent and paternal employer who are cynical about the team, such as Stan above.) Many of the younger group have been with Hephaestus ten years or more, long enough to develop the bonds of loyalty and commitment that the older ones have. Attitudes are a matter of generational location and a change in the cultural production of loyalty and solidarity, a result of the erosion of industrial society and of the traditional, organic solidarities that provided cohesion.

According to middle managers:

Todd: The concept of Team Hephaestus is absolutely imperative. I don't think we'd have made it if we hadn't brought it in, and got everybody on board.

Si: You know, we were doing very badly back in the late 70s, early 80s – I don't think most of us realized just how badly we were doing. We'd been used to the early 70s especially when there just seemed to be so much money around. Back then . . . there was so much money around that if you had half a good idea you could get money to develop it. And the bonuses, you wouldn't believe the bonuses. And we used to waste a lot . . . But people got lazy, and there was so much bureaucracy, and we had just grown too fast, like we were out of control. I think if the new culture hadn't been brought in, we would have lost it.

Team meetings

The team structure organizes everyday work operations and regulates everyday workplace relationships. While there was broad consensus that it was a good thing, that it was the most successful innovation of the new culture program, it did not always work in its meeting form as well as individuals reported it to work for them. The meetings manifested all the new language and problem-solving processes, but they also featured traditional hierarchical, paternalistic authority, competition, bickering and political posturing. At the same time, meetings also displayed the team members' strong commitment to their product, and their desire for the customer to be satisfied – or to appear to be satisfied.

It was a common occurrence in the Iris Team meetings for several hours to pass during which problems were discussed and ideas for solutions or ways to proceed were debated. While everyone present was entitled to contribute, the actual effort toward problem-solving was usually left to a small group of about four or five, almost always the same people. Most of the others at the meeting would either report information and describe the problem to be addressed, or say nothing at all. On several occasions, after hours had been spent on a set of problems and an effort at team decision-making had been attempted, the Chief would make a unilateral decision to resolve the problem. If that decision met with any disagreement or complaint, he would typically exercise his authority by employing a traditional directive tone of voice and statement:

Steele: We're going to do it that way, because I say so, and I'm the boss, okay? And that's the end of it.

Statements such as this one were generally accepted, often with displays of relief from the meeting participants. There would be a bodily shuffle and re-adjustment, a rustle of papers, and a joke or two at the easing of the tensions of indecision and uncertainty. On occasions when the Chief did not attend the Iris team meetings, the mood in the meeting room would be lighter with more joking, more coming and going and less direction in the discussion (although an agenda would officially be guiding proceedings). Occasionally Ken, the Second-in-Command, would act as authoritatively as the Chief and make similar decisions to break through a blockage. But usually Ken would comment on the absence of the Chief with some irritation and the meeting would drag on, often apparently fruitlessly. Few people would contribute and some would tend to nap or do other paper work.

At the same time there were also collective displays of genuine interest and fascination in a product. Occasionally someone would bring to the meeting some material samples of problems and possible technological solutions. Everyone would gather around and the mood of the meeting would visibly change as contact with the materiality of their product was re-established. There was a group identification with the product that transcended the particularity of individual responsibilities. The role of the authoritative chief would appear to contradict the rhetoric of the team, the flattening of hierarchical structures and the appearance of collegial egalitarianism. However, the chief and most of the other senior team members did not regard authoritative unilateral decision-making as a problem. As the chief told me: "Hephaestus is not a democracy. We're a business operation. I'm responsible for this product team, and I'm accountable. So I make decisions, and they do as I say. Of course we go through the whole group process, and I rely on those guys, especially my managers, but I'm the boss."

The team is a vehicle for the expression and communication of ideas and information, but it is not a democratic structure of employee decision-making process. While the concept of team is employed among the white-collar workers to provide the appearance of open input and shared decision-making, team behavior actually resembles, especially during meetings, the "family" that is the model used for the manufacturing-line workers and other lower-ranking employees. The team-family consists of siblings who compete with each other for the attention and recognition of the chief-father. Among themselves there is a fairly high degree of familial

119

good-natured banter and underlying competition. None of them reported socializing with each other outside of work. Many of them adamantly rejected the idea, as one senior manager of the inner Iris team put it: "Never socialize with people from work. First cardinal rule." A generation before him typically did socialize with people from work. Toward the chief-father there is an element of familiarity coupled with deference. Each of the senior six members of the Iris inner-team always know where their fellow members are with respect to the chief, and the opportunities or rewards they receive from him. There are often jealousies and allegations of favoritism from the chief – these expressed in interviews – and subtle competition over the seating arrangements in the main meeting room.

Mary-Kate: A few of them have made it known to me, and well, a friend, she happened to hear some of the other guys talking and . . . she said that one of them made a comment about that I hadn't deserved it (a promotion). And she said, "What are you talking about? You were singing her praises last week and now this week all of a sudden she doesn't deserve it." So luckily I had her stick up for me, but there were also people that wouldn't talk to me for a year. And we go to the Iris Team meeting, and we'd talk – he's never talked to me outside.

One man, Vinny, always arrives at the meeting a little ahead of time so that he can sit at the corner of the conference table. The position at the corner of the head of the table is implicitly reserved for the chief. Even if the chief does not come to the meeting his place is left open, in case he arrives late. Occasionally a visitor from out of town would unknowingly take the vacant, unlabeled chief's chair. While the meeting participants seem to regard the faux pas as too minor to point out, it none the less appeared to have an effect on the comfort level in the room. There was more shuffling and some consternation as the familiar interactive patterns were somewhat altered.

Team meetings are invariably long, arduous and intense, conducted under fluorescent lighting in a usually cramped room, with tensions and anxieties rarely well-disguised. The purpose of the meeting is to share information, discuss and assess on-going problems, to make decisions about these problems and to develop strategic options. The problems are not always major ones of a technological or technical nature. Apparently minor problems of shipping and delivery would recur frequently and be discussed in the same way over again while some of the team members were aware of this and would sigh in boredom. But this apparently minor matter did not get resolved. People expressed mixed views about their attendance at these meetings that occupied hours out of a day, several days a week. Many members reported that they tried to attend only the portions of the meeting that were especially relevant to them. But this was not usually possible for the senior members, as in keeping with the team concept of integrating all aspects of a product's development, they were required and expected to know what was going on across the product's development team. At the same time, many people reported enjoying the Iris meetings. They liked the political exchanges, intrigue and being privy to information and corporate gossip. They also enjoyed the status that attendance at the inner-team meeting provided.

The meetings also serve latent purposes, particularly as a competitive arena in which individuals seek to display their knowledge, problem-solving skills and ability to get their deliverables out. They are also opportunities for some to display personality characteristics that differentiate individuals from the rest. The majority of the meeting attendees speak very little – they report and listen. A small number of inner-team members assume control of proceedings and discourse. For the rest, team meetings were a matter of disciplined endurance, sufferance, tolerance and interest (the latter indicated by the very act of being present). In conversation with individuals, I found that such displays were regarded as part of the daily work performance. They are displays of the team concept irrespective of the quality of team work performance. Their productivity may also be measured in their cultural function. They are symbolic aspects of production.

In addition to the two main Iris team meetings there were a number of other team meetings of the staff of the six senior managers under the Chief. Most of these meetings overlapped in personnel and were often attended by various senior managers. In particular, the early morning "Sunrise Meeting" held at 7.20 a.m. every morning, was formally an information and problem sharing meeting where sub-teams report to each other progress on developments or various technological or technical problems. The Sunrise Meeting had a character of its own. Held before dawn for most of the year, this meeting was immediately a display opportunity. Its participants, apart from a few senior Iris managers, were employees with various technological responsibilities. The meetings were quick, competitive, cathartic and also vehicles of sustaining motivation and maintaining solidarity. People were not supposed to leave these meetings feeling too good, but to feel slightly admonished and motivated to work even more productively today.

Disciplinary practices

Like most organizations Hephaestus has a system of formal disciplinary rules and procedures for employees who do not perform as required or who breach some other institutional rule of behavior. In addition to those formal and visible disciplinary practices the Hephaestus team-family culture contains informal, or hidden, disciplinary practices that form part of the everyday network of power relations and systems of control. It was common practice for someone, sufficiently senior to be attending the Iris team meetings, who had failed to perform well or to produce their deliverable to be reprimanded at the team meeting by another member or by Ken or Steele, the Chief, himself.

Another disciplinary practice was the self-initiated confession, most evident in the Sunrise Meetings. Employees would report, with expressions of culpability and remorse, their failures, delays and mistakes. More serious errors were punitively criticized and the offender would apologize again and promise to improve. The matter, however painful for the person responsible, is usually then considered dealt with. However, blame is not always well taken. Occasionally, an offending employee in his own ego-defense would blame others in the team or another team for the problem. Usually, however, these public admissions of fault and displays of remorse and promises to do better next time serve to alleviate guilt and failing, and to build group harmony and solidarity.

The Sunrise Meetings are latent displays of an elaborate system of ritual devotion to the company and of loyalty to the Iris team and its product-development mission. Members show each other, and the company, their commitment and dedication and their willingness to make personal sacrifices in the ability to arrive at work before dawn. These meetings were also a subtle differentiating structure between men and women. Commonly, there would be no women present. Women with family commitments find it prohibitively difficult to attend these dawn parades. Many of the women were painfully aware of the differentiation and the significance placed upon their lack of attendance.

The discursive disciplinary practices that acccompany the formal structure of disciplinary procedures operate on an everyday, ever-present level, and the rules and expectations appear to be more commonly understood than those of the formal structures. People fear having their failings displayed in front of their peers and team leaders during these meetings, and the repercussions of disapproval or criticism, more than they fear punishment for breaching other company regulations. This is illustrated by a case in which a number of employees continue to participate in an electronic-mail distribution list in a subject area that the company had officially decreed to be inappropriate for Hephaestus employees and ordered that it be discontinued. Senior managers claimed that it was difficult and time-consuming for the company to track individual electronic-mail users of a particular network, and usage therefore continued. If an employee were caught using the banned network a privately administered formal warning might result. Employees reported little fear of this disfavor in comparison to that instilled by the wrath and reprimand of the Team. Furthermore, it was also commonly believed that if the company really wanted the networks shutdown it could do so immediately.

Employees are not as afraid of the corporate bureaucracy as they are of their own team or "family." Again, this is reminiscent of Ouchi's (1981) emphasis on "clan control" in which members are disciplined and constrained by internalized rules of acceptable group behavior. In this way the corporate disciplinary apparatus is decentralized. It is now more immediate and everyday, as it is among the traditional industrial manufacturing and clerical workers. While this decentralization is consistent with the idea that autonomous work teams should be empowered to make their own decisions it also ensures that a localized disciplinary apparatus is maintained with little overt intervention on the part of the corporate bureaucracy. A culture of discipline is established and the employees police themselves.

The decentralization of discipline enables deeper levels of identification with the company as employees assume the authority and identity of disciplining executive-father. The chain of supervisors, the overt structures and rigid lines of authority of traditional industrial workplaces have gone. They are replaced by the new flexi-structured, "soft" (or "dotted") lines of management and the filial collegiality of the team. But power, control and discipline, however transmuted, have not gone, rather they now operate less overtly in the emotional and intra-psychic domain. The new disciplinary practices are processes of "colonization" of the employee self (cf. Habermas 1984, 1987, on the "colonization of the lifeworld") that completes the process of acculturation into the new Hephaestus Corporation.

The disciplinary apparatus is mitigated and legitimated through the rhetoric and simulated emotionality of the Hephaestus team and family. Employees find themselves in, and give themselves over to, the hoped-for familiarity, sociality and stability of the team-family. The need for the social – for feeling part of a purposeful entity, for feeling valued and useful – is approximately met and people continue to work and produce the company's products. The immediacy of the fear of peer and team discipline, and the panopticon design of the cubicle work spaces, allow few avenues of dissent, and few places of retreat at work from work. Employees are immersed in a constant, everyday process of discursive colonization – they are shaped and trained into the new desired Hephaestus employee. They must relinquish industrial habits that include the tendency to find avenues of retreat and resistance against the company in occupational solidarities and in factional loyalties (such as those that Kanter (1977) describes among secretarial employees).

The new team-family displaces and compensates for the loss of those older forms of identification and solidarity. As employees increasingly refer to themselves, not as physicist, engineer, computer scientist, but primarily as a Hephaestus employee with a job designation indicating team location, they close off avenues for retreat and distinctiveness within the Hephaestus culture. Without a union or a professional association, and only the official Hephaestus social or sports club, employees find that there is nowhere to go (at work) except to the team's simulated sociality and relative psychic comfort.

Counter-culture

The efforts of individuals to develop ego-defense strategies in the face of corporate colonization of the self, and the benefits as well as the costs of corporate culture, are fully addressed in the next chapter. There were, however, few visible efforts at collective counter-cultural or dissent strategies among the white-collar employees. The combined effects of the social technologies of workplace layout, the close proximity of employees to their managers and teammates, and the immediacy of the team culture, seem to have militated against organic efforts at establishing a counter-culture or for sites and practices of resistance among Hephaestus employees. Furthermore, in the pre-team 1970s Hephaestus had prohibited the gathering of three or more people in a private office or cubicle, and employees were urged to report to their managers any conversations in which talk of union or group interests transpired. (Some of the older employees remember this event, but most do not.)

Most of what I interpret as efforts in a struggle against the dominant culture and its colonization of the individual life-world, increasingly mediated through team and family structures, were private and not collective. The strong tendency of the employees – except the blue-collar and younger technical workers – not to socialize with each other suggested a wish, later confirmed in the interviews, to escape the Hephaestus workplace culture during outside hours. Many of the informants, except the very senior, said during the interviews that their willingness to talk with me was in part prompted by the wish, as one person put it, "to talk to someone about what really goes on here, to the people that is." The personal struggle against the prevailing culture was often expressed in terms of people rigidly compartmentalizing their lives. Even though most spent long hours at work, they regarded that as simply a requirement for the job, not as some form of habit or a compulsive adherence to duty or an addiction which it more closely resembled. Instead, they expressed a desire to spend less time at work, where few of them reported feeling "most fully themselves" and they wished to "try to develop other things in my life outside of Hephaestus".

The most common form of dissent or resistance was the retreat into privacy and defended out-of-work lives. One 42-year-old senior manager, on whose office walls are displayed huge, larger-than-life color posters of his children, puts it this way:

Luke: I don't like being here . . .we've talked about that before. I think one thing I can say is that I don't feel as though I'm working for

Hephaestus. I'm working for my family. The only reason I'm here, even when I was single, is because I have to work, to make a living. Now it happens to be for the family, my family, but the thing that motivates me to work hard, is to work better and better for my family.

Catherine: Has there been a conflict for you between the strong culture of teamwork here and your own personal family?

Luke: Yeah. I don't get excited about just teamwork. I don't have fun because I'm working in a team. I'd rather be my own man. I'm here to earn a living. Now with all this business throughout the 80s about teamwork and everything, Hephaestus has never stifled real hard work (of individuals). If they ever did then I might get dissatisfied. I'm a Republican, not a Democrat. My philosophies are individual in nature. I'm trying to do good for myself, I'm not trying to help anybody else. I think I agree with half of what's meant here (about teamwork). And I work very hard for this company, but it's not for the company, it's for me.

Catherine: But you've given 60 or 80 hours a week for most of the last 20 years, and your family, and yourself, have fewer hours . . . how does that work out then?

Luke: I'm doing it for them. To make sure that I do a good job for them, not for Hephaestus.

Some forms of collective practice are evident, such as the Black Caucus and the Women's Caucus, and electronic distribution lists (DLs) that explored special-interest-group issues and lobbied the company for increased anti-discrimination procedures and advancement opportunities. These groups, including the electronic ones, tend to function as support groups where people air grievances and gain understanding from each other. They seldom exert much impact on the daily life of the company, but they do act as protectors and defenders of the minority employees, and in that sense operate as collective buffers against further psychic assault.

As it is seen by a young African-American man:

Paul: The one thing that maybe I have learned is – this could be just maturity and basically being on the inside and seeing changes in Hephaestus – I think that people have misconceptions about the corporation . . . I used to think that the corporation did things for their employees and now some things are happening in Hephaestus . . . You are a tool that the corporation uses for the shareholders of the corporation and that's who pays. You are just a business tool and you have to look at yourself as being a business tool and every change that the corporation makes is for the corporation's benefit and not for the employees' benefit.

Paul goes on to comment on the current policy of encouraging managers to value "diversity" which, in essence, means greater ethnic and gender diversity than has previously been represented in the composition of the workforce of Hephaestus Corporation.

Paul: And, like I was saying that Hephaestus feels that managing diversity is something good, that is not because they want us to get along together in the world, and work together. But everything is based on the bottom line . . . greater productivity.

He rationalizes it in his understanding that this is simply "the way the world is." "That is what we are here for – we are a tool, and if you realize that you are a tool, and used and paid as a tool, then there is no problem."

Paul's account typifies the lower sense of loyalty and dedication to Hephaestus that is apparent among the younger cohort of professional employees. His clear awareness of the limits of his commitment and his instrumental view of the company and his place in it is only in part attributable to his personal experience as a member of a racial minority and to a consciousness of representing diversity within Hephaestus culture. His highly instrumental orientation toward the company is an example of a rationalized, adaptive strategy of self (see Chapter 6), that remains personal and not collectivized. It is not a counter-cultural strategy. Although he was a member of the Black Caucus, he did not see that group as having a major influence in shaping the culture of Hephaestus, he viewed it rather as a watchdog. Paul's views were echoed in part by others of his minority group and by some non-minorities in the under-35 cohort. Older men who had been passed over for a promotion that they believe was rightfully theirs, reluctantly tend to display some cynicism but rarely express a desire to treat the corporation as instrumentally as it treats them. Most employees, irrespective of age, gender and ethnicity, want to go along with the team, and to derive the semblance of satisfaction and community it provides. But there is a more cynical reservation about the effectiveness of team and its language among the younger cohort. They wish to retain at least the possibility of not working for Hephaestus, and working for something they imagine to be better.

THE DISCOURSE ON CHARACTER: THE HEPHAESTUS PERSON

Hephaestus promotes an elaborate set of "customer requirements," including among them the desired characteristics of the generalized ideal Hephaestus person. Generally, official discourse on the Hephaestus character promotes the values of diligence, dedication, loyalty, commitment and the ability to be a team-player, to be adaptive and flexible, and to be a good, somewhat conservative, citizen. It also promotes the commitment to excellence in the company's product and in customer service. Persons who might deviate too far from the local socially-constructed norm would be eliminated from the Hephaestus culture. Or they would self-select out. Most of the employees believe they possessed these qualities, or had developed them during their years at Hephaestus (again, they believe, the rationale for Hephaestus valuing and retaining their employment). They had become "appropriate" and good Hephaestus employees, therefore, they believe, the company must retain their services. The vast majority live in the Rusty River suburbs, the men are married and report various family-related community involvements. Employees who are homosexual believe it necessary to keep their sexual orientation a very private matter. Many employees report church involvements and a few have involvements in city youth programs (other than Hephaestus sponsored ones), or other community activities.

Diligence, dedication, loyalty

The archetypal Hephaestus employee is one who is unquestionably hard-working, who is dedicated, loyal and committed to the company and its products, and is willing to go the extra mile for the company and for his or her team. These qualities are best displayed in the practice of the correct language forms and in the service of long hours at work. Like the new language, the long hours were assumed to be a requirement of the job. But many hours during the day are spent in unproductive or diversionary activites. The extended hours, in themselves, in most instances are not required for the job to be done – what is required is the *display* function that the long hours symbolize. Many employees made references to people commenting on whose car was seen in the parking lot on Saturdays or Sunday mornings. The details matter. Some employees report that they want everyone to know if they have bought a new car so that it would be recognized in the parking lot on the weekends. Everyone seems to know when others arrive at work in the morning and when they leave. While among the exempt employees time-keeping is not strictly observed, there is a highly accurate informal perception among the managers and employees of each team member's hours of work habits.

Mary-Kate: I try not to but sometimes I come in Sunday mornings. I usually find I get more done on Sunday mornings because there are not as many people here.
   I think the workload here is very high so it is almost necessary, but I also feel cheated by having to work on the weekend so I try not to and there is – I feel bad about leaving when I have to leave every night and I know most of the guys are here later, but I also think that I work more efficiently than most people because I know that I only have a certain amount of time I can spend here. I also do a lot of work at home after the kids go to bed.

127

Employees are proud of their long hours and the displays of devotion and commitment they represent. For some, whose family commitments make extended hours extremely difficult, there is apology and regret for such poor displays. One senior woman engineer and manager with three young children expresses fears that her inability to arrive before 7 a.m. each morning is affecting her credibilty and respectability among the inner Iris team members and some of her own team members.

Mary-Kate: It's a trade-off between how much time I am willing to commit to Hephaestus and . . . I don't spend enough time with my kids. Hephaestus' culture is very much oriented toward it being, like, working more hours means you are more committed. Which I don't believe is the truth, but it is the reality, so if I can't, if I'm not willing to give that much, I am going to have to sacrifice becoming a [very senior post].

On the other hand, for some, early mornings were easy:

Donal: I'm an early riser, I get here at six in the morning, and my technical program manager (like Bill Y.) was also an early riser and we would have good technical discussions at 6 o'clock in the morning, before the Sunrise meeting . . . I've always done this . . . The family always just accepted it as part of Dad's job.

Other everyday displays of dedication, commitment and loyalty appear in the voluntary display in one's office of company posters and slogans, the use of company coffee mugs and the purchase of Team Hephaestus tee-shirts, caps, toys and other items.

The adaptable, flexible team-player

In addition to these personal qualities, the individual must also be seen to be a team-player and to possess the abilities to be flexible and adaptive.

Vinny: We had seen a number of different things like that [the new culture] come along . . . Hephaestus has always been very progressive and very interested in trying things, but the way I looked at it was every new gimmick that came along. But this [new culture] really was a lifestyle change. It was more than just they paid lip-service to it, and they showed they were committed to it in the long haul. So you better get with it or get out. If you can't cope with change this is not the place to work. For me, it was just a matter of, tell me what environment you want me to work in, and once I saw the company was really committed to working in this style then I was committed to it. I adapted to it.

Another example of the desired Hephaestus character on display is an incident in an Iris Team meeting, not atypical, but particularly poignant because the person involved had recently reported to me a crisis in his job and his wish to seek early retirement. The Monday Iris Team meeting had been proceeding for about three hours. The chief, Steele, was present but he was not sitting in his usual place. The news of his VP promotion was out and he was preparing to withdraw from most of his involvements in the Iris Team in three weeks. His successor, Tiffins, had arrived. He slipped quietly into the meeting room, although everyone noticed he was there and guessed who he was. The chairperson introduced the new chief. A discussion about customer service deliverables ensued. Andrew, a man known for his skilled work with customers, began to speak to follow up on a matter from last week's meeting.

Andrew: I want to talk about last week's deal with Centacorp . . . I got pretty beaten up in this meeting last week . . . and I went away feeling kinda beat, but I want to say that I took action, and the install went flawless . . . So I want to say "Thanks, Team."

Andrew's behavior and speech followed the normative cultural script superbly. He accepted his "beating-up" the previous week and took action to produce the desired result. That he had been humiliated in a rather hostile group attack the previous week, had simply to be absorbed by him, and turned into action. He also did the right thing in his confession to the meeting in front of the new chief. It was a simple, everyday display of the desired Hephaestus character reinforcing the official discourse and building team solidarity during a time of leadership transition. His comments were greeted with smiles and "You're welcome" from the chairperson and his teammates. The out-going chief chuckled warmly.

Another feature of team-playing flexibility is the ability to relocate from one office cubicle to another. Employees told me that it happens alot and "you just have to go with it." On one occasion I was looking for someone in his cubicle. He was not there and the new occupant said, "He's gone somewhere over by Joe." When I found him, he explained that he moves around a lot. "It just happens. Everyone does it." In response to my question about how it just happens, and who decides, Jerry replied that: "Someone, usually Steele, I guess, decides that someone needs to be near someone else, and the person just moves – overnight." Ostensibly, such relocations are for work organizational reasons, to get people who are working together on a project located near each other. But relocations can just as often occur for "social" reasons, that is, someone might have their own cubicle or office when they don't manage people, and they must exchange with someone who does and who needs relative privacy. According to Jerry, "It has a lot to do with perception. People won't listen to, or take much notice of, someone who doesn't have the right office, or the right furniture in their office (that is, wood furniture)."

In the interest of maintaining relative harmony in the team one must be willing to relocate immediately if so directed. The pecking-order in the team is not disguised by first-name familiarity, family-style bondings and close physical proximity in the office layout. Individuals implicitly know that, but rarely discuss it. Jerry was aware of the importance of the accoutrements of office, and he admitted that he often carries his briefcase with nothing in it, "Because, well, it means something, you know, it tells people something about me."

Self-control

The new Hephaestus employee is now required to be more aware of his or her emotions, and, as a good team-player, those of others. Officially, as part of the policy to encourage and value diversity, the majority group, white, middle-aged men are trying to become more aware of the place of women and minorites and typically held attitudes toward them.

Vinny: At Hephaestus it used to be acceptable to be emotional up until the new leadership evolved. It was an accepted way of reaching a decision was who yelled the loudest or who was at the highest level. Generally it didn't stop me – if I got yelled at I would yell back and if somebody was at a higher level I didn't care, I still yelled back. That is often how meetings were conducted and how decisions were made, until someone at a high enough level sent the decisions to me, and everyone punched three.

Catherine: So did PQ effect some change in respect to that style?

Vinny: Absolutely. That is no longer acceptable in negotiation. By the way, I was pretty good at that, too! . . . Obviously, women were pretty disadvantaged in those days. Very difficult days for women in business . . . And women in business are anything but emotional. Women are typically less emotional than men here . . . and that is because they [women] are accused of being more emotional.

Karen: I think that I should be more professional at work . . . I have a reasonably quick temper and can be sarcastic and get frustrated with people. I would like never to express that at work. I really think that you should very seldom resort to being angry . . . I think that one should be on an even keel at work and that is the highs and the lows . . . I should approach launch meetings the same every Monday, and if there's an issue on the table then I should not get emotionally involved in it. I should be able to stay dispassionate and just evaluate it and decide what ought to be done, without getting angry at this group who didn't do what they were supposed to do.

Karen wears steel-grey suits and participates clearly and evenly in the meetings. She was always in attendance at the Iris meetings, and some

130

other regular meetings. I never observed the anger (or warmth) she fears expressing in the workplace.

DISCUSSION: THE NEW CULTURE, SOLIDARITY AND PRODUCTION

The installment of the new culture is uneven and incomplete. Employees' language and behavior manifest contradictions, denials, confusion and variable internalization. Hephaestus vigorously continues its campaign to establish and embed its new culture and to promote the new Hephaestus image. It aspires, as one of its current slogans says, to be "one of the most innovative, productive and admired companies in the world." The official reasons for developing the new culture stem from the company's perception of its need to respond to the changing market conditions of the 1980s and 1990s. Hephaestus was encumbered by a structure of management and organization of work that were no longer effective. Its rigid hierarchical structure did not facilitate the forms of relationship necessary for harnessing employee knowledge and creativity. The new Hephaestus introduced structural changes, but more importantly, it designed a new culture and set in place social forms that were qualitatively different from those of the old Hephaestus.

At the same time, Hephaestus, like most other large corporations in the 1970s and 1980s, was vastly expanding its internal deployment of advanced technological systems. During that period, as the management literature and trade fairs of the time confirm, corporate leaders were concerned about serious problems of employee resistance to the new technologies and their fears about job losses and workplace reorganization. As indeed the new technologies did influence these changes, the corporation moved to compensate for those effects. The new corporate culture that provides the *affect* of community, involvement and self-development seeks to reintegrate employees after technological and organizational change and to compensate for the loss of older industrial and occupational belongingness and identifications.

The new culture, officially, allows for employee involvement in production and management processes in unprecedented ways. Diversity and creativity, strategic problem-solving, the pursuit of excellence and total customer satisfaction are Hephaestus' new organizing principles. The "learning organization," as the company calls itself, has regained its place in the global market, productivity and profits are up and Hephaestus continues to develop technological innovations and new products. Employees officially report high levels of satisfaction and identification with the company. They value and promote the team concept and are proud of their company and their products.

But there is another, deeper layer beneath this official story. Hephaestus

Corporation is endeavoring to create a new culture and a new social organization of the workplace in response to the erosion of the social organization and culture of industrial society. Manifestations of the erosion or transformation of modern industrial culture have been elaborated by social observers for some years.[11] It is the crisis in the *social* that is the new crisis in post-industrial production. It is not simply a crisis in the market, or of technology, knowledge and skill, as is commonly claimed by corporate leaders. The new cultural discourses of production as manifested in the corporation's designed culture are now as essential to production as labor and machine technology were in traditional industrial production.

The task performed by these discursive practices of production is the creation of a simulated social sphere that provides the semblance of solidarity and cohesion (and denies alienation and exploitation) which is necesary for production to occur. The social relatedness and *affect* of belonging and collective meaning-making are necessary for production to take place. These conditions, although generally denied in industrial production (and hence the problems of alienation and anomie) were none the less by and large satisfied by occupational belonginess and class solidarities in industrial society. The designers of post-industrial corporate culture no longer deny the necessity of relatedness and belonging for production to occur. They implicitly recognize these needs in their design of a "caring" corporate culture. A culture of feeling good at work by having apparently meaningful and energized team and family relations generates a simulated sociality that ensures the necessary human effort in production continues.

Displacement of industrial solidarities

The old discourses of industrial production – typically understood as ideologies that include traditional class locations and identifications, traditional relations between capital and labor, management and unions, and occupational stratifications – are diminishing in importance in post-industrial conditions. In traditional industrial society class-based formations, including the union and not the company, provided much of the social sphere for the workers. Industrial workers knew they were in an unequal and antagonistic relationship with owners and managers of capital (whose own solidarity was found in their owning/managerial class and identification with the company). There were other social forms of solidarity – religious, regional, ethnic – in industrial society, but social class (even when not consciously recognized) provided a primary source of identification and solidarity.

In the workplace the company generally expounded a unitarist viewpoint that sought to integrate the workers into a unitary operation with shared goals and fortunes. But integration was not essential. Worker identification with the company was slow and variable. The persistence of alienation and incomplete identification did not present serious problems under the old order. Only when large cracks in the modern industrial infrastructure began to appear with the event of both revolutionary new technologies[12] and the cultural changes in modern society, was a much more vigorous campaign required by industry to win employees' hearts and minds. Industrial ideologies, including the labor process, enabled industrial production to operate within a contested social sphere. Likewise, industrial solidarities formed by class and occupational identifications played their part in a functional industrial society. The social sphere, necessary for production to occur, was already present.

Among the many social consequences of capitalist economic class structure, occupational stratifications became everyday sites of social and class identification and were an essential structural component of the production apparatus. Industrial workers indentified themselves, and were socially identified, by their occupation and the place of that occupation in the hierarchically structured organization of work. Labor unions were established on the basis of trade and occupational categories and much of their everyday activity, especially at the workplace level, was concerned with the protection of relative privileges and the maintenance of demarcations between and among different occupational categories. Occupational differences (which were also gendered) were as distinct as the structured divisions between management and labor.

The ideological apparatuses of industrial capitalist society provided the appropriately acculturated industrialized worker, who, despite systemic conflict and organized contestation of the rules of the productive apparatus of industrial work, knew those rules and by and large lived within their bounds. Industrial enterprises did not have to provide additional social forms, such as a deliberately designed workplace culture, because the social relations of capitalist production had successfully provided them in the class cultures of a distinctly class-stratified society. The promises of modernity, of progress, rationality, science, education, and consumption, mitigated the lived experience of class contradictions. The belief in social rationalization and in upward mobility provided a primary integrating societal goal.

In turn workers organically generated their own cultural forms and experienced a certain continuity between work and social life. Indeed work was part of everyday social life, despite occupational and class hazards of alienation and exploitation. Ideological maintenance of the relations of power and exploitation was assisted by occupation and class identification which provided a sense of belongingness and solidarity that compensated for everyday experiences of alienation in an occasional assertion of class solidarity. Notwithstanding systemic class conflict, everyday antagonisms and periodic eruptions of industrial discontent, a tense societal stability was maintained in a contested social sphere in industrial society. But that began to irrevocably change under the conditions of advanced industrialism and the crisis in modern culture. The post-industrial corporatization of culture requires and facilitates the erosion of a contested social sphere. It requires an undifferentiated familial culture to counter the disintegrative impulses of the dismantling of modern industrialism that includes a no longer "manageable" contested socio-political sphere.

The advent of post-industrial material and social technologies and the decline of industrial social organization has led to some unintended consequences. Important among them is the reversal of the labor process. Specialized, fragmented and often deskilled and degraded industrial work is being transformed. Advanced automation technologies, advanced information technologies and the integration of work tasks produce more complex, skilled and unspecialized work tasks. The subsequent reorganization of the workplace to serve these technological developments is occurring with the construction of new workplace cultures. As a result, more complex and rewarding work is attractive to employees and their commitment and dedication is more readily acquired by the company. At the same time, however, a polarized corporate workplace[13] without the intricate divisions of labor of industrial society, and with a requirement for flexible technologies and workers, and structural unemployment, hastens the erosion of traditional class and occupational identifications.

Furthermore, in the United States the systematic campaign to defeat organized labor has not just led to a potentially more agreeable and productive workforce but has unexpectedly resulted in hastening the erosion of an important element in the solidarity of industrial society. The effort to divest unions of their social and political power has made precarious the social solidarity function they once provided. While the "damage," in the corporate view, that unions have historically caused has now, by and large, been eliminated, the social solidarity function of the union must be appropriated by the corporation. The social integration provided by occupations and professional identifications was similarly provided by an economically integrated working class and its remnant political agents.

In disempowering the unions and, importantly, dismantling their social functions, which enabled production to occur, corporate society is faced with the unexpected task of having to create an alternative identificatory and cohesive locus for its employees. The corporation must now win the social-psychological space emptied by the fall of unionism and occupational solidarity. That is the task of the new architecturally designed corporate culture. It has succeeded among the older traditional middle class whose social and religious socialization was simply appropriated and added on to the corporate value system and organizational forms with which it is consistent. But it is struggling to win among the younger generation more acutely influenced, not so much by the fall of unionism and the absorption of class identifications, as that was well in advance before their time, but by the demise of the modern social sphere more broadly. In these post-industrial conditions, the societally-provided social forms and aspirations of the grand narratives of modernity can no longer be assumed to be reliable, or apparent.

Simulation of the social

The new designer culture of Hephaestus Corporation furbished with the sentiments of team and family, and diligent and dedicated employees is not primarily created by its participants. But, none the less, their engagement with it produces the everyday form of workplace culture. The designer culture is a simulated culture. Occasionally this simulated but not cheaper version of what was once in industrial society a more organically created culture (mostly in the politicization of class-based resistance and dissent but also in occupational pride of craft and skill) is recognized by its members. But even when that happens, there is little possibility for dissent, because, it is believed, "It's all we've got" and, "We would've lost it anyways without the new culture." The new culture creates a simulated social sphere which compensates for the lack of the social (of collective meaning-making and of traditional workplace relationships which notwithstanding their oppositional nature provided functional solidarity) and of organically created cultural elements.

The corporate-simulated social displaces and obscures alienation and exploitation in the culture of team and family as it simultaneously substitutes for the solidarity and relatedness of traditional industrial social relations. It covers over the conditions of industrial work and "business as usual" that have been retained in an iron infrastructure which has not yet given way. It also exerts new forms of control that are disguised and denied in the processes of employee internalization and identification with a caring corporate employer. Employees identify with their own team and family (and consequently the corporation) rather than their occupation. They believe, or want to believe, that they are needed and valued in a familial, caring relation to each other, that they are "all in this together." They are "smart" believers developing "smart" technologies. They have not been "duped," as some earlier industrial critics might suggest. Rather, they have been *reasonably* convinced of the merits of organizational reforms and affectively attracted to the ethos of familial caring and belonging not offered by typical industrial companies (except small family-style operations retaining pre-industrial forms).

The new culture absorbs the *affective* as well as the residual structural elements of class formation and identification. In its effort to design

135

employees into team-family members there is a necessary denial of the corporate retention of core industrial relations of power and control in the newly-polarized structure of work. Hephaestus makes over old class-selves and reconstitutes them in its own image. At the same time the structural reconfiguration of former class and occupational groupings in the polar structure of the corporation squeezes out residual class consciousness and agency. Most employees report that the union is no longer missed.

Production requires more than the elements of capital, labor material and technology as industrialism's engineers believed. It requires a "social" or community sphere. The social-psychological need of employees for relatedness is also required and now implicitly recognized in the new corporate culture. Industrial production operated in a contested, tense, yet by and large stable social sphere. The new designer culture and its designer employees create a simulated social sphere that meets the need for relationship and solidarity. In the absence of an authentic, contested terrain of the social, a simulated social has a tenuous hold. Competitive production in the global market is at risk of failure because the social cohesion that industrial production could rely on, and reproduced, is crumbling away. People no longer believe, or behave, as they once did in "traditional" modernity. A new generation of employees faces conditions in society and in work that their predecessors did not.

The corporate designer culture represents the corporate struggle against a fear of postmodern, post-industrial entropy, and towards a revived industrial integration. It simulates a cohesive social for employees to feel the semblance of community and therefore to give their energies, knowledge and emotional commitment in production. It is an effort, against Weber, to harness *generalists with spirit*.

Without it, people would still show up for work for instrumental reasons. They would give only their half-hearted effort, and would retain in a defended privacy, the potential of their knowledge and skill. Passion, spirit and creativity would remain guarded, contained and displaced elsewhere in out-of-work private lives. Employees would not go the extra mile and provide the extra smile that Hephaestus now believes is essential to competitive productivity. Production in Hephaestus might still occur to some extent without the new culture, but the advanced technological developments that require sophisticated and shared knowledge work in a globally competitive market, and the passion necessary to "delight the customer," would fail. Hephaestus production would, therefore, ultimately fail.

As the new technologies integrate and informate more and more of the production process the social technologies are similarly organized to facilitate the integrated flexibility and *potentially* democratizing capacities of the new technologies. It is indeed possible that employees could appropriate the new culture to transform the institutions of work in other ways.

136

But the new corporate culture has been overlaid on a deep iron infrastructure that has not yet given way. The logic of industrialism struggles to survive the postmodern impulses challenging its dominance. What is happening now is a nostalgic restoration of industrial solidarities, and pre-industrial mythical memories of family and belonging, to hold together the social sphere and to ensure production for the time being. It is an effort to shore up the corporation against the effects of wider cultural changes that are now upon us. The new corporate culture and its manufactured post-occupational solidarities, as currently manifested, do not herald truly new forms of social life beyond industrialism. Corporate post-industrial culture is only an interim one.

6

DESIGNER EMPLOYEES: CORPORATE CULTURE AND THE PRODUCTION OF SELF

This chapter now turns to an exploration of the effects on the self, or the processes of "personal identity" (Hewitt 1989) of the experiences of working in the Hephaestus Corporation workplace. My discussion of the self implies something more than personality, although this category can provide important avenues into deeper (metaphorically speaking) psychic structures and processes.[1] There are clearly desirable traits, values, attitudes and behavior that the official Hephaestus culture encourages. But these features are aspects of a character discourse, described in the previous chapter, rather than of personality type. I explore the effects of the discourses of the new culture, of which the character discourse is one, and social processes (particularly the categories of team and family), and of practices of discipline and integration. But the effort in this chapter is not so much to consider these practices in distinction from each other, rather it is to explore the effects of their collective operation as corporate discourses on the self. I wish to explore the affective and psychic consequences of the new Hephaestus culture on Hephaestus employees. From there I consider the features of generalized manifestations of the self invoking a Weberian ideal-type schema (see Parsons 1968).

The core of the analysis of my observations among the contradictions and a few idiosyncratic variations that people displayed and reported is that there is a duality operating in the effects of the Hephaestus organization. The basis of this duality is the process of an effort at *defensive production and maintenance of the self*, poignantly displayed in the cathartic disclosure of the interviews, and what I call a process of *corporate colonization of the self* (cf. Habermas 1970, 1984, 1987), which is the endeavor and result of the new program of acculturation that is making the "new Hephaestus employee" in order to serve the requirements of the new forms of production and the new styles of corporate organization. Individual experience of relative psychic harmony or accommodation is correlated with the degree of effectiveness of, and complicity with, the processes of corporate colonization. This chapter explores and analyzes the elements of this complex duality and its implications. The first part of the chapter describes cultural processes of the self and the general effects of the corporate culture on the self. The second part analyzes the corporate patterning of the self under three clusters of characteristics and strategies. The last section assesses the relationship between these selves and social formations.

CULTURAL PROCESSES OF THE SELF

Fitting the self

The psychostructure (Maccoby 1976, LaBier 1986) of the Hephaestus workplace – that (in my use of the term) is the result of the discursive practices of culture, organizational structure and material production – selects and shapes in the employee certain kinds of orientations that achieve an appropriate fit between the requirements of the organizational culture of work and the character of those who work there. The emphasis here is on appropriate fit with the requirements of the organizational culture and not so much with the requirements and conditions of the work itself, as expected under traditional industrial conditions (Kohn *et al.* 1983, Kohn 1990). The person's values, attitudes and general orientation must correspond with those promoted by the organizational culture. Consequently, specific traits and attitudes that are useful to the work and the team are stimulated and rewarded. Traits and attitudes that are unnecessary or that impede the processes of the workplace culture, and therefore of production, are thwarted and suppressed. Individuals who display more of these corporately undesired features tend to experience higher degrees of intrapsychic conflict, discomfort and alienation than those more disposed to, or more willing to comply with, a congruent fit with the corporation's desired character type. The options for the self under these conditions are few.

Ronny: I wasn't as competitive as most people. I was more laid back. I figured that I am not one of these people, that I don't like to play their games just to get ahead . . . But it is a harsh reality, because I found out that since I am not playing the games I am not getting promoted as fast as everybody else. I had a manager who had a problem with me, because I try to do everything good, so that if there is a problem that might take somebody else ten minutes to solve I may spend an hour or two on it because I want to learn more, and basically it is that other people just blow-off half of it and do one or two things and they look like they did everything, because they make themselves look that way . . . A lot of people will cut corners to do things and get their job done, but they didn't do it right, but they say the right things, and they look good. That goes into competitiveness too, because there are ways of cheating as a way of getting ahead. It's deceiving, and looks are deceiving . . . After a while you kind of lay back because you get tired of being shot down for whatever reason.

Another employee reported that qualities she possesses in her style of work and interpersonal interactions are not recognized as contributive to team work and productivity. In particular, she felt that her low-key approach and intuitive ways of understanding people and processes were considered irrelevant.

Angie: I'm a very quiet person. I get things done in an interactive way, like I try not to make negative comments. There is too much negativity here and I think that it's a habit and it destroys people. But most people don't notice, but they feel it, and that's why there's so much tension here. So much noise . . . I have a gentle style of working with people, and I am creative, and I look for creativity in other people. And I see it in people that the company doesn't see it in. And I try to nurture it and to make life in my group better here . . . I believe in management by caring, but that's not what it is here. It is task-orientated and judgmental. PQ [the new culture program] is kind of fake. It can be manipulated to make it look good.

I believe that quality is about making the best decisions for the day rather than in how much is accomplished. I have been doing this, working like this for years, and you don't get promoted for what I do . . . And I feel like Hephaestus has tried to kill me.

Angie thought that her own immediate staff felt good about their group because she encourages them to dismantle the barriers between work and personal life, and to allow problems to run their course rather than be solved immediately. But she feels a heavy personal cost for her divergent style and is now trying to find ways of integrating and sustaining herself. Her coffee mug on her desk bore the slogan: "Eat, drink and be quiet."

More commonly reported among employees was the problem of speaking out.

Tom: I try not to get into trouble at work. I have learned my lesson over the years . . . I was never scared. I was brought up not be scared. But you get into trouble. My managers always told me I have too much to say, I ask too many questions. And it gets you into trouble. Like I say, I learned the hard way. Sometimes it still slips out, and I got to watch what I say. I have learned basically to shut up because it is safer and you can't get into trouble if you don't say anything.

Tom learned that his tendency to speak critically, to "ask too many questions," was an unwelcome and discouraged trait. The differentiation between desirable speaking up in the participatory, problem-solving process of team organization and undesirable speaking out was usually left unspoken and assumed to be implicitly understood by employees. However, when the boundaries were crossed, Tom was reprimanded for asking too many questions and warned against being a troublemaker.

Management in industrial organizations has long regarded employees speaking out too often or too critically as a problem. Industrial disciplinary practices usually managed to control or eliminate this problem. But in the new participatory culture and the diminished hierarchy of the new corporate organization speaking up and contributing is now valued and encouraged. Employees must learn the difference between acceptable and unacceptable verbal commentary in these new conditions. An implicit censorship continues to operate. The company expects employees to learn the subtle rules governing discourse and to acquire the desired corporate characteristics by means of which they will be internally regulated. Appropriately acculturated, self-censored employees will know automatically the difference between welcome speaking up and troublemaking speaking out.

Another employee, more senior than Tom, recalled that he learned very early on that his quick and insightful comments about corporate practices and managerial decisions were regarded as troublemaking.

Tim: It was like, and I can remember it now, that I used to have a lot to say, that was before I became a manager, and I was told that that would have to stop. If I was going to stay with Hephaestus I would have to learn to watch my ideas, and what I would say . . . And then, well, when they brought in PQ, all of a sudden we were supposed to have things to say, and they put all these suggestion boxes out. Like, that was how we were supposed to have our say, ha!

Tim regarded the PQ program as having a great deal of potential. He reported that he felt frustrated that his colleagues were reluctant to take the opportunities it availed. As a manager now he was in the position of urging his own staff to speak up and to contribute to team problem-solving processes. Despite his own earlier experience of being warned that he had too much to say, and his awareness of the sudden turn-around in company policy regarding spoken contributions, Tim did not grasp and was not sympathetic to the reluctance of his group to seize the new opportunities. Employees perceived a fine line between welcome and unwelcome speaking up. Many chose not to risk crossing it. Another value orientation that similarly contains contradiction and generates ambiguity in the discourse on team behavior and values is expressed by an employee who finds that features about herself, that at first glance would appear to be consistent with team cooperation, are paradoxically disadvantageous.

Opal: I often think that because I'm a very outgoing, nurturing, supportive person it causes conflicts . . . I need to be more directive, and not let people take me for granted or assume that I'm always going to be there to help them. That's my way, if you need help, I'm here to help you. So I really have to watch it. It's difficult, and I have to really watch it, because as I say, I am the kind of person who wants to help and make sure things are going the way they should. One of my co-workers does it all the time. He gets himself into trouble because he wants to help everybody, to make sure everything goes right. And it's like, in a way being a helpful person is good for the team, but it's not good for me . . . and I have to watch it.

The disciplinary apparatus embedded in the new culture acts to eliminate or contain undesirable features to achieve appropriate fit between employees and culture. It also operates to encourage and stimulate certain traits that are deemed to be desirable and useful. Like many employees, David noticed that he has become more aggressive during his years with Hephaestus.

David: I am like a lot of Hephaestus people. I am a control-taking person, and that is very common here. It may not be a good trait, but it is common, and I'm very aggressive and in control. I like to be in control all the time . . . I think Hephaestus values aggressiveness as a customer requirement.

Vinny also believes that his ability to take charge and to be aggressive is valued in Hephaestus. Vinny is a manager of a group of employees colloquially known as "the Pumas." The Pumas are field engineers who are responsible for solving technical problems in machines located in customers' sites that the technical representatives are unable to solve. Most of their work is done over the telephone where they act as technical interfaces between customers, technical representatives and subsystems engineers. The Pumas are required to be aggressive, fast-thinking and willing to make quick decisions and take action. Vinny, a former Puma himself, has found that his tendency toward aggressive behavior and quick action has been encouraged and rewarded.

Vinny: When I came here, and I've been here 23 years now, I had absolutely no training whatsoever. I didn't come with a college degree in engineering like most everybody else . . . But I had good instincts. I grew up in a really tough neighborhood here in Rusty River. I went to high school where I was a minority, so I think with that background, decisions and so forth come to you a bit easier. You are used to making them five times on your way to school. Whether or not you are taking the right street or whether you should walk around this person or shove them out of your way . . . That is where I think my confidence and self-assurance come from. And the other thing is that it gave me a good sense of not looking back and making a split decision, and if it is not a good one, you can't agonize over it. You made it and you live with it, and you just hope you do better next time.

And so I had good instincts and I've used them here. Pumas have to be able to act fast, and that's the way it is in Hephaestus.

Vinny's skills and "instincts" were encouraged and rewarded. His lack of academic qualifications, in his case, were compensated for by his ability to take risks, act aggressively and make decisions. Vinny's background is an unusual one among Hephaestus employees, and it is one that Vinny remarked as having discussed with no other Hephaestus employee prior to his interview with me. But notwithstanding the irregularity of his (class) background, his skills have been readily received, appropriated and enhanced. The new culture continues to value these abilities, although now somewhat tempered by the use of more moderate and moderating language, and a retraction of openly aggressive macho interaction styles. Employees must think and act aggressively but not appear openly aggressive.

Transfer of learning

Studies by Kohn and associates (1983 and 1990) show that a transfer of learning occurs in the domain of work from one's occupation to one's personality. Transfer of learning is evidenced in Hephaestus employees by a process of internalization of features of the Hephaestus character that appear in their lives outside work. The transfer is not just of *occupationally* associated skills, orientations and values (as Kohn emphasized) but of cultural characteristics that transcend occupational ones as the latter diminish with the increasing dissolution of occupational specificities. By complying with the new culture's requirements of appropriate attitudes, behavior, and self-presentation, Hephaestus employees internalize particular characteristics, values and practices that constitute their selves. The Hephaestus culture seeks to work over pre-existing forms and experiences and to reconfigure earlier patterns of work in the employee into the new desired form. Hephaestus designed employees are the appropriate "new" employees. What is happening here is more than an assumption of a corporate organizational role; it is the internalization of the values and practices of the new culture and identification with the company over and above previous occupational identifications as those older forms of identification are displaced. The new culture produces "designer employees."

Some resistances to complete internalization and identification, and inconsistencies in the transfer of learning are discussed in a later section. Here I discuss elements of the culture that do transfer into employees' out-of-work lives. Some employees are aware of some of these transferred learnings. They report the effects of the new culture influencing their behavior and social interactions outside of the workplace.

Paul: There are the things about attitudes and thinking processes that Hephaestus says we should, like we should be like . . . the thinking processes, and the way that you attack things like problem-solving, and you start to do that every day, and you start to do that in your personal life. For example, I was out in the hall at home the other day and I was saying to my wife, that is a "quality of return customer requirement," and I say, I have to have the requirements. Because she said I did something wrong that she didn't want me to do, and I said, you didn't get me the requirements . . . After a while it becomes, like part of you. And you can't stop yourself from talking that way. But I think that also sometimes you do like that and you don't even know you're doing it.

The incident that Paul reported was an example of his treating himself and his wife as customers, the desired interaction style of his workplace. The language and behavioral expectations of the team workplace culture, and its marketplace source, were transferred into his everyday orientations outside of work.

Tim: My behavior has changed and, my wife could tell you more about this because she has mentioned it to me from time to time that "you have changed" and I am self-conscious about it and I don't like it.
Catherine: What are these changes?
Tim: Well, like maybe being more aggressive, yeah, you have to become more aggressive to do a good job as a manager, and I don't like it. It carries over to my home life . . . Let me give you a typical example, that is just so true. I used to get a call (in the office) from my wife about this or that, and if she interrupted me at a particular time that caught me off-guard, I would continue on just like I would here . . . in the same objective manner . . . overbearing, cold. And when you are on the job, it is almost impossible not to become this instrumentally rational person and that is how you get things done, and you get into this very structured way of thinking, and it is not just doing it, it's you are totally engrossed in this instrumental process. It's like *I* am not really there. And my wife, she really notices it, and she doesn't like it. She says she doesn't like that person on the phone when I am like that . . . She says it's like she doesn't recognize me . . . And if I could I would not be like that, because I don't want to be that. But you have to be like that here. You have to let go of all those other things about yourself, like nice things, to be 100 percent productive; that's what they want here.

Similarly, Opal, who has been with Hephaestus since she graduated from college seven years ago, reports some of Hephaestus' influence on her:

144

Opal: You have this vision, that you don't want to play into it. You think there's a way to get around it, and to be morally and ethically correct. But things change. Things that you don't expect to happen, happen, and you get this different perspective. Somebody else gives you a different perspective of why you're doing that, and it doesn't seem so bad . . . I think they've changed me a lot. I think I've become maybe less trusting, a lot more observant of the things that go on around me, a lot more aware of how much the politics of an organization really change the organization.

I think I've been able to take a lot of what Hephaestus has taught me and apply to other areas of my life. And I think that has made me successful in other arenas. Hephaestus is very good at teaching. Their whole (PQ) is a process you can take anywhere and be able to produce quality output. I think I'm able to do that in any of the other organizations that I'm active in. It's an advantage . . . I think the main thing that I've picked up is that everything is profit motivated, really. For the most part it appears to me, and maybe this is just when I look at things in a global sense, even outside of Hephaestus, the bottom line comes down to how much money somebody's going to make . . . If you can find out what people's motivations are, where it hits them financially, sometimes you can start to break down the issues. I've never really thought about that much.

Catherine: Do you think you've taken on some of that?

Opal: Yeah, I do. I guess maybe I've become more like customer focused. If I buy something at the store that when I take it home I'm not happy with, then now I will go right back and say I'm not a happy customer, that my customer requirements haven't been met, and I will want them to satisfy me. I'm like that now, because I'm like that here. And I'm much more concerned about the bottom line all the time. I start to see everything in those terms. And I guess . . . is that normal?

Not all the new cultural characteristics are readily or completely internalized. The process of transfer of learning occurs slowly over time. At the early stages of the introduction of cultural changes, resistances to change and to new demands on employees are more readily observable. While transfer of learning does occur, some elements of the culture that employees are aware of are submitted to scrutiny and some degree of control by employees. Opal's ability to apply Hephaestus' customer-requirement model to a commercial interaction outside her workplace was a learned ability that she was pleased to have gained. Tim's and Paul's examples described characteristics that neither welcomed. They both expressed the wish to watch their behavior and attitudes that are valued at work, and not in their personal lives. Other employees, however, report that they were the same outside of work as they were at work; that they noticed no variations in their behavior, attitudes or values. Some welcomed the increasing congruency between their work self and their outside-of-work self.

Karen: Yes, I am the same every place . . . I like to be the same . . . I think you should be consistent and I like to be even

I have taken everything that I have learned at Hephaestus because I think it's good, and it's the right way to go . . . And I basically don't have any conflicts with any of it (PQ) because it's what I believe too. And I've just tried to become more like it wherever I am, because I like to be on an even keel . . . And I think these values apply everywhere.

Mary-Kate: I am not one of these people who tries to be someone at work that they're not. Some people are two different people. They have a work person and they go home and it's a totally different person. I'm pretty much the same all the time.

Still another describes with difficulty a case of being unable to access self-understandings or differences of view and value personally held, and to scrutinize aspects of the "learning culture" in which he is immersed.

Ken: I was talking with my wife last night about the new organization and I told her that I thought Sam was going to go. And she said, "don't you want to go somewhere?" And I said I don't really want to go anywhere. I'd just as soon get the thing [the Iris machine] finished and get some rest. I haven't had any rest. I have always been on a product that has had to get out the door, in the last fourteen years not one rest.

Catherine: Is this a new feeling of awareness for you? With the re-organization, and the changes here, are you becoming more aware of some things?

Ken: Well maybe a little bit. Mainly financially.

Catherine: How do you feel in yourself about these changes, about Hephaestus? . . . How much do you feel that you're being yourself here?

Ken: I don't understand the question.

Catherine: I'm just trying to find out a little how you feel about yourself here at work . . . Do you think that you are the same kind of person at work as you are outside of work, like at home or when you're doing other things?

Ken: Hmm, I don't understand the question.

Catherine: Well, sometimes people say that they have a "work me" and a "non-work me." Do you think that you are the same, act the same, feel the same, have the same attitudes, values, when you're with your family or in other social circles outside of your working life?

Ken: Hmm . . . I don't act the same. When I'm outside of work I'm not in charge . . . My wife has to do everything, so I don't have to be in charge but that has its downside because I'm not as important at home as I am at work.

146

One of the concerns that we both have is that I'm getting kind of dull; I don't care if we go out or not, and I show no initiative in that regard . . . I always want to stay at home.

I don't feel too good about that. But the job has to get done. The job is going to be done here pretty shortly and we will see whether I change. Maybe it's too late! ha!

Processes of resistance

Other elements and processes of the new culture that are not generally observable by employees cause doubt or dissent that is repressed and denied. Psychically disturbing effects of some of the new cultural elements that are not immediately displaced by team-family compensations can cause deep internal resistance. Among the most typical resistance reactions was the cessation of employees' social activities with each other outside of work in the midst of heightened team-family intimacy at work. Most employees reported remembering spontaneous socializing with other employees before the introduction of the new culture. While most reported that they believe in the new culture and feel warmth and commitment toward their teammates and a faithful dedication to the company, they also reported that they wish to "escape the place" after hours.

Bob: We're here with each other all day, long days . . . And I like these guys, but when I go home I want to be away from here. I want to be with my wife. I don't want to have to talk about Hephaestus all the time. It's like if ever we do get together, like at the Christmas party, all we talk about is work and who's doing what, and that's what we talk about here all day. So it gets to be too much.

Colin: This place is too close. We're here too much, and basically, even Tom, and he's like a friend, not a friend exactly, . . . we get on well, but I don't want to see his face when I'm gone from here.

You might've noticed that the walls are close here . . . you can't walk straight down the corridors if somebody's coming toward you . . . You always brush up against people. And it's well, they're okay, but it's like too close. We're always in each other's faces . . . And even if you have your own cube, you can still hear everybody, and they can hear you. Like I know when Lynn (she's three cubes down) is talking to her boyfriend. So who wants everybody to know your business?

Some also reported, with pride, that they believe their workmates socialize with each other but they do not. The others, such employees believe, are conforming to a workplace cultural process that they assertively choose not to be a part of: "After all, they can't make me, can they?" The wish of these employees to withdraw and to hold back somewhat, is an effort to resist the totalizing program of the new culture and to defend some realm of privacy from workplace encroachment. Their ability to exert some control over socializing outside of work enables them to express resistance to Hephaestus' intrusion into all areas of their lives. The workplace sociality and team solidarity do not transfer to their out-of-work lives. Some employees revealed or reported that they wished me to know that they were different, that their views were unusual in Hephaestus. They continued to strive for a sense of identity not completely tied to Hephaestus.

Bob: You won't hear anybody say what I'm saying. I'm not like most people here, and I have my own opinions, and they're not typical . . . I could say that you will not hear anybody say this . . . You talk to some of these others here and they will say the same things. The only person who's different around here is Stan and everybody knows that.

My own perception was that there is little idiosyncratic variation, but rather a homogeneity among views and values and a conformity of self presentation. The new culture discourses on the ideal Hephaestus employee promote such homogeneity despite the espoused valuing of diversity. As the language practices and values become everyday parlance and employees act out the desired characteristics, most become adapted to the role of the ideal Hephaestus employee. But their assertions of difference enable some unconscious wish for resistance to be satisfied to some degree.

A former tendency for occupational groupings and specialists to (legitimately) have different opinions and views, and to assert them in a competitive manner among each other, has largely given way to inter-team competitiveness, not over occupational expertise and distinctiveness, but over productivity and "teammanship." (There are annual competitions for the best team, best team reports, best presentations.) While competitiveness and differences in views and styles among occupational groupings have diminished, some minor regional differences are visible and a source of joking and teasing, especially between the East and the West Coast. By and large, individuals wished to sustain a personal view of their difference and they tended to assert that in the privacy of the interview. Some developed their wish for detachment from the forces of the prevailing culture into images of themselves that reflected that wish.

David: I tend to be a loner and I like my own projects, and I work silently on my own projects . . . I am known for the fact that I easily interact with people but I choose to be a loner. They know that they can give me a task and leave me alone and I'll do it. And I will do it whichever way I want to do it. I will do it . . . in many instances, I will go and talk to someone, like today I needed some specific information so rather than getting a group together and talk to them in a group, I will go to an individual and get that information. And so I don't always go by the team, I will still do things my way . . . At home I work on engines of old cars because it is a challenge to me, and I am not competing with anybody else, I am competing with myself.

David believed that his personal working style was (to some extent) inconsistent with that promoted by the new culture. But he believed that it was permissible for him because he still did a good job for Hephaestus. He was also an older employee and not on a management track. David wished to be known as an individualist who could interact well with others but who was also (still) a scientist with specialized skills to contribute to Hephaestus. David was unconsciously accommodating himself to a situation in which he was not the specialist physicist that he had believed Hephaestus had appointed him to be and in which he had no managerial authority. His resentment toward Hephaestus for this disappointment was dissipated in his self-narrative of individual contribution and autonomy. His efforts to maintain a distinctiveness of self and working style were strategies of resistance and defense against the encroachment of corporate culture and control in individual lives.

In sum, the processes of assault and diminishment of self, described by the critical theorists (from Marcuse (1962) and colleagues of the Frankfurt School, who influenced Maccoby (1976) and Lasch (1978) in turn) continue to occur. But these processes are more sophisticated and less discernible by the employees who, paradoxically, also derive satisfaction, a sense of relatedness, relative meaningfulness and higher productivity, from participating in the new corporate culture. They are participants in their own self-production in collaboration with the corporate processes of acculturation and identification. The new culture is sophisticated and multifaceted. It is credible, attractive, apparently social, and perceived as desirable by both managers and employees. Acculturated employees participate in the simulacra and derive a good enough meaningfulness from its busyness and routines. At the same time the processes of truncation of self, of delimited possibilities for psychic development and awareness (as Ken's comments above typify) and a social life delimited by production continue to occur. These are the outcomes of the corporate colonization of the self.

The self and the team: psychic accommodation

The new organizational forms and cultural practices alter the expected acute forms of bureaucratic and technocratic rationalities characteristic of traditional industrialism.[2] Post-industrial work that integrates formerly fragmented work and reputedly increases employee involvement and responsibility establishes organizational forms that alter the acute forms of bureaucratic and technocratic rationalities of industrialism. The processes of assault on the self in industrial conditions were apparently more acute and evident because of both the degradation of work in conditions of fragmentation and deskilling and the intensification of impersonal, rigid bureaucratic authority systems that controlled white-collar as much as blue-collar work. Notwithstanding, or perhaps because of the visibility of oppressive forces, there were somewhat stronger measures of self and class defense provided by the psychostructures of industrial society's forms of social solidarity and belongingness that included unions, occupation, and regional (as well as historical) identifications.

Similar processes of psychic assault and employee exploitation, without fragmentation and deskilling but with increased anxiety associated with the new complexities of post-industrial work, now seem less severe, less problematic, and indeed increasingly denied. The company and the employees implicitly regard the psychic discomfort of anxiety-making complex and responsible work as transitional, and as individual problems that will be managed by successful group processes and human-resource management. Psychic discomfort is implicitly accepted as an inevitable aspect of corporate acculturation of employees in the new culture of quality, service and global competitiveness. It is normalized and legitimized by the new culture as it is at once denied.

In portraying the workplace as a team and family, employees project their anxieties and injuries onto the group team and gain some anxiety relief as a result. Employees unconsciously recognize that it is in their psychic interests to believe in and belong to the team. The new culture discourses mask, and largely mitigate, the continuity of the entirely commercial and exploitative nature of the corporate enterprise and its new burdens of increased work anxiety inherent in integrated, intricate work that crosses the old boundaries of occupation and professional solidarity. Increasingly, but not conclusively, the new culture's effort to establish team bonds and emotional commitments among team members is effective. The team-family culture bolsters a fragile corporate self formed under the influence of traditional hierarchies and weakened by the cultural narcissism of advanced industrial society (Lasch 1978, 1984). It provides compensatory affect that enables an acutely ambivalent and conflicted self to feel relatively whole and in purposeful relation to others. In giving up the struggle for self-defense and self-maintenance against the corporate colonizing assault, and unfulfilled by the promises of consumer gratification, the employee is rewarded with psychically harmonizing benefits in the affect of belonging, of being valued and being productive.

The new corporatization of the self is more than a process of assault, discipline and defeat against which employees defend themselves. It is a process of colonization in which, in its completion, *assault and defeat are no longer recognized*. Overt displays of employee resistance and opposition are virtually eliminated. Corporatized selves become sufficiently repressed to effectively weaken and dissolve the capacity for serious criticism or dissent. The burden of greater work anxiety and a reactivated guilt (as narcissism gives way again to compulsiveness (discussed below)) overwhelm the capacity to dissent. Instead criticism and disagreement are channeled into the production process through team processes of speaking up, brainstorming, problem-solving, and "critical thinking."

While employees are encouraged, and wish, to believe in the team, and while it does serve as a mechanism for collective anxiety containment, the team does not shelter and protect. The team turns on members who fail to deliver. The action of anxiety displacement is simultaneously projected back onto the offending individual who introjects the disapproval and criticism of teammates as self-admonishment and renewed guilt. Anxiety relief and reparative teambond are only minimally maintained. The individual's confession of failure to the team provides some immediate anxiety relief and psychic comfort. But the burden of guilt is not displaced. Rather, it is returned by the collective recognition of the offender's fault reflected back to the offender as guilt. Thus the offender's anxiety relief is only temporary. Confession results not in reconciliation but in renewed guilt. The corporate self, like his archetypical Protestant bourgeois predecessor of industrial capitalism, redirects guilt into more vigorous efforts to work ever harder. Salvation, once again, is gained through "works" and not by "grace" alone.[3]

An incident occurred at a Sunrise Meeting a few days prior to an important product development review meeting. (This is a review conducted by senior people from outside the Iris Product Development Team (Iris PDT).) Tensions had been running high for several days and tempers were fraying. The meeting, chaired by Felix, starts as usual. Reports are delivered, problems discussed and various people nominated or volunteered to take up action items. Ken Boyes then arrives and takes charge of proceedings. "Come on guys, solve the goddamn problems," he urges them. He tells them they can't wait, that launch is upon them and that if necessary they should "bypass procedures," meaning that the procedures of customer requirements that guide official problem-solving processes should be ignored (in this instance) to achieve the desired results. This is followed by disorderly talk and loud discussions. Suddenly, Joe, an engineer, who is half-standing, half-crouching on the floor of the over-crowded meeting room, is blamed for a specific major problem. Boyes tells Joe that they should have had the deliverable two weeks ago and it is not acceptable to have such a delay. He admonishes all of them for their lack of urgency and informs them that they will fail the test (the product review) and then "there'll be trouble." Joe admits some responsibility for the delay of his deliverable. Murmurings against him reverberate among the other participants in the team meeting. The others wish to deflect Boyes' anger at the team onto Joe.

At this point, Joe tries to defend himself. He cannot physically stand his ground in the crowded room and is forced to move up and down in an obviously disadvantaged position. He gets very angry, he does not wish to accept the blame being laid upon him and he fights back. Lacking support from his teammates, he resorts to blaming company procedures for the delay. It is not his fault, he argues, because he followed the rules of PQ. The angry exchanges continue until Boyes tells them, "that's enough now." At the end of the meeting a still angry Joe tried to continue the discussion among his colleagues and to criticize the PQ procedures. But his teammates withheld understanding and team forgiveness and Joe did not gain the anxiety relief he sought. His teammates, however, had displaced their own discomfort at the reprimand and tensions, and left the meeting, still anxious, but with some relief that their scapegoat Joe had shouldered the wrath of their leader and the burden of punishment.

The younger cohort (under 40) manifests variable internalization of the new culture values and behavior; hence the concerted corporate effort to win over this group. The younger cohort was raised under cultural impulses that included a post-war generational struggle (enunciated at the time by activists and intellectuals) against some of the psychically and culturally oppressive traditions of modern capitalist society. Notwithstanding some of the successes of that effort in breaking through cultural oppression, and despite radical efforts to renew and transform public life, the more defining outcome of that endeavor in America was a resulting culture of narcissism and a retreat from the public institutions of life. This event, enmeshed with a tide of other social forces (discussed in Chapter 1), contributed to the decline in cohesion of other grand narratives of modernity.

Similarly, as Lasch (1984) argued, the influence of the superego, while not declined, has altered into punitive compulsion without the modification of the ego-ideal and the promise of forgiveness through good works and success in the performance of one's "calling." This generation, characterized by narcissism, is reluctantly acculturated into the corporation. Somewhat unexpectedly it has been easier for the new culture to take hold among the older group of employees.

The older group has unconsciously recognized the cultural artifacts and organizational psychostructures reminiscent of an earlier (secularized) Protestant culture of industrial capitalism in which they were raised. The younger cohort has been influenced by the culture of narcissism to a greater extent. The new corporate culture seeks to reintegrate all of its employees, now diverse in age, gender and race, into a restored Protestant corporate culture of dedication and deference to the company (superego), sober moderation and self-restraint, and a relentless compulsion to work. One is called, again, not so much to serving God and one's fellows through occupational vocation, but to dutiful service and devotion to the company that has usurped the place of community and occupation.

While the younger cohort expressed, and I observed, more resistance and cynicism, most of this cohort none the less *wished* to believe in and belong to the team. The corporate ethos nurtures employees who are "smart believers" – people who are well trained and highly skilled in the broad domains of production and organizational processes who at the same time believe in the promises and sociality of the new culture. It also, strategically, retains provisions for individual contribution and reward alongside the team sentiments and egalitarian beliefs such as, "We go up or down together, team" that was often announced at meetings. The team rhetoric dulls awareness of contradictions and exploitation and mutes the cool, ruthless corporate restructuring that does not care for the employees. Paul, typical of the younger cohort, expressed a clear awareness of the corporation's strategy and its approach toward its employees. At the same time, he too wished to believe in and be part of the team.

Paul: You're a tool, that's all you are. And if you know that's how the corporation treats you then it's okay . . . You can kind of deal with it, and you know exactly where you are.

Team – I think it works to a great extent. I feel part of it. I like the idea and the concept of team . . . Hephaestus always comes up with these work culture concepts that try to improve productivity . . . PQ was one thing that I think was absolutely worth its weight. In terms of, you have everyone thinking – I worked at Hephaestus before PQ, so I can see some of the differences when they implemented PQ, and now everyone speaks in the same terms and it is easier to actually get your work done. You know what is required of you and what is required of someone else in simple terms, so there is no more miscommunication. So I think it actually works great . . . Once you learned it, it became second nature and you began practicing it without even knowing what you are doing.

The new culture is an elaborate adaptive strategy for both the corporation and its employees in the conditions of post-industrial production. Industrial forms of work organization are no longer effective or appropriate. Post-industrial work requires and precipitates new forms of work organizations. The team-family is a multi-purpose entity. It is an effective organizational structure in that it allows for integrated knowledge work to be performed and disseminated, and it also serves as a collective corporate site of anxiety displacement. For the company, the deliberately designed corporate culture is a way of generating, at least internally, a sociality that is eroding and fragmenting in post-industrial and postmodern conditions, and which gravely risks the end of capitalist industrial production. It resuscitates an old form of industrial solidarity – it is a new manifestation of an old form – that provides a credible social sphere in the semblance of warmth, caring and belonging.

GENERAL EFFECTS

Like the self processes, the general effects of working in the Hephaestus culture affect every person, manifested in various ways. The subsequent discussion explores the ways in which these general effects are patterned in particular ways to create discernible types of self options among Hephaestus employees.

Ambivalence

The most obvious and pervasive effect of the experience of working in the new culture is a condition of ambivalence. Ambivalence is a manifestation of an incomplete internalization of the new cultural values and behavior. Among the most common displays of ambivalence is the expression of the wish to find sociality, even intimacy, with the people one works alongside for ten hours a day, and the desire to escape them after hours. At work, employees wish to cooperate with the practices of the new culture and they especially want to get along with and enjoy the company of their team-mates. They want to belong to the "winning team Hephaestus" and to share vicariously in its glories. At the same time, they cannot completely dispel doubt in the manufactured social relations of the workplace.

Formal grading structures have been altered to a flatter team structure, resulting in fewer opportunities for upward advancement. Competition is now more complex and at the same time regressive. Teammates compete with each other for the attention and favor of the manager-father. Favoritism and political maneuvering were present in the older-style bureaucracies but the more elaborate structure encouraged impersonality and some protection from advancement by nepotism. The flatter, closer team-family structure covertly revives nepotism and interpersonal suspicion at the same time that it overtly promotes egalitarian teammate cooperation and overriding commitment to the product.

At an unconscious level employees both collude with and resist the simulated sociality of the team-family. They suspect that the workplace is not a family, but are confused and frustrated by the rhetoric that claims it to be so, and their wish to believe it. The confusion that results from this contradiction and the inability to address it, since it is incompatible with the official model of team-family, is transposed into yet another anxiety.[4] Many employees wearily express the wish to retreat to domestic life, usually marriage and family, and to find a less commercial sociality. Most express ambivalence in the same breath as they express devotion and commitment:

Donal: I would like to get the hell out of here, I would like to leave Hephaestus . . . because I would like to go into another mode, to enjoy life. But I have a commitment too, you know, here. It's real strong . . .

154

And I like it here. I don't know what else life would be like . . . I think a lot about leaving.

Gordon: I think that if I put my 30 years in I have done my part. But it's such a big part of my life, it's why we live here . . . And we have this place up on the lake, and I like to go there . . . And I find that I think about retirement . . . It's funny . . . But I want other things away from here. But Hephaestus has been good to me . . . I guess I don't know.

Technical and blue-collar workers have retained a stronger class-based remnant of an organic social life at work. Many of them continue to socialize with each other and play company-organized team sports. Some of them also report the typical industrial workplace diversion of playing practical jokes on each other, of minor production sabotage for entertainment and of "taking out" the manager. None of these practices was reported, or observed, among the white-collar employees. The manufacturing-line workers experience greater relative satisfaction at work and about themselves, they are not as burdened by the desire to climb the management hierarchy, as that is an inconceivable proposition, and they are not as competitive. They are generally well paid and they have their union that is still able to negotiate collective contracts and agreements on overtime and other conditions.

It is the white-collar workers who feel more aggrieved and conflicted toward the company. They are more defensive because they have only an imitation, company-provided, sociality. They suffer the confusion and frustration of ambivalence because they can not yet fully believe in the simulacra. The anxiety generated by this ambivalence is one of the major influences on the self in its unconscious choice of a psychic option for survival in the new corporate culture. The self must contain ambivalence to a tolerable level. This containment requires strategic ego defenses that characterize the particular self option of the corporate employee.[5]

The personal struggle for self against absorption and dissolution in the encompassing vastness of the corporation was not only not collectivized, it was struggled for alone through the paradoxical course of the expression of loyalty and dedication at work and the effort to escape and find detachment outside of work. Ambivalence is an effect of the paradoxes embedded in the new culture. Employees repeatedly expressed the desire for Hephaestus not to dominate every facet of their lives and shape who they believed themselves to be, but at the same time they continued to give everything of themselves to the cause of the company.

Sally: I gave the very best of myself – *of myself* – for 23 years to this company, now I want something else in my life. I want a relationship with a man, and a good life outside of work. You know, Hephaestus was everything in my life – it probably still is, but I want it to be less now . . . I still come in here by 7 a.m. every day. Some days I'll come in even earlier, like 6 a.m. And I still come in most Saturdays, but not Sundays any more. I've stopped doing that, at least. But, I wake up . . . I guess maybe it's a habit, but no, *I* do it . . . You know, it's like I've been on automatic-pilot all my life! And that's exactly what this place wants you to be like. You give 120 percent of yourself, and then one day eventually, you kind of wake up and you wonder about your life.

A deeper source of this prevailing ambivalence are the deep contradictions of a consumer culture in which Hephaestus is embedded and of which it is an agent. Employees are required to be self-denying, hardworking, cooperative team players committed to cheerful service and long hours of work. At the same time they are required to be self-seeking consumers who find gratification of an endless hierarchy of needs in the consumption of mass-market products. The corporation's effort is not only to obscure and deny this cultural contradiction in the twin goals of industrial capitalism (cf. Bell 1976), it is to win back employees from an unintended over-indulgence in the gratifications of compulsive consumption. The corporation urges an ever more complete process of identification with the corporation and its familial culture which displaces ambivalence into guilt. The contradiction is repressed and simultaneously maintained by the dialectical process of employee guilt and consumer gratification which generates acute anxiety that fuels the cycle.

Discipline and corporate "civilization"

In the course of the interviews and observations I heard and saw many incidents of failures and mistakes and of personal squabbles among employees. But at the same time I observed the ways in which the team and the language practices of the new culture exerted strong integrative forces upon the employees. In the insistence of the team culture that employees must get along together in a team and family-like manner, and that problems must be resolved through communication, lest they exert an adverse effect on productivity, the new culture produces an effect of *forcing* the semblance of more mature behavior and accommodations that traditional workplace cultures did not require. For instance, I neither observed, nor heard about, instances of feuding, blacklisting or vindictive practical joking typical of industrial workplaces. Similarly, overt racial discrimination is rare and overt sexism less commonplace.

The provision of structure, purpose and sociality in work subsequently enables primary, functional mental stability. In addition, the new requirements of the culture that insist that employees must conform to the cultural values of cooperation and sharing of knowledge and skills open more avenues in which employees may perform well. Employees can display their talents and abilities not only in their knowledge work and productivity but in their team and group skills. Through their commitment to and identification with the team and the product that is greater than themselves employees find a reason (that is rewarded) for the struggle to improve themselves and to become the "new Hephaestus employee." In the reification of the team-for-the-product, employees find the associated status and rewards to be sufficient motivation to behave appropriately and to become the "mature" corporate citizens the company desires. The reification of their collective knowledge, embodied in the machines and image of Hephaestus, acts as a mirror that reflects back to employees, not just the grandeur of Hephaestus, but images of their own status, cleverness and virtuosity in productivity. Such gratifying images are confirmed in the rewards of high pay, which enables and justifies their consumption. In an everyday sense employees believe that the company has improved them, has brought them up to the levels of maturation and citizenship ascribed to the company.

Pat: You know, I've really changed since I've been here. I've been here seven years now . . . I've had to really get my shit together. This place has really made me work, but it's also made me, you know get to work with people better, like to get along better, and not to fight . . . And I've got to stick at things too, and learn to see the other person's point of view. Hephaestus is really strong on people getting along together . . . it makes people behave better . . . I used to be a very distrusting person. I never trusted anybody and I was always, like, leery of people I worked with. But I'm not like that now. I've learned to open up and to communicate and I guess I trust the team. I believe that we are all very committed to what we're doing, and if you know that you're dedicated then other people know it too and you get things done as a team.

Vinny: I used to be one of those guys . . . that used to fight and yell a lot . . . and it was pretty rough in those days, but we all did it, so there was always tensions running pretty high . . . We're much better now. We don't do that anymore. And we know how to deal with problems and communicate. So you have to learn, and you have to learn how to get along . . . and I think we treat women and minorities much better too. Before you didn't used to get anybody taking notice of them. I have to say I've learned, and my attitudes have changed.

Hephaestus culture offers employees a corporate "civilization" which provides them with purposeful working lives with structure, legitimacy and the semblance of meaningfulness and relatedness. It provides a reason for the struggle for corporate-style maturation (at least in the public expression of their selves). Abiding by the values and practices of the corporate culture brings out the best in employees in terms of their rational knowledge, technical skills, productive capacities and inter-personal skills. However, this civilization and psychic cohesion is, paradoxically, accompanied by costs to the self that include the persistence of a deep frustrating ambivalence, acute anxiety, and the exaggeration of "appropriate" characteristics at the expense of unnecessary characteristics such as nurturance and patience. Social defenses, including regression, are commonplace. Importantly, the revival of nepotism as a result of the restructuring of bureaucratic authority, in which advancement is secured by vying for the senior manager's paternal favor as against the impersonality of formal employee review procedures[6] typical of industrial bureaucracies, distorts the maturation and filial cooperativeness officially extolled in the new culture.

Hephaestus' effort to shape employees into model corporate citizens and excellent technological producers is achieved under conditions of denial and distortion. None the less, adaptation to the new corporate culture, within the broader constraints of contemporary capitalist culture, provides some benefits to employees. With the increasing precariousness of other sources of (healthy) self-formation, in family and school, and the decline of other modern sources of social solidarity and value, the compulsive, compensatory identification with their work products (as production team) shapes and structures employees, it represses and civilizes them and provides normal functioning psyches. Having a job to do, being responsible to the team, being effective, dedicated and team-identified occupies their consciousness, disciplines their minds and bodies and provides a working, adequate, necessarily repressed, but not so bad, psychic stability.

Teamwork requires, much more than did old industrial hierarchies, a greater degree of agreeability and congeniality that is read as maturity. Infantile demands and acting out still occur, especially in meetings, but outside of meetings more overtly immature performances are discouraged by the group process, and people learn to behave "more appropriately." Most of the over-40s men and women could all remember the days when it was quite acceptable and common behavior for managers to slam doors, to shout at each other and their employees in corridors and offices, and for personal falling-out to have ramifications for individuals and work groups. In suppressing and eliminating from daily workplace life these remnants from undisciplined industrial anger, the corporation has replaced a former outlet of work tension, and manifestation of conflict, with the "kinder, gentler" style of interaction that glosses over deep tensions and the capacity to revolt. The "good Hephaestus employee" relinquishes the right to anger for the appearance of corporate-style maturity. Recall from Chapter 5, the pride with which Si and Merv (and others) reported that they have "never gotten angry at work."

Beneath this apparent maturity, and mystified domination, are typical social defenses, neurotic anxiety displacements and obsessive compulsive behaviors. Unconscious processes such as juvenile sibling competitiveness in team meetings and "primal horde" type behavior such as scapegoating, group attacks and "killing-off" aspirant leaders occur. Corporate-style maturity is a functional, enforced maturity, a corporate "customer requirement" displayed mostly in public. Obsessive compulsive behavior is commonplace, clearly more so than the overtly aggressive acting-out more typical of a previous generation. The contradictions inherent in the team model, in the imitation of the ("good") family, that are located in an irreducible structural condition in which egalitarian team-family rhetoric cannot displace the inequalities of employee–corporation relations, are internalized by the employee not just as everyday tension, but as anxiety that cannot reach resolution. Corporate-style civilization is not quite "good enough" (cf. Winnicott 1960).

Delimitation of psyche

The psychostructure of the new Hephaestus workplace endeavors to provide, albeit unevenly, the fundamental sustaining requirements of the self: autonomy, competence and relatedness (Deci and Ryan 1991 – see Chapter 3). Corporate culture promotes the self requirement of competence necessary for production. Autonomy is provided in the facility for broader use of skill and judgment, and relatedness, as I have argued above, is provided in the simulation of a caring and familial team. However, these second two self requirements are implicitly regarded as auxiliary requirements of the productive workplace. An over-emphasis on competence, more visible in the post-industrial corporate workplace than in traditional industrial workplaces, results in the manifestation of certain workplace neuroses. Under typical industrial conditions a drive toward deskilling and extreme routinization generated an oppositional struggle by workers' movements against competence deprivation. At the same time these movements provided both compensatory competence in the act of resistance, and satisfied relatedness and belonging needs in the social solidarity they generated. The psychic costs of competence and autonomy deprivation were more apparent than those of relatedness (and produced concomitant industrial neuroses). In post-industrial corporate conditions the problem is relatedness, and hence the project of the new culture to at least simulate its satisfaction. The typical neurotic defenses of denial, chronic anxiety and compulsion are the everyday legitimate neuroses of contemporary corporate workplaces.

Obsessive compulsions are "normal" neurotic behaviors that are freely facilitated, and expected, by the corporate culture and internalized as individual characteristics. Some employees acknowledged their obsessive compulsions and believed them to be individual "personality traits", rather than culturally produced defenses within the workplace. For many, the training seminars and management courses they had attended encouraged and confirmed this belief. Being able to label their own personality type enables employees to explain and excuse a range of behavior and styles.

The corporate culture produces, legitimizes and normalizes the everyday manifestation of workplace neuroses. Such manifestation ranges from the minor forms of pacing, shaking, finger tapping, handwringing and blurting out in meetings to the compulsive routinized alignment of pens, papers and desk items in ordered patterns, or other personal ritualized movements. Some employees reported, or intimated, in interviews compulsive thought patterns and private compulsive rituals that I did not observe. For others, neurosis is manifested in compulsive hyperactivity that may or may not produce valuable results for the team or for themselves. Employees, when questioned, did not appear to notice any of these behaviors among their co-workers.

These manifestations of obsessive compulsive behaviors are features of the process of corporate colonization of the self, and represent an incomplete stage in this process. They are a psychic reaction to ambivalence, corporate cultural contradictions and the desire to displace mounting anxieties. Obsessive compulsive behavior and excessive alcohol consumption (but not to a clinically dysfunctional level) are two commonly reported reactions. Donal, a senior manager, is, by his own admission an "obsessive type." Donal's few after-hours activities that are spent in leisure for himself include taking a walk in the park or around the golf course near his home. But these walks are invariably dominated by Donal's obsession with collecting stray golf balls. His collection of "a couple of thousand" was acquired during these walks when, he reports, he will scramble around hedges in search of a golf ball he has seen. His wife, he says, will no longer accompany him on his walks because of this minor yet irritating compulsive behavior. When the weather is too bad to walk, Donal reports that he drinks "maybe too much" at home. Donal does not remember being a collector of objects prior to his years with Hephaestus.

At work, Donal's obsessive compulsive behavior is confirmed and rewarded. Donal arrives at work by 6 a.m. every day, and leaves after most other people have left. His job involves complex responsibilities in marketing Iris products and in team management. The job includes, not unexpectedly, a responsibility for the quality of certain components of the Iris machine that requires considerable attention to detail. However, he told me he often upsets his engineering staff by being overly involved in specific details of the development of technological components for which his staff are responsible. His staff complain that he "breathes down their necks" and that he cannot delegate. He wants to know every detail of development in the machine technology and to make decisions on the process even when such decisions are formally delegated to task engineers. Donal's twelve-hour days are self-inflicted but he believes them to be a requirement of the job and in keeping with the ethos of the company.

Donal has been regularly promoted and is highly regarded for his productivity and commitment. His obsessive compulsion is exploited by the company and construed by Donal as a personality trait that is desirable and "normal" at work. Donal's obsessiveness, which is problematic in his personal life, is welcome and rewarded at work.

Donal: This is a "killer job," this is a total job, a 70–80 hour week job . . . But I think when I took it I was ready for the commitment, the time commitment, and I was ready to take on the responsibility – that's what this job is about – and I liked working for Steele. He knew what he was getting with me – we've worked together before and he knew he could count on me . . . We're both kind of driven . . . But there's no other way to get this job done. You have to be driven, and you just have to be like, obsessive.

Donal, more than most, is aware of his compulsive obsessiveness, and he says that he wishes he could be different. He both resents and admires the company for its abilities and products. But he wishes to retire early, "Before it's too late to have other things in my life." However, his wish to retire early and to regain sacrificed parts of himself that he quietly mourns, amounts to only another voice in the litany routinely recited by senior men. In the next breath, Donal restores his normal orientation:

Donal: Work means a lot to me, and I think that work should mean a lot to the people who work for me. And I want to see people interested in doing things that matter for the company. Work has to matter. I must have one hundred percent.

THE HEPHAESTUS PATTERNING OF THE SELF

Duality: defense and colonization

The dual processes of colonization (the corporate program of acculturation) of the new Hephaestus employee, and of ego defense, occur continuously and simultaneously. Corporate colonization of the self takes place with varying degrees of resistance and struggle as I describe below.

The new culture is an effort to revive an old Protestant bourgeois self with a strong superego that will once again goad employees into hard work, devotion and productive service, and away from self-indulgence, rebelliousness and cynicism. But only half of the bargain is kept by the corporation (hence injury to the self, both traditional and "new"). The rewards to the self that a wise and benevolent parent (and therefore a healthy superego) provides in satisfaction through achievement and material comforts in moderation are no longer guaranteed by the corporation. Hard work and productivity (which were the means toward salvation) are not guarantees of security of employment, of promotion or of high status and fellowship formerly consistent with the Protestant bourgeois citizenship ethic and provided for, more or less, in traditional industrial white-collar organizations. Hard work, productivity and dedication are now increasingly rewarded only in the *affect* of team recognition and solidarity. Employees who are encouraged to believe in the promises of the new culture and who believe in the exemplary citizenship of Hephaestus Corporation deny the possibility of a breach in these implicit promises. When such a breach occurs, they experience shock, disbelief, devastation and disorientation in their lives. The bargain they have contracted, and which they believe the company to have likewise contracted, is controlled by the company and may be honored or breached at its decree.

Andrew is a senior executive in his fifties. He has been with Hephaestus for more than 25 years and has given the company, he believes, the best of his abilities and dedication. Andrew had believed that "Hephaestus could do no wrong." He had been influenced by the Jack Nicias ethos and had warmly embraced the new culture program since its inception. A few weeks before he talked with me, a major crisis had erupted in his team and in his work. A request that Andrew had made to the company that he believes would have resolved the crisis was refused. Andrew believed the severity of the crisis would mean that he would have to resign.

Andrew: In essence, I went to see Dick [his manager] and shared some of this with him, and he said, "Listen, I don't want you to leave." But quite frankly, if the outcome of that conversation would have been, "I'm sorry, but this is the way it is" . . . then today would have been the day that I would have turned in my letter saying that I am leaving. So to me it was a matter that if the issue didn't get resolved, then there is no question that I would basically have to leave in terms of trying to maintain my own personal sanity.

There were a few moments when I was like, "Oh my gosh, this is, this is serious," how am I possibly going to make those decisions. This is really big-time stuff . . . There were some hours in those few days I said, I am not sure if I can handle this . . . I have never had a nervous breakdown. I don't know how close I came to one. But there were certainly moments when my ability to function was impaired a lot. I took time off work, but I couldn't do anything.

Andrew told me that his considering early retirement over this crisis was not only traumatic but completely unexpected. He had never thought it would happen to him. As he recalled the event and his feelings, those feelings of shock and betrayal by the company arose again.

Stan is another example of an older man who had to come to terms with a shocking realization of a breach in the company's implicit promises to its highly productive and dedicated employees. Stan had reconciled himself to his retirement in advance of its event. He recalled the disappointment of the realization that he had been passed over for the promotion that would have confirmed his status and value. He was shocked to realize that he would go no further in Hephaestus even though he had been groomed for executive success as a young chief engineer.

In his latter years Stan had become an outspoken, yet agreeable, critic of Hephaestus' various cultural programs and new language practices. He performed a role for the team in which he gave voice to views that many others silently held, but in their adaptive self-protection, kept to themselves. In team meetings Stan was the one to make jokes that expressed humorous cynicism or disbelief in the official rhetoric. Such jokes were tolerated from Stan, but unacceptable and ignored when made by a younger employee or an "on-track" manager, such as occasionally ventured by Jerry. At meetings where opportunities for amusement did not avail, Stan usually napped.

The Hephaestus self

In the complex process of corporate colonization that offers promises and obscures contradictions the self simultaneously struggles in various ways, and with variable success, for a defensive self-protection, and assertive self-maintenance against those processes. The process of corporate colonization generates psychic strategies or self-styles[7] for employees that fall broadly into three clusters: *defense*, *collusion* and *capitulation*.[8] For many employees, the psyche's limited choices in this process of corporate colonization of the self are best dealt with by a process of collusion. The colluded self, discussed below, is the ideal designer self. The corporate patterning of the self also produces employee responses in which some adopt other strategies of defense or capitulation. The new culture's continuing effort is to win over these self-types to the ideal type. These three clusters of self options are described and analyzed below.

The self is affected by the processes of the new culture in two ways. It is assaulted, limited and diminished at the same time that it is comforted and sustained by the promise of the self-requirements of belonging, productivity and individual reward – the latter are the promises, expressed in corporate industrial terms, of the new culture rhetoric. They compare directly with the self-requirements of self: autonomy, competence and relatedness (as elaborated by Deci and Ryan 1991). Autonomy and competence are more readily maintained in carrying out the tasks of work. Relatedness is much more problematic. In Chapter 5 the problem of relatedness was considered through the ways in which its collective satisfaction in the solidarities of the modern phenomena of class and occupation is being eroded and displaced.[9] Erosion of industrial solidarities underlies the importance of the installation of the new culture. Psychic requirements of competence and autonomy are not as much in need of bolstering or repair, as these requirements largely continue to be met, but they are at risk of failure when relatedness wavers. Relatedness, upon which autonomy and competence flourish, is increasingly precarious and erratic in post-industrial conditions. The new precariousness of relatedness is an important unintended consequence of the corporate triumph over industrial culture and the erosion of organic solidarities of complex interdependence. My intention here is to describe and analyze the manifest effects of corporate colonization of the self, and the elements of self collaboration with that colonization. The latter refers to the ways in which employees consciously or unconsciously go along with corporate integration in return for perceived benefits to the self.

Each "self-type" described here contains some elements of the behavior and strategies of the others. They overlap and intertwine. But there is discernible a prevailing set of features that lend to analytical clustering of these strategies in three basic categories. This clustering does not necessarily firmly locate particular employee selves in one or another category; it represents general tendencies of self strategies. Individual employees may adopt one set of self strategies for a period of time, and later adopt another. But my findings suggest that defensive selves appear to maintain that strategy, or some may adopt a capitulated self strategy. Defensive selves are unlikely to adopt a collusion strategy, although that may happen after a crisis event. I propose that the third category, capitulation, is emerging as the prevailing type.

The self in capitulation refers to a form of negotiated psychic settlement or surrender with the colonizing culture of the corporation. It is especially common among the younger cohort and is also adopted by some older, former defended selves after they perceive themselves to have reached the limits of their careers with Hephaestus. Capitulated selves, may, over time, become colluded selves, as the corporation wishes them to be. My effort in describing these general self-strategies, refers to "normal" psychic reactions. I am not attempting in this analysis to deal with psychic disorders or to describe psychotic elements in the organizational culture itself. The following categories of defense, collusion and capitulation represent discernible distinct options for the self of relatively normal employees.

The defensive self

Some self-defense and protection strategies are employed and displayed by each of the various self-type groups. But for some employees defense is the prevailing characteristic in the everyday manifestation of the self. The defensive self is characterized by displays of multiple and various forms of small-scale resistances, retreats, rationalizations and blockages. The defensive self (more than the other types) expresses, or unconsciously manifests, confusion, fear, anxiety and ambivalence. Defensive selves tended, in the privacy of the interview, to criticize the company and their former or present managers. They reported memories of bad experiences in their working lives at Hephaestus and various affronts to their self-respect, self-worth and abilities. Some expressed dissent but most remain in the psychic quandary of ambivalence that does not reach the catharsis of dissent. Many sustained elaborate fantasies about living and working elsewhere.

Defensive selves were especially ambivalent about the quality of their working life and they were resentful of the demands and intrusions Hephaestus made on their lives, but they none the less continued to work hard and serve long hours, to try to be teamplayers and be proud of their products. They were uncertain and often fearful about their future. They wished to retain a belief in possible options for themselves lest Hephaestus fail to honor its implicit promises. One typical defensive self is Jerry, a young engineer and manager with an outstanding record of achievements in the company. Jerry suffered a heart attack a few years ago and he resents the conditions in his job that contributed to his illness. He describes himself as "driven" and extremely hard-working and he knows that he is a "fast-tracker" and highly regarded by peers and seniors. Jerry carries a burden of ambivalence and resentment that he could not express in the workplace. He acknowledged with surprise the unexpected catharsis in his interviews with me and he welcomed the opportunity to talk about many things that "never get talked about here."

Jerry: I don't expect you'll hear many opinions like mine . . . I don't really go along with a lot of this new culture thing. It's not all it's cracked up to be. You get a lot of people paying lip service to it . . . people use the right language, but they don't live up to. I find it irritating to work with.

Jerry, by his own admission, is totally obsessive about his work: "When I'm alone, I'm at work. I live to work."

At the same time Jerry is angry about the 60–80 hours a week he works. After his illness he had tried to reduce his hours but "they've crept up again, somehow." He is also critical of others, particularly senior men, whom he regards as "company men" and who don't "know who they are anymore." "This place will suck you dry if you're not careful. It happens to most people here. But I'm not going to let it happen to me."

Jerry is aggressive and outspoken in meetings. He is defiant about limiting his attendance at meetings, which he feels "are a big waste of time, most of the time." At the same time he is devoted to technological excellence in the Hephaestus products. He is excited and "totally absorbed" by technical problems. He says the company is not as great as everybody makes out and he likes to explore the possibility of establishing his own business "some day." At the same time he thinks Hephaestus products are great and the company is leading the world in its technology. He displays the President's Award for employee excellence on his wall, along with his patents.

Jerry is in a constant and fierce process of self-defense against the processes of corporate colonization. His awareness extends only to cynicism about the new culture and acting-out with his senior colleagues. He comforts himself with the compensations of being smart, highly productive and on the fast track. But he suffers in his health. The impossible goals he has set for himself (projecting them onto the company, so that he believes it has set them for him), are an inescapable burden which erodes his health and well-being. As a consequence, Jerry resents the company and has adopted an elaborate defensive stance against it. Furthermore, he defends himself from his unconscious projection of excessive, relentless demands with compulsive work habits and high productivity. At the same time, the corporation exploits and exaggerates these beliefs and Jerry is regularly given more work and responsibilities.

An additional complication in Jerry's case, is that his father had been an engineer with his own highly successful business. His father, Jerry reported, had traveled constantly, furiously "burning the candle at both ends" and was always highly motivated and extremely successful. He never, apparently, suffered health problems or failed to do what he set out to do. Jerry also reported that his father was proud when Jerry had joined Hephaestus Corporation, but that he ultimately admired people who had the resources to succeed in their own business. Jerry's present condition may well result from a complex transposition of his own superego into the superego manufactured by and embodied in Hephaestus Corporation. Under these conditions, the subtle relations of control and exploitation by Hephaestus are unfettered and unrecognized. Rather they are internalized by Jerry and his only psychic recourse, while in covert collusion, is a fierce defense.

Jerry's case is an example of a "frantic defensive" self. There are two other main types of defensive selves: "introverted" and "resistant." Introverted defensive selves are less overtly visible than frantic defensives. They tend to avoid conflict and acting-out performances and they do not engage in company or team politics. They are manifestly agreeable but seldom excessively so, as are their colluded colleagues (described below). In the interview, introverted defensive selves tended to express critical views about the company and similarly reported bad experiences and crisis events. They seek to defend themselves against an intensification of the daily corporate assault on the self while at the same time appearing not to be defensive. Many will find ways to protect or control their own everyday workplace space and to personalize and harmonize their immediate working environment with, for example, personal furniture and the playing of quiet classical music in their cubicles. Whenever possible they avoid meetings, work travel and social events.

Angie is in her forties. She has been with Hephaestus for sixteen years. Angie has a disability which she attributes largely to industrial conditions in the Hephaestus workplace. She believes that Hephaestus has, in effect, "tried to kill" her. She feels that while she works hard and enjoys her job, she has rarely been recognized for her skills and creative working styles, and that she has suffered personally from working in the vastness and "fakeness" of the corporate culture. She also believes that women especially suffer in such an environment.

Angie: I have the golden handcuff sensation, that I'd like to leave, but the security and benefits are such that I'm not sure I could adjust my lifestyle. But I'm continually re-evaluating my position with Hephaestus . . . I used to be more like the typical Hephaestus person. I was task-oriented, judgmental and I didn't have any real appreciation of the contribution of individual people. But now I am not like that, and it's not because of the new culture here, it's because of what I've read and studied in my degrees outside of here.

I haven't really been influenced by PQ, well, not in a positive way. It's a very punishing approach. They don't typically, I think, select people into management to make this PQ work, they already have them there, and they are like good old boys, hierarchical and structured. I feel offended by it, not only that they expect people to change so dramatically, but they're not accommodating – that this is difficult to do. They simply say: "Let's do quality." It's just kind of against the whole thing anyway . . . I'm not quick to volunteer negative views. I don't want to be too negative about it, but I have my own views, and usually I keep them to myself.

Angie avoids meetings. On one occasion she was required to attend the main Iris Team meeting in the typically crowded conference room. She sat next to me and whispered her comments and reactions as the meeting proceeded. She reported to me that she felt uncomfortable with the physical proximity of the predominantly male bodies in the room and the defensive position in which she believed the few women in the room were immediately placed. She felt threatened by the meeting atmosphere and over-exposed by the fluorescent lighting in the room. She asked me if it was usual for a group of five or six men to do most of the talking in the meeting that typically consisted of about 25–35 people. She was not surprised at my affirmative reply, but appeared to retreat into a protective demeanor and she did not verbally contribute to the meeting. After the meeting, Angie reported to me that she "couldn't wait to get out of there" and that she was glad that she did not have to attend those meetings every week. She could not imagine having to attend them every day.

Angie's manager confirmed with me that she was a highly capable employee and that she interacted very well with her own group. Her manager believed she should go far in Hephaestus, but doubted that she would. "Those kinds of people don't really do well here. She's just not visible enough. Or aggressive. I've seen it before. That's how I used to be, but I've become instrumental and aggressive now."

The "resistant defensive" self displays most of the characteristics of fellow defensives. But like the introverted defensives, resistant defensives are less clearly visible than the frantic defensives who make little secret of their stance. The frantic defensives are more likely to feel more sure of their employment security and to know that they are valued by the company. Or they may simply be less able to contain their desperation. Their compulsive productivity and native creativity are valuable assets for the company. Resistant defensives are more akin to their introverted defensive colleagues. A major difference is a gendered one. Where the introverted defensives tend to be women, resistant defensives tend to be men and ethnic minorities. The other distinction is that resistant defensives tend to be unspokenly defiant. They are minimally agreeable. They do their jobs well, but they go along with the new cultural requirements in only a minimal sense. They are stolid, detached and measured. They routinely take lunch breaks (most salaried employees do not). Their defensive strategies are not as fierce as those of the frantic defensives but, unlike the introverted defensives who tend to retreat, they may speak out or act out on particularly threatening occasions.

Tim is in his early fifties. He has been with Hephaestus for over twenty years. Tim is highly educated in a field not immediately relevant to his job in Hephaestus. Although he is not on an especially high grade he manages a large group of staff. The anomaly in his grade and level of responsibilities aggrieves him. Tim's predominant strategy is that of defended observer. His rare ability to observe and analyze what is going on in the company and its culture provides him with a psychic comfort that in turn assists his wish and ability to resist it.

Tim:　I suppose in one sense, and I'm not sure if this is true, but I would have to work extra hard, or at least I took care to do my work so that it was acknowledged as being above average; to protect myself and to show them [management] in my way that I was superior to them . . . There was a lot of frustration, but it never occurred to me to become one of them.

But somehow . . . it was a combination of things . . . And another thing was the new culture, I thought, gee, if ever this is the time to become a manager, when they want to make those (PQ) changes. I saw the opportunity to do some democratic things that I wouldn't have dreamed of earlier . . . I was self-conscious in one sense when I stepped into this formal role, but on the other hand I was feeling engrossed in doing things differently . . . In the end, I don't think I changed the job [of manager] a lot, not as much as I would have thought . . . I found, no surprise really, that you can't really make significant changes in the relationship of work without changing the structure. The structure hasn't changed at all.

Early on in these three years I did very radical things. I wanted to create a democratic workplace, and I had things like we would make group decisions and like I would refuse to stand up in meetings, and I was conscious of this. And I knew I was being misinterpreted as being a new manager not being able to cope and afraid to make speeches . . . And all this time, like I was trying to make my group – I would refuse to say "my," I said "our" group – a democratic team . . . I've just about given up on it particularly because the pressures of the job consume me and I just don't have time . . . It has been a real problem. I used to wake up in the middle of the night. But it's eased up . . . I don't give a damn about the company.

I have got to the point where I am really thinking, am I doing the right thing? . . . I say to myself now, well, forget it, and in the total scheme of things, things are better. But I am sure it is not healthy. But that wouldn't be enough to take care of the subconscious problems caused by not following . . . I don't know, I get myself confused.

I have always stood back and looked, "Look at this silly game." I have been part of it, but I have always been able to stand back and know that you are a player.

Tim's master self-strategy is a defended resistance to further acculturation to the company. He has tried to conform to the new culture and to realize its potential for humanizing the workplace, but he believes he has seen through its hollow rhetoric. He maintains his ego defense in rationalizing the material necessity of his employment, and assumes the role of the detached observer.

The colluded self

The option of collusion, of which there are basically two types, "compulsive" and "passive," is characterized by compliance, dependence, ambition, manipulability and, for the less senior, over-agreeability and visible displays of total dedication and identification.[10] The colluded self experiences little discontinuity between work life and out-of-work life. There is an effort to avoid and deny intra-psychic conflict by compulsive displays of complicity with the corporate culture. Colluded corporate selves manifest a *compulsive optimism* in their beliefs about the company, its products and their future within it. Compulsive optimism is a psychic buffer that filters competing messages and impulses. It allows the colluded self to structure and sort its responses and construct consistent interpretations. The self-option of collusion brings about an immediate displacement of the psychic conflicts of defense that Jerry displays. The (unconscious) wish to identify with and obey the corporate superego requires the psyche to repress defensive individuation through independence and to exaggerate dependency and conformity. Historically, the "organization man" of Whyte's (1956) analysis was the model promoted by extensive hierarchical bureaucratic organizations. Although collusion is the self-option that the new corporate culture implicitly promotes and rewards it is no longer the "best" strategy for the psyche. Post-industrial conditions that include the integration of knowledge and production functions and flatter hierarchies no longer guarantee the rewards that the former colluded self expected. As a result the relatively simpler process of collusion among white-collar employees apparent in traditional corporate organizations is now more difficult to procure.

An example of the colluded self is Karen, an engineer-manager in her thirties responsible for a world-wide project. She wishes to be known as an employee who is highly competent, entrepreneurial and totally dedicated to her work and the company. Karen reports that she believes that the company is the "best in the world" and she is committed to continuing that excellence. Karen wishes to be a vice-president someday and says she will do "whatever is required" to achieve this goal. Her personal style of gender management is to wear steel-grey suits which evoke the traditional stereotype of the high-flying corporate man. She appears measured and highly disciplined. She readily employs the desired corporate language and reiterates its slogans at every opportunity. In meetings I observed her to be tough, resilient and at times combative and ruthless. She told me that she "plays politics," networks and "can be very aggressive" and she believes in the company and its products. The walls of her brightly fluorescent-lit office are adorned with company posters and slogans.

Karen: I feel proud of this company . . . But there are some things here, like I've seen people get rewarded for disorganized behavior . . . There is too much fuzzy thinking, it's not organized enough . . . I wish Hephaestus was more organized.

I guess I would say that Hephaestus runs my life . . . I like being at work, it's where I feel most in control, and most fulfilled . . . I guess I can't work 90 hours a week forever. It's perfectionist, isn't it? My manager has told me to do less and to stop taking all the responsibilities in the world. But I like having 99 percent of everything correct

I'm the same kind of person at home as I am at work. Unfortunately, I think so. Sometimes I wish I wasn't! But you're like this all day, I guess it gets to be like hard to be any other way . . . but I like to be the same . . . I think you should be consistent and I like to be even.

I think the way we work here is good. They were already doing PQ when I came here, but I think we've got a ways to go. But we're learning . . . It's the meetings that don't do it well. How often do you hear them use the process? We don't use it enough. Sometimes we only remember to use it if somebody speaks up and says, 'Hey, what are we doing here!' That's often me.

Karen expresses and displays an unwavering commitment to the product. She believes that Hephaestus technology is the best in the world, and if Hephaestus gets its work organization right and its employees sufficiently organized, it will lead the world in the business. Whenever there were discussions at team meetings about details of the technological development of the product, including issues and problems that worried the design scientists, Karen would bring the discussion around to an upbeat tone by reminding her teammates of how great their products were and the progress the company was making. She deflected doubt in the product as quickly as she dispelled doubt in herself. In keeping with the company image of being a risk taker and possessing a youthful vigor, Karen believed she possessed the same qualities: "I'm a risk-taker, and I'm willing to do whatever it takes, and that's what makes this company great, and that's how you can succeed here." She believed she was on track for becoming a Vice-President and she had established good political connections to facilitate that. Her narrative construction of her experience with Hephaestus contained none of the harsh or troubling experiences many other employees reported in the privacy of the interview.

Karen: When I came in [to the Iris team] the field was just starting to get interested in the product and we needed to do demos and show the machine to customers . . . I was the closest thing they had to a marketing manager so I decided that I best learn how to demo the machine. That would be a high visibility thing that wasn't getting done by anyone else, that was a very conscious strategy. This could be a politically good thing to do. It was beyond my wildest hopes, I ended up doing it for about eight months but it was one of those holes that I thought was like stepping into a pothole, but really it was kind of an oil well and the good news is that there was oil there, and it was really deep.

So far, each move has led to something better. Going to marketing was what gave me the skills to take the launch team job which has been very beneficial to my career. And being willing to make those moves is why it all turned out right and it is working very well. And that's one of those things that is great about Hephaestus, because that's how the company is, and that's how you can succeed here.

Through aligning herself closely with the goals and strategies of the corporation and adopting them as her own, Karen eliminates the psychic conflicts experienced by selves struggling in defense against those same corporate strategies. She manifests a strong belief in the corporation and represses doubt, that momentarily emerged when she spoke briefly of her young child whom she "hardly ever sees," into compulsive dedication.

A little older, more senior and with more years of experience with Hephaestus is the Chief of the Iris Team, Sam Steele. Sam exhibits many of the same characteristics as Karen, although more discreetly and in a form now somewhat tarnished. Sam's experience has tempered the compulsive optimism displayed by junior colluders, but his ambition and political acumen ensure his total dedication to the company and its strategies. As a senior team leader (now a Vice-President) Sam is an agent of corporate success and has aligned his own success with that of Hephaestus. Sam joined Hephaestus more than twenty years ago as a young college graduate. He moved rapidly through grades and gained broad experience including an international posting. He returned to the Hephaestus plant at Rusty River to take up the position of chief engineer for the Iris Team. It was a position that he had aspired to and it occurred "at about the right time," although everyone knows that he is young for an incumbent in such a senior position.

Sam: A lot of people are passionate about the product so I think what I have discovered in my own experience, is that if you seize or assume responsibility, it seeks its own equilibrium. People are always looking for leadership at some level, at all levels.

I looked around me and I saw people in management positions and I said to myself, I could do this. I could do that. My ideas were as good as theirs. I was about twenty years old then. And I guess I began to set myself goals in this company. And I have achieved them.

Sam could recall a difficult period in Hephaestus, prior to the introduction of PQ, in which a product went out with major technical faults and had to be recalled. A lot of people lost their jobs over that incident, but Sam came out on the winning side and advanced. He welcomed the introduction of the new culture, especially as Saffron, an American rival company, was "killing us." His ability to work extraordinarily hard, to make decisions and to move with the company helped his rapid advancement. Sam is untroubled about whether or not his team and senior managers like him. He is concerned with productivity, decision-making and "doing what's best for Hephaestus."

Sam: I would say that what I am criticized most for is the fact that I think I am right all the time. I think that in the last five years I have really tried to conquer this, because it has been that I am not right all the time . . . I

172

have kind of dampened what I call my arrogance, in the last five years I have really consciously addressed it.

I don't like conflict. I really don't like it, so I try to beat it. I don't like it when Ken gets angry in meetings, I don't like those performances, and they will have to stop. I can see everybody getting uncomfortable with it. And I don't believe in getting angry like that . . . There are other ways to deal with things.

Sam believes that by perfecting the procedures laid down in the new culture program such displays of conflict can be eliminated. He believes that if everyone was "doing what's best for Hephaestus" these problems would go away. Sam appears to be a firm, tough-minded decision-maker who is unwaveringly confident in his own judgment. At the same time he is completely entwined with the corporate culture and the goals and strategies of the company. His cool fierceness and air of personal detachment mask a deeper dependence on the company that feeds and rewards his ambition and reinforces his need for recognition, achievement and control. His collusion is not, at first glance, as obvious as Karen's, because he has eschewed the personal gratification of popularity and ingratiation with his colleagues for the sake of higher satisfactions in increasing power and control. The deeper his ego-identification with the company, the more distorted and controlling his own wish for control becomes. Sam's wife summed up her observations of her husband throughout his twenty years with Hephaestus: "Sam is unable to control his ambition," and that characteristic has been both the source of his success and the flaw in his character. It is also the feature that has "dictated" the lives of his family as well as Sam himself: "I sometimes really worry about him . . . when he puts on his business uniform he is a different person. But, that's who he is *most* of the time."

The other type of colluded self is the "passive colluder." Passive colluders manifest most of the characteristics of the compulsive colluder without the former's intensity and vigor. They comprise largely an older cohort, including retired employees, who committed themselves at an earlier time and have remained identified with the corporation. All their experiences, memories and observations are constructed glowingly and contrary impulses are denied with a smile. Passive colluders expressed little awareness of the possibility that anything about the company might be different from the way it is. Unlike the compulsive colluders who can consider, however momentarily, a critical view, the passive colluders are uniformly disinclined to express contrary views or to imagine divergent possibilities. They speak reverently about Hephaestus and they seek a vicarious glory through its image in the marketplace and in the world. Some who have been financially successful through timely investment of Hephaestus shares during the now passed days of employee profit-sharing

173

expansively praise the company and express considerable self-satisfaction for their association with the company. For the passive colluders, Hephaestus represents an incarnation of the great god of benevolence and prosperity who makes wondrous technological products. They serve in complete faith and untiring dedication.

Si is a man in his early sixties. He had worked for Hephaestus for 27 years before retiring three years ago. Si has recently re-joined Hephaestus as a contract employee in a group that develops training and service curricula for the Iris products. Si reported that he had not enjoyed his retirement, that he missed Hephaestus too much and he was eager to return. Although no longer managing his own group or involved in developing the latest technological systems in Hephaestus machines he does not mind his quieter, lower-status job. He feels honored to be able to return to service in Hephaestus.

Si: Hephaestus always struck me as being a very personable company that cared about me, and not about their product so much. It's very very strong. They always gave you the impression that you were more important than their products. Even when Jack [Nicias] left, it started going down hill, but the real concern for employees is still here present today. They really care.

When we learned how to work as a team, we could problem-solve everything. And it was amazing, really . . . Once we went into the revolution, we really started doing exotic things . . . I was working 70–80 hours a week, sometimes 90, but it was just part of the job, and we did whatever was needed to get the job done. But it was great, it was great. We were running before we could think . . . Hephaestus wants you to keep on learning. Like we went on all these 'sensitivity' classes . . . you had to be able to separate people from work. You had to learn to click on and click off.

Because, I really think that coming to this place and doing some of the things that I was working on, and things like the President's Award, and things, made the difference between me being 'Joe Doke's average' and being somebody, and I really feel that I am somebody, and I was somebody.

Both types of colluders identify with the Hephaestus superego and derive a relative psychic integration in knowing that their dedication and unwavering commitment are welcomed by the company. In blocking the capacity for doubt that serves as an anxiety relief of the unconscious fear of failure (of belief), passive colluders displace anxiety through ritualized devotion and repetition of the official cultural narratives. Psychic discomfort is thus diminished and contained and identification more readily ensured. Si, and others like him, become the ritual bearers and protectors of the new cultural forms. They often take the role of meeting chairpersons and facilitators because they can be relied upon to employ the correct language forms and to operate by procedural rules. They regularly monitor deviations from correct PQ procedure and keep everyone on track. They are also involved in staff training and inducting new employees, and they often act as consultants to designated staff training and development specialists. They tend to display company posters in their cubicles, wear its slogan-bearing sweatshirt and cap, and carry its coffee mug.

The capitulated self

Other critical studies of bureaucratic institutions have similarly argued that the self is under a process of siege and assault (Baum 1987, LaBier 1986, Maccoby 1976). The processes of siege in the new corporate culture, although somewhat less immediately apparent because of the deflective, compensatory device of the cultural construction of sociality, continue to operate. But a new form of compensation for that siege is emerging in the form, not of defense, but of capitulation. For many, the capacity to defend against the assault on the self, and the psychic energy required to sustain such resistance, have been sufficiently weakened that manifestations of resistance are becoming rarer. Many previously defensive selves, who resisted the psychic option of collusion, are now worn down into capitulation. They seek to compensate for the assault by (unconsciously) negotiating a settlement that provides sufficient psychic stability and integration derived from the relative comforts of a simulated culture and familial team. There are two basic types of capitulated self, the "pragmatic" and the "reluctant."

Capitulation contains elements of both defense and collusion, but both are restrained by strategic, instrumental pragmatism. In coming to a settlement, capitulated selves are able to maintain a sufficient sense of self-boundary that is less vigilantly patrolled than that of the defensive selves. At the same time they adopt an air of "cool" self-control and an element of ironic cynicism toward the company. The cynicism acts as a defense against the possibility that capitulation might collapse into collusion – the positioning of the self sought by the company. Ironic cynicism protects against both commitment to the company, which requires self-denial and dedication, and its further encroachment into the private realm of (relative) individual choice and apparent self-determination. It enables an illusion of measured self-distancing that regulates their relationship with the company. Capitulated selves sense when it is beneficial to believe, and yet retain a capacity to disbelieve. They know how to present an image of themselves as appropriate Hephaestus employees, how to play the game, and when to retreat. They are pragmatic, strategic selves. They expend considerable psychic energy in dampening the desperation of both the defensive and colluded selves.

Paul has been with Hephaestus for ten years and he now manages a group of ten people. He has degrees in science and computing engineering and he is now studying toward an MBA at the University of Rusty River. His current job is the "software interface to the program" that includes developing and auditing software functions in the new machines. Paul is well-spoken, impeccably dressed and carefully presented. He thinks about his job and his future a great deal, and he believes that he is managing his career and will control his future.

Paul: I think about my career a lot. I think that it is like I have my own time schedule . . . And if you write it down you can see if you are getting the things that you need so that when the time comes to change assignments, you can see if you can make that happen. So it's like between you and them. You as an employee have your agenda and your manager has his agenda . . . You are the vehicle that he gets his objectives accomplished by.

I am a tool and going to MBA school and supplying the corporation . . . You're a tool that the corporation uses . . . I don't think that is wrong. That is why I don't have a problem with it. That is just the way it is. But people just do not understand, and they often times get hurt because they don't understand it. They think that the corporation doesn't care about them and they thought the corporation cared about them at one time, and now it does not care. I said, well, they never cared about you. The reason they want to keep you healthy and stuff is so they can keep you working . . . I am saying, realize that it is what the corporation does to you, and that it is just the way it is . . . Things at work don't really get to me because I stay focused on myself and my career. I'm only a short-timer here. That is the direction I am setting my goals for, so it is like I am saying maybe I won't work for Hephaestus one day.

It does not control my life. I think that I work for a different purpose. I would say that I work to make my pleasure times more pleasurable and not the other way round. I don't work to have pleasure.

Paul wishes to maintain his own sense of control and destiny. He wishes to benefit from his experience at Hephaestus, to cooperate with its culture and production project and at the same time maintain an air of calculated, "mellow" detachment that enables him to keep his options open. Paul is proud to report that he never gets angry at work, and that he keeps himself "cool." Paul's declaration that he "knows what the corporation is" enables him to maintain an attitude of apparent indifference. In his view, recognizing that the corporation is morally neutral and adopting a correspondingly morally neutral view toward the company are all that is required of

176

employees to successfully accommodate to it. It is a stance that defiantly resists the new culture's religious impulse to revive an ethic of self-sacrificing dedication and devotion. At the same time, it is an accommodatory stance that ensures the employee will not contest or dissent from the goals and programs of the company, despite his assertion of private independence.

Paul's belief that he could walk out of Hephaestus next week provides a defense against the need for a more pronounced defensive self strategy. It bolsters his wish to believe in his own self-security and confirms to himself his capabilities and marketability that are transferable beyond Hephaestus. Capitulation enables a "mellow" and self-satisfying air of self display. It provides the illusion of independence and self-control as it at once defends against the knowledge of a corporate colonizing influence on character, values, lifestyle and habit.

A more primary, less sophisticated capitulation is that of the "reluctant capitulator." Reluctant capitulation is characterized by resignation, inner conflict and the appearance of an awareness, not of control, but of having traded off the self. Yet the reward for the trade-off is still perceived as the way for the self to secure gratifications and status in the achievement of corporate-induced goals. It is the option favored by former defensives and disenchanted colluders. Defensives contrive numerous rationalizations about their participation in the Hephaestus culture. They enumerate the attractions of pay, benefits and professional opportunities as strong reasons for their working for Hephaestus. But they are more resigned to the personal trade-offs extracted from their services in terms of surrendering competing personal value systems and commitments, such as family life and non-work activities. This group most resents the long hours of work but none the less serves them.

The reluctant capitulators have more doubts than their pragmatic colleagues, who filter doubt through the constant effort to maintain mellow equilibrium, but they similarly derive psychic comfort from giving up the more costly struggle that defensive corporate selves engage in. But they are unable, usually as the result of an experience of severe disappointment or disillusionment with the company, to give themselves over to the dependence and comfort of collusion. A further factor influencing this self-strategy arises when an employee experiences significant conflicts with competing commitments such as children. Corporate women with children seem particularly likely to manifest this self-option.

Mary-Kate has three young children and she holds a senior management position in the Iris team. She is known as a quiet person who is extremely competent and very hard-working. She delivers her "deliverables." Mary-Kate expresses conflict about the demands the company places on her with respect to her family. She knows that accommodating her family life to the demands of the corporate schedule is the price of her senior position and her high career prospects with Hephaestus. The conflict troubles her a great deal, but Mary-Kate has moved psychically from a defensive position, which she (unconsciously) believes would hold her back from the advancement that she seeks and values. She must be seen to be willing and committed and not reluctant, or constrained by expending psychic energy in defense. Yet the gravity and imminence of the conflict with her family life preclude the option of collusion for her.

Mary-Kate: After I had been here a couple of years I was sure I was going to be a Vice-President some day. And that is what I want. And now . . . I am not sure I want it any more, even though I think I have the potential to get there, I am not sure I want it any more because the commitment is so great.

Before I had children I thought I could do it all. I thought I could work full time and have kids. But I realize it is too great a personal expense. It is important to me to spend the time I do have, or don't have, with my kids . . . I feel guilty all the time. The hardest thing for me is to find balance. I'm always trying to balance everything. And usually I just feel pulled in every direction . . . But I work as hard as the guys do. Maybe I'm not here at 6 a.m. like Donal, but I would say that I work better, more effectively, than they do . . . I have been picked as one of the top Hephaestus leaders in the next decade. And so I know I can do it. I guess I want it all.

Capitulated selves no longer recognize, as the defensives continue to, the ongoing processes of disciplining and corporate shaping of self in their dedication to their own ambition and securing their own status. Like the colluded selves, capitulated selves are accommodating to corporate colonization, but their accommodation is filtered through a further mechanism that interprets such acculturation as serving their own self-directed interests and goals. They wish to believe they have retained an assertiveness and self-control which, if they so chose, would enable them to leave Hephaestus and go elsewhere. Maintaining and asserting such a belief in itself provides an immediate self-gratification. Capitulation is a self-option that appears strategic and rational, that appears neither defensive nor collusive and that allows one to be "mellow." It is, however, just as much as collusion, a psychic option of the *latent narcissist*.

The capitulated narcissist (somewhat less obvious than the colluded self) derives sufficient psychic stability from association with the company, and glories in the reflection of himself in its image, but maintains a fragile belief in, and an image of serving, his own self-interest and advancement. At the same time capitulation is also the option for the disillusioned believers and wearied defensive selves. It is the option that is more precarious for the stability of the company than either of the other two. It is, therefore, the option the company wants most to win over – to win over narcissists and unbelievers to a rehabilitated older form of a believing, hard-working, dedicated, Protestant bourgeois self imposed across old class and ethnic boundaries.

DISCUSSION: CORPORATE DESIGN AND CAPITULATED SELVES

The former, industrial experience of siege especially for the working-class self, was resisted in more organized and collective ways through the compensatory solidarity of class and occupation loci. Now that those solidarities and their benefits have gone, compensation needs to be found elsewhere. It is found in accommodation to the new culture. Capitulation, therefore, is emerging as the prevailing self strategy. This represents a significant departure from industrial bureaucratic culture, in which employee selves opted either for the protection and comfort of occupational solidarity or for the conversion of allegiance to the corporation. The modern self is both a product of modern industrial society and necessary for consumer society, as it is at once a problem for class control – a central problem of industrialism. The modern individual, agentic self of bourgeois culture was also a class self.

Modern industrial society produced class-selves that were bounded by class-prescribed limits of agency and power, and that generated class-based forms of solidarity. The problem of control of the individual self lay in the contradiction between promotion of bourgeois notions of selfhood and concomitant citizenship, and the maintenance of class distinctive selves in which working-class selves were denied by the bourgeoisie the fullness of the self requirements of the bourgeois self. Such selves, while protected and defended by their own forms of solidarity, experienced a class-specific assault in a colonizing force that ensured the aspirations to selfhood were controlled by the production needs of self-sacrifice and disciplined compliance to a higher managerial class of authority. Thus producer selves were maintained as a class distinct from consumer selves.

The working-class self of industrialism, through the forms of occupational and class solidarities, typically engaged in a more overt contest against the mechanisms of industrial oppression that characterized industrial workplace culture. The capacity for resistance was found in the traditional forms of industrial solidarities which had emerged in response to the imposition of the early Protestant ethic of worker and citizen of the eighteenth century and which became, for the working class, an expression of solidaristic resistance against it. But advanced industrial capitalism's requirement for mass consumption eventually undermined an oppositional working-class culture. The promise of consumption (as citizenship) integrated the working class. Furthermore, identification with the employer bourgeois self, who was disciplined by manifest or latent religious practices, precipitated the collusion among corporate employees evident in later industrial conditions (as described by Maccoby 1976 and Whyte 1956). Under present corporate conditions, class-based resistance is evident only in a remnant form among the defensive selves. The displaced remainder opt for capitulation and consumption. Now it is the narcissist who is under siege in the corporation's effort to discipline her and win her back to the rigor and restraint of its culture of production.

Capitulation manifests an element of conscious as well as unconscious giving up, trading-off and rationalizing defeat. The strategic self, successful in surviving in the corporate environment, but still constantly under disciplinary siege, lives in a defended privacy and defended out-of-work life. Capitulation contains anxiety sufficiently to enable a credible self-rationalization based on a familiar American pragmatism. But it delimits the self as it obstructs and truncates fuller psychic development and maintains narcissism.

Design flaws: unintended consequences

The "ideal" corporate self is a neo-Protestant bourgeois self who displays the virtues of the character of classical Protestant culture but is bereft of its full rewards. Yet, once again, an unintended consequence of corporate capitalism is the narcissistic consumer self (superficial, dependent, self-indulgent) that has been only partially modified and "civilized" by the sensitivities encouraged in the new culture's language and inter-personal behavior specifications into a simply strategic self able to blow with the winds of corporate change to wherever self-gratification is perceived to be most immediate. Despite the corporation's concerted effort in its new culture program, the secondary narcissism of late capitalist culture (Lasch 1978, 1984) has not yet given way to the corporate designer self in which self-denying hard work and renewed dedication to the company prevail. The promotion of the ideal corporate character of self is an effort to win back the "ideal consumer" – the chronically anxious narcissist seeking fleeting gratifications in consumption. Yet the advanced capitalist mode of production is completely unable to reconcile its deep cultural contradiction (cf. Bell 1976) of the continually self-gratification-seeking, anxiety-displacing consumer self and the self-disciplined, self-denying, hard-working employee self dedicated to the corporation and its culture of production.

Even more than the corporate culture's simulation of the social sphere to promote the "normal" relatedness of human interaction in shared activity that is necessary for production, the corporate culture attempts to manage narcissism at a deeper psychic level. The corporation's elaborate effort to create a workplace team-family enables the *primary* narcissism of the family to be offered as a legitimate and noble alternative to the acquisitive, self-seeking consumer narcissist. The new corporate culture, while

180

endeavoring to displace the *secondary* narcissism of the self-gratification-seeking, infantilely rebellious self, allows for the compensatory device of a reactivated, romanticized notion of the family to inadvertently serve corporate pathologies in providing a primary narcissism in the nascent undifferentiation of family.

For more psychically troubled selves, "normal" processes of family bonding and the exclusivity of family are distorted by the corporate simulacra into provision of a narcissistic gratification through reflection of oneself in the similarity of kin. Under these conditions family bolsters and accessorizes the chronically weakened individual self in its provision of "normal" and legitimate primary relations. The new corporate culture establishes a replica of family relations and bonds that enables the corporation to promise individuals the psychic rewards of primary narcissism as a trade-off for relinquishing the immediate gratification of secondary narcissism. The corporatized, emptied-out self is compensated instead by the gratification of nascent undifferentiation from the company as mother and teammates as siblings. In so doing, the simulated family not only provides a substitute sociality, it feeds the pathological tendencies of the employee products of corporate culture toward a narcissism that mocks ideal family life of reciprocal bonding, commitment and, through maturation, an openness to communitarian public life.

For the employee self of the designer corporate culture capitulation is, therefore, a strategy that sufficiently preserves narcissism and private individualism and, at the same time, eschews the social and facilitates its demise. It looks like the strategic compromise between the desperation of frantic or defiant defense and compulsive collusion. For the so-called "New Age person," which new corporate culture is often reportedly aligned with, it is the ultimate rationalization and denial of corporate power. Capitulation enables the individual to maintain sufficient psychic integration and stability to continue the cycle of production and consumption.[11] It is the option most favored by the younger cohort. Most of the older employees exhibit an unhappy mixture of defense and collusion.

Old class-selves and the narcissistic personality that crosses historical classes, are being made over into corporate teammates. The teammate-self directed into family-style cooperation and renewed compulsiveness (to displace secondary narcissism) in dedication and hard work, is encouraged into the habits of a vague and superficial self-awareness that enables an old invocation of guilt to reappear as reasoned self-restraint in the service of corporate goals. Confessional teammates are admonished by each other and their leaders and (partially) reconciled to the company team to renewed efforts in production. The corporation revives and restores the Protestant cultural forms that have been obscured and faltered under the culture of narcissism of advanced industrial society and its therapeutic salvation. But it does not honor the rewards promised by the Protestant tradition, even

181

under Calvin's harsh regime of self-denial and unceasing service. No longer guaranteed the rewards and the accoutrements of one's "calling" in non-material "blessings" and salvation, the new corporate self finds gratification for this elusive chronic disappointment in renewed consumption.

New, designer corporate culture is a first cultural moment in post-industrial society. In the panic of a prospective epochal shift that threatens the fabric of modern industrial economic and social relations and that will lead beyond industrialism, post-industrial corporate capitalism moves to revive and rehabilitate earlier forms of social organization. It invokes vague, but not disintegrated, social memories of a Protestant ethic that ensures production through self-restraint, rational submission to higher authority, order and dedication to duty (work). It is a corporate effort to fend off and defy the *fin de siècle*, *fin d'industrialisme* decadence of a rampant consumerist narcissism which advanced industrial capitalism unleashed.

7

REVIVALISM, SELF AND SOLIDARITY

RE-COLLECTIONS

I set out in this book to address two primary questions. The first is an exploration of the effects of the discursive practices of post-industrial work on self-constituting processes. My intention, in approaching the new work as a discursive or symbolic practice, is to emphasize a shift away from the fixation with the materiality of work in industrial societies and in typical industrial studies. It is not my intention to privilege discourse over the materiality of production, but rather to illuminate communicational practices in work, especially the practices of the "new" deliberately designed culture and new organizational forms of the post-industrial corporation, and to demonstrate their increasing importance in shaping employees through their experiences of work. I have endeavored to describe and analyze these practices and to discern their patterning of working selves in corporate, advanced technological conditions.

The second question, implicit throughout, is an interest in the forms of social solidarity that selves, acting in emerging new social conditions, may create. It is a modernist sociological interest that gazes upon these emerging conditions with a lens and tools formed in an age that is passing. But like work, the problem of social solidarity endures beyond modern industrialism. It is a question that my effort to address in this chapter is able only provisionally to answer. Instead, social solidarity in diffuse, disunified, plural postmodern conditions becomes a vast new problematic. Most immediately, as the corporation takes over, at least for now, a primary cohesive locus of modern society, as an unintended consequence of its triumph over a no-longer seriously contested industrial capitalism, it leaves open the public spaces formerly distinctive of pre-modern and modern society. Post-industrial corporations can electronically generate productivity and financial exchanges simultaneously across the world. The central urban space where market and public life were historically conducted is now increasingly irrelevant. The city, once central not only to capitalism, but civilization from classical times to modernity, may well be rendered redundant in a post-industrial, postmodern society. Modern, negotiable solidarity will no longer hold in the conditions of dispersion, decenteredness and corporate global networks.

I wish here to review the first question and the main theoretical propositions that are developed in this book, and to return later to the question of post-industrial solidarities. But first, a brief disclaimer on the limits of this study, and a reminder of the limitations of its methodology.

I have offered in this study of corporate selves some categories for understanding the processes of self formation effected by the experience of contemporary corporate work. Although I have used some psychoanalytic constructs, particularly narcissism, I have not developed primarily a psychological theory of the self at work. I have appropriated, as Lasch (1978, 1984) does, a psychoanalytic construct for a *social* analysis. I have taken a social view that favors an analysis of the influences on the self that are supplied by society and culture. But I do not subscribe to a view that the self is composed only of social inputs. The person, first and foremost, has a body that determines her physical being in the world. Similarly, the multiple psychological, and social, processes that occur in self-formation prior to and outside of the culture of work are acknowledged but not attended to in the analyses of the self offered in this study. Other theories of self and identity may attend more fully to the nascent psychological, and biological, conditions of self development. But even Hewitt's (1989)[1] substantial theory biases the social, following Mead, in his "personal identity" and "social identity" constructs. With Hewitt, I share a view that the self is a social product and process, not a solely biological entity nor a narrowly-conceived psychological response system impelled by environmental forces.[2]

But unlike Hewitt, I do not rest my analyses of the self entirely upon the tensions operating between the bipolar axes of communitarianism and individualism, optimism and pessimism, conformity and rebellion.[3] I have emphasized the effects of an active corporate culture on employee selves, but the variation in individual self-strategy in "choosing" a psychic option among the basic categories of defense, collusion and capitulation, may in part be attributable to each person's response to the relative strength of the sets of opposing forces in their personal biographical histories. My analyses have not attempted to describe the historical biographical sources of personal variation and specificity of experience at work. I have attempted to make general propositions about selves affected by the practices of contemporary corporate work which I have drawn from analyses of data gathered from my field study of work.

Neither do I offer an analysis of national character, a peculiarly "American" type of self that is central to Hewitt's effort. A corporate character of self crosses national boundaries as freely as the expansion of capital and the export of corporate culture. The globalization and uniformity of multi-national corporate culture is of much more importance to my analysis than the retention of national and ethnic cultural distinctiveness. Employees of Hephaestus Corporation, for example, use the same new culture manuals and technical manuals, adjusted only for the vernacular, that are in use in every country of the world. Employees follow the same dress code[4] in Hephaestus, IBM, GM Corporation, and so forth, all over the world. The globalization of corporate culture will have significant effects beyond the historically-specific national experiences of individual countries, including the United States of America. Although ethnic, religious and regional identifications will remain important, the decline of the nation-state and the rise of the multi-national corporation will exert considerable influence on the production of culture, and social and political structure, everywhere.

These questions and projections call to mind the recurrent problems I share with other social researchers undertaking naturalistic enquiries. In particular, the issues of validity, reliability and generalizability in studies such as I have offered in these chapters remain problematic. Social researchers[5] influenced by anthropological traditions and the ethnographic genre in sociology, following the Chicago School, have devised caveats and disclaimers that, although not resolving the scientific question, carefully seek to "justify" qualitative enquiries. Their appeal to the systematic rigor with which qualitative research is designed, conducted and interpreted, and which differentiates ethnographic writing from "mere naturalistic description" (Bulmer 1984), to validate the ethnographic method and its scientific endeavor, is invoked again here to "authorize" the study I have elaborated in these chapters.

I am aware of the contingencies of epistemological bases and analytic categories. But I have, none the less, sought to demonstrate systematic interpretation of the data and to construct a rational narrative while not seeking to "prove" the interpretations and theoretical propositions I have developed. I am reluctant to assert the authoritative voice of the modern scientist (Clifford and Marcus 1986). Rather, I wish, in postmodern vein, to make a somewhat more modest invitation to the reader to accept that in my rigorous adherence to the data and its "natural" validity, and in the systematic construction of interpretations, I have offered a credible analysis of work and selves in contemporary corporate conditions.

POST-OCCUPATIONAL WORK, POST-INDUSTRIAL SOLIDARITY

I argue in these chapters a theoretical proposition that we are witnessing the transformation, if not demise, of occupation. Occupation has been a definitive category of social organization in industrial society, and a pivotal discursive construct in our analysis of industrialism. Specialist occupations, with codified bodies of knowledge, skill, standards, and customs of practice, are declining. Persons from expert professions along with those from trade and service occupations are being transformed into multi-faceted, pan-occupational team players in the new corporate organization. The elaborate division of labor and the specialization of function that made occupation a compass point in the indication of social status and role, and a primary locus of cohesion, as well a site of practical solidarity in the factories and cities of industrialism, has ceased.

Many other studies have reported and documented changes in the world of work particularly with respect to the impact of advanced automated manufacturing technologies and advanced information technologies. Similarly, analysts have considered the effects on the subsequent organization of work notably the manufacturing changes facilitated by Just-In-Time production systems, quality circles and other employee involvement programs. Again, changes in the composition of labor forces and the relative proportions of workers in economic sectors, and the consequent debates over skills requirements (see Chapter 2) are well documented. More recently, some analysts note the rise of many new jobs in the post-industrial service sector and there is growing attention to corporate organizations guided particularly by an interest in developing and managing "competitive cultures." Yet amid the voices in the debates on skills, flexibility, management levelling, quality, restructuring and cultural change, there is a consistent failure to recognize a profound shift in the actual categories of work and work organization that affects the employee, and the organization: that of occupation.

The transformation of occupation in the corporation and the emergence of post-occupational work in corporate practices of team and "family" groupings is affecting the composition of a post-industrial self and will affect the forms of social solidarity in society after industrialism. In the meantime, notwithstanding the dramatic changes in industrial production, culture and society, industrialism is not yet over. The revival of industrial ethics in production and the industrial character of self, as exemplified in the corporate revival of a Protestant employee self, will ensure that work-based solidarities, although this time company-appropriated, will endure for some time yet. Social organization *beyond work* awaits further transformations in the productive sphere and in the postmodern patterning of human beings that allows for a creative post-production mode of being human – a matter beyond the scope of this book.

At the present time, though, we are already witnessing the disappearance of many typical industrial occupations[6] (signalman, switchboard operator, welder, typist, insurance underwriter) as their functions become obsolete under the integrative capacities of new automation and information technologies. Furthermore, we can observe the amalgamation of other skilled occupations, as I have demonstrated occurring at Hephaestus Corporation, into generalist pan-occupational jobs known by their company-specific designation, such as "customer test interface controller" and "Iris product supply/demand schedule controller." Moreover, in workplaces where unions still play a role, *enterprise* unions (rather than occupation- or trade-specific unions) are emerging in implicit recognition of this development. The specificity of single trade and occupational unions typical of industrialism will, I believe, soon become a thing of the past. The place of occupation as a specific social category in the historical industrial production of class, and of the self, is diminishing. The integration of knowledge and function, precipitated and facilitated by the advanced information technologies of this era, has rendered specialization obsolete, and generalization the new uniform requirement. In turn, this development has broken down the social bondings that occupational status provided, which again in turn, have been taken over by the identificatory processes of the new corporation.

In Hephaestus Corporation itself, its former specialists in mechanical and electrical engineering, computing sciences, physics, chemistry, mathematical sciences and so forth, are crossing former professional demarcations and performing a range of duties in the team structure that promotes team responsibility for product development. Recall the case of David, the former Ivy League physicist who joined Hephaestus believing and expecting that the company wanted him for his specialist scientific expertise. David, by his own admission, was reluctant to recognize that after the early 1980s "cultural revolution," as many jokingly referred to the PQ program, the expectations of his professional performance and contribution to the company had profoundly altered. David was expected to "learn the business" of the entire Hephaestus technology, and to learn the business of management. Unlike the majority of his cohort, David did not gain an MBA degree and he did not advance through the ranks of management, the primary route to promotion and seniority.

As it happened, the nature of David's work has changed without his gaining seniority, and with his relinquishing his specialist role as research scientist. David had lost both his professional locus of identity and solidarity as a physicist – he no longer published research papers and no longer attended conferences of physicists – and he had not found compensatory bonds as a generalist technologist on a sub-team, or as a manager. While he was, officially, part of the wider Iris and Hephaestus team, he was regarded as an "individual contributor" who compensated for his sidelining by maintaining his own sense of himself as an expert physicist in his current job as an advisor and consulting troubleshooter to product development sub-teams. David presented as an "introverted defensive" self.

The majority of David's cohort, and more especially the younger ones coming up behind him, were more readily adjusting and accommodating to the demise of their professional designations. Recall Hal, the "principal information systems consultant" who held a view that welcomed his breadth of responsibilities from software development to financial planning to marketing. At the lower end of this pan-occupational *and* polar corporate structure are the manufacturing workers who, although more traditionally and rigorously controlled in their work tasks, are gaining the job skills of their workmates on either side of their own work station on the line.

Of even more importance to my consideration of the transformation of occupation, is my proposition that post-occupational team work generates a replica of the social solidarity bonds that are necessary for production to occur, and that have been rendered precarious by the erosion of occupation and spontaneous class-based (whether conscious or not) social cohesiveness. As the company takes over the social solidarity provided by the culture of occupational specialization with its "fellowship" of the guild implicit and residual, and for some still overt in the union or professional association, it becomes the locus of worker identification and the source of one's work appellation, rather than one's occupation. It is in this action that *workers* become *employees*. An employee becomes one who describes herself as: "I'm an Hephaestus employee, on the Iris team" rather than as: "I'm a physicist (who works at Hephaestus)."

The erosion of these industrial influences on the self has opened up an arena for significant corporate influence on self-constituting processes. Most immediately the demise of occupation and the rise of post-occupational team work have facilitated the turn toward the company for identification and solidarity, and have opened up conditions for the self-responses to manifest in the strategies and circumscriptions of the self types that are described in the Chapter 6.

THE SIMULATED SOCIAL

The demise of occupation is not a deliberate corporate strategy of the new culture – it is an unintended outcome of corporate restructuring instigated by technological change and the new corporate culture. But the new sociality, provided in the culture of team-family, the use of the shared new language and the espousal of the new company philosophy of Total Quality Management and globalization, is. The corporation has moved, not only to compensate for the demise of the old industrial sociality, but to create in its new sociality the means by which employees accept the outcome of its restructurings launched at the beginning of the 1980s. The restructurings include not just the comprehensive new culture but the material changes of wage freezes, pay cuts, forced early retirement packages, general cutbacks in benefits and conditions and downsizing in the ranks of line and professional employees. These changes reflect the corporation's belief that it cannot be globally competitive with older bureaucratic models of management still in place. The corporation's new designer culture provides a solidarity locus that compensates for the demise of former industrial loci. At the same time it provides the means by which the material conditions now discarded – job security, graded career paths and explicit assurances of retirement and health benefits – are accepted and legitimated.

In compensating for the loss of occupational solidarity brought about by the dissolution of traditional industrial occupational boundaries, the corporation's new culture creates a new social sphere. I wish to point out that my argument does not extend (for the moment) to professions outside the corporate workplace. Such professions and trade occupations are still intact and continue to occupy an important place in social structure, but they too are exposed to the encroachment of para-professionalism, which erodes their privileged terrain and contests their claims to exclusive ownership of distinct bodies of knowledge and expertise.[7] The democratizing capacities in the new information technologies are fast facilitating this trend.

The new corporate social sphere is a simulated, artificial social world that provides in its team-family structure the semblance of the relationships, loyalties, values and attitudes of family life and sports-team energy. The human need for social relatedness is met through this social sphere in the workplace and the human energy required for production subsequently becomes available (production follows satisfaction, near enough, of relatedness and belonging) and is simultaneously harnessed by the corporation. From the vantage of the corporation, ensuring that its employees' social-psychological need of relatedness is met simultaneously ensures that corporate production occurs.

Hephaestus Corporation typifies the culture of the new corporation. It is the new corporate workplace, the simulation of the caring, purposeful, related family of nostalgic, pre-industrial myth. It provides a simulated community that is manufactured for a vital function of production. It is the reification of the displaced hope and desire of a diminishing, increasingly colonized self – a self that in its emptying is re-filled and re-stored with a replica of religious virtuosity and, for the more pathologically troubled self, the comfort of a resurgent primary narcissism. The new Hephaestus employee becomes somebody in his association with the reified company and through performance of his team-family work role. The employee also finds gratification in a sense of giving, a devotion to an entity greater than herself and her ordinary, narcissistic, anxiety-ridden life. In believing that Hephaestus will reward them for such selfless effort in cooperative team work and company devotion, employees find the comfort of the echo of an old calling, and the semblance of community service.

However, that *semblance* and the rhetorical proclamation is the extent of the company's honoring of its side of the bargain. The grand vision of this neo-Protestant[8] ethic is unfulfilled. The belief that Hephaestus rewards employees for selfless effort and dedication is often blatantly disconfirmed. The simulated community they serve does not reciprocate on a reliable basis. The bonds of fellowship and mutuality through occupational specialization (calling) and interdependence (community service) are contradicted by a regressive sibling rivalry, nepotist patronage and advancement, and elimination of job security and benefits. The new, restructured corporate conditions in which a new designer employee might practice his neo-Protestant ethics actually prohibit the realization of that ethic. The discordance of the ethic and the conditions is, however, denied and obscured under the rise of the simulated team-family that is intended to take care of the primary need for relatedness following the displacement of the solidarity role of occupational and class solidarities.

The corporation's provision in the corporate family for an alternative (primary) form of narcissistic gratification, allows the cultural pathology to be legitimized and functionalized for corporate production, whereas secondary narcissism with its socially disintegrative impulses is not. The pathological condition, therefore, is not healed or resolved, rather it is normalized, affirmed and integrated in corporate culture and organizational practices.

In the workplace, primary narcissism promoted by the deliberate creation of family-style structures and relations both meets the "authentic," or normal, human need for relatedness and purposefulness, and accommodates, by its compensation, the pathological condition of secondary narcissism that pervades the wider culture of corporate capitalist America. Production is thereby, at least in the interim, still ensured while greater efforts to restore a neo-Protestant culture of work and character of employee are underway. Outside the workplace the confused, capitulated self, who aspires to be strategic and active, not only wishes, but is also compelled, to resume its compulsive consumption habits to sustain capitalism and to compensate for the anxiety of the schizoid tensions at work – real relatedness and real family against imitation corporate-designed family relations, and compulsive work.

CORPORATE SELVES: DEFENSIVE, COLLUDED, CAPITULATED

The corporate self "opts" (unconsciously) for a self strategy that best enables it to deal with the conditions in which it finds itself. I have not attempted to explore self-constituting processes for individual selves drawn from realms of life prior to and outside of working life. But, as I have demonstrated, the psychostructural conditions of the institution of work, in this case of the Hephaestus Corporation workplace, exert powerful influences on employee selves. The defensive option for the self describes a self that is burdened by a confusion that results from the doubt and resentment of feeling torn by their association with the corporation and their adoption of the role of Hephaestus employee. The defensive self would rather be somewhere else, living according to their own self-narrative of who they are, or might have been under other conditions and circumstances. But they are attracted and tied by the package of financial rewards (even as that package relatively diminishes) and the kudos (that is compensatingly exaggerated) of association with Hephaestus. Their strategies of defense include elaborate rationalization as a mechanism for deflecting their own guilt for a sense of self-betrayal. But most of their energy is expended in fighting off further corporate encroachment and containing their anger and ambivalence.

Defensive selves are not a new type of corporate self, even though the particular manifestations described in the previous chapter refer to the new conditions of Hephaestus culture and display accordingly some innovations and developments beyond those of disaffected employees described in earlier studies.[9] The defensive self has internalized what Weber called the "disenchantment" ([1919] 1946) of bureaucratic life as the triumph of instrumental rationality epitomized in the corporation permeates all areas of life.

The colluded self, likewise, has a source in earlier bureaucratic corporate conditions. But under those earlier conditions of the passionless impersonality of traditional industrial organizational hierarchies, collusion was rather a matter of simple conformity. The cultural and moral conditions of corporate institutions operated in greater congruency with those of the wider industrial capitalist culture in which its employees had been formed. The current manifestations of collusion with its characteristic compulsive optimism and its evangelical espousal of the values and behavior of the new culture are a distinctly new form which result from the altered conditions of the post-industrial corporation. The new colluded self is no longer permitted to be quietly compliant and dedicated. Rather, the new employees must be, as the popular management writers Peters and Waterman (1982) urged that they become, "charged up people" who "feel great" and who are "unleashed" to become "winners" for the corporation and for themselves. In its ideal corporate form the character of the new corporate self is a colluded self: dependent, over-agreeable, compulsive in dedication and diligence, passionate about the product and the company. The colluded self is comforted by primary narcissistic gratifications of identification with a workplace family free of the older attractions of occupation and class based solidarities.

In its less than ideal form, the other side of the emerging character of the new corporate self is that of capitulation. In capitulation, the self negotiates a private psychic settlement with the corporate colonizing power, which implicitly recognizes but denies the processes of discipline, enforced self-restraint and evangelical optimism – a wearied surrender[10] on negotiated

191

terms. The capitulated, strategic, pragmatic self produced by corporate culture does not foreclose the possibility of counter-corporate cultural production. But the conditions for such alternative production are increasingly less conducive to employee initiative. The possibilities of action are reduced as employees' previously semi-autonomous loci of solidarity and protection are taken over by the totalizing corporate culture.

REVIVALISM AND RESTORATION

Manifestations of religious faith and behavior have long been evident in bureaucratic organizations as have organizational myths and values by which organizations structure and order everyday life and retain the allegiance and commitment of their members. The current manifestations of these religious features in Hephaestus Corporation represent a particular reinvocation of religious rites to provide not only structure and meaning, but legitimation for corporate changes that irreligious, or disbelieving, employees would find unacceptable. The secular revival of early modern religious forms in corporate culture extends more widely than the manifestation of values and interaction practices. Patterns of religious expression as well as religious form and organization are pervasive.

In addition to adherence to company-designed and promoted values, beliefs, attitudes, and behavior, a religious expression is evident in the company's and the employees' regard for their products. In surrendering identifiable (and occupationally specific) personal interest in personal contribution to the technologically complex products, and according the product the status of an entity or life with a history and a future that transcends individual or sub-team efforts, employees reify and venerate the product. As the company is held in revered esteem by almost all employees (even the defensive ones) the product is similarly accorded a mysterious quality in its ascribed ability to outlast even the most long-serving employee, and to be nurtured into an apparently limitless trajectory of more advanced and sophisticated capability.

Technologists on the Iris team held the usually explicit assumption that the problems surrounding the product at its present stage of development would simply be solved in a matter of time. It was just a question of "unlocking the secrets" in the technology to enable further development to occur. Of course, this is a typical modern scientific view and not at all peculiar to corporate technological work. But it is a view that is encouraged and harnessed in the culture of Hephaestus, and serves the company's interest in retaining dedicated and committed employees in pursuit of that technological holy grail.

The company is similarly reified and imbued with mythical characteristics and qualities as employees described in Chapter 5. Notwithstanding the somewhat cynical views and fears among defensive employees, some of whom criticize aspects of the new culture program as gimmicky and patronizing and who eschew too much allegiance to the company, they too imbue the company with powers of control over their everyday lives and futures and are fearful of its power. At the same time they are in awe of the company's global expansion and influence. The religious character in its secular manifestation is the structural and cultural form of the organization. The rationality embedded in the structure corresponds with that valued and aspired to in the order and restraint imposed by traditional religious structure (by no means only Protestant). The cultural form in which work is equated with virtue and duty, and value is measured by productive performance, is the more typically Protestant form.

Promotion of the secular religious character, and not just economic need, ensures that people come to work every day and perform to their utmost in the service of the company's goals. Faith and commitment, dedication and devotion beyond the call of duty (or even the requirements of personal advancement) are elicited and sustained by the corporation. Religiosity – belief and practice – is the sustaining organizing principle of Hephaestus Corporation. Faith is most simply displayed in belief in the product, the values and wisdom of the company and in its work principles: teamwork, excellence and customer satisfaction. Practice is seen in the unquestioned willingness to put in routinely long hours, to display agreement with and commitment to the values of the culture, and, generally, to serve for many years or leave without complaint when no longer required.

The corporate self, whatever its predominant self strategy, and in which-ever cohort – the older and faithful and the younger and cynical – displays devotion to the company through active participation in the ritualized practices of sunrise meetings and various team meetings, by using the language of the corporate culture, and adopting the company-desired styles of interpersonal interactions. Employees routinely recite the official discourse in their expressions of regard for Hephaestus as benevolent, caring, solid, the paragon of citizenship and the exemplary employer. Most of them report that Hephaestus is, as it seeks and claims to be, a family, and they treat each other at work like family. They believe, or at least act out an effort to believe, their ascribed roles and corporate identities.

The family metaphor – that is, the bourgeois family – is the everyday shopfloor organizing principle. It is the family that ensures that everyday organizational principles and procedures are adhered to, that authority is obeyed, and that people carry out their assigned tasks. Family mutes and disguises the rigidity of an authority structure that is as much in place as in traditional bureaucratic organizational structures. Family encourages work-ers to believe that they are valued and that they will be taken care of by a benevolent parent. It also, at least rhetorically, allows for the possibility of conflict and squabbles among "siblings" and for their resolution to be adjudicated by their manager. The team, similarly, promotes the sporting analogy, the aggressive, goal-oriented effort that moves out from the nurturance of family to fight competition in the external environment. Both metaphors aim to encourage members to put aside personal issues and grievances for the sake of the greater glory of the success of the team and the solidarity of the family, which they have already been acculturated into believing will dispense honor and reward upon its individual members.

The new culture manifests a revival of an old form of social life, and an old monolithic work ethic, upon which modern industrialism was socially structured. But this revivalism is not a simple restoration of classical Protestantism, although its cultural virtues – temperance, diligence, prudence, moderation and methodicalness – are surely extolled as the desired character of the new Hephaestus employee and embedded in its work ethic. In the neo-Protestant corporate culture there is the additional American "Southern-style" revivalism with the sexual energy of evangelism, charisma and conversion displayed by the corporation's leaders and promised to its employees in exchange for faith and work. Hephaestus has taken to heart the pursuit of "excellence," as defined by Peters and Waterman (1982) (and similar management writers), which sets out to create a culture that generates "the magic of the turned-on workforce" and a workplace that provides for the establishment of "meaningful relationships" in the intimacy of the team-family.

The new designer employees of this neo-Protestant evangelical culture must appear "highly charged" with sexual and emotional energy that is expended in the totalizing culture and the meaningful relationships of work. Work as intimacy collapses a former distinction between self boundaries and economic production, an old distinction between the private and the public. It is the total integration of human being and human doing for production, and a further triumph of instrumental rationality. In this restoration, the new culture is only a new, and exaggerated, manifestation of an old industrial form. It does not make the leap forward from the iron culture, as technology has, into a social form that heralds a future beyond the cultural and psychic constraints (for surviving successful corporate selves), and the economic and social failures (for the world's majority) of industrial capitalism.

Marx long ago pondered the question of a cultural restoration [1852](1978) after a revolution he hoped would render deeper and enduring social changes. The revolution that is now taking place as industrialism (in the organization of work and production) is surpassed by a form of production that bears little resemblance to that of industrialism, in which information technologies promote global communications and a "decentering" of the workplace, presents many possibilities. But the architects and promulgators of the new corporate culture, so far, have read only with alarm the signals of possibilities and new practices enabled by advanced technologies, and a creative critical challenge to the meta-narratives of modern society. The reaction, embodied in the new culture as I have shown in Chapter 6, has been to bolster a flagging ethic and a fragmenting self by resuscitating the cohesive forces of a modern, Protestant superego and culture. It is an eleventh-hour effort to undo the excesses of compulsive consumption that industrial capitalism set in motion.

Juxtaposed with the corporate project to establish a neo-Protestant ethic of work and commitment is another post-industrial technological development. The deployment of advanced technologies which alter the nature of work and reorganize the workplace, is facilitating the emergence of another new condition of post-industrial production, what I call the "decentered workplace." Information technologies have enabled the dispersion of productive work to cross international boundaries. And a loosening up of trade restraints and protective legislation has enabled a global market for sectors of skilled and knowledge workers. Furthermore, advanced IT and work reorganization are decentering the workplace in even more complex ways. The corporate workplace now extends beyond the shared workplace site of the corporate tower or manufacturing plant typical until the early 1980s. A growing sector of corporate production functions does not necessarily require employee attendance at an actual worksite in the company of others. But, whether one is working by modem, cellular phone and fax machine from one's livingroom, or from a trans-Pacific jet, the medium and the product of one's work are still controlled by the ethics and values of the corporate culture.

A physically decentered workplace can sustain the corporate culture through its ability to manage remote employees by the requirements of productivity and customer orientation. However, the simulated sociality of the workplace culture is not required or effective and the remote employee might therefore be able to maintain her relatedness needs through primary or other than workplace social relations. Yet there is also evidence that the corporate sector is building corporate lifestyle enclaves in which employees live, work and recreate within a planned physical community that has diminishing ties with the nation-state in which it is located (Reich 1991). In part because of the globalization of knowledge work and the mobility of corporate employees these new cosmopolitan (but not urban) "symbolic analysts" who may or may not have company-specific employment security, acquire a general corporate cultural identity which is, when necessary, transferable to a particular corporation.

The operation of the "decentered workplace" may apply not just to employees in remote workstations but to the "workplace within" (Hirschhorn 1988). Although at the present time there are few corporate employees working from remote personal locations, they, like their on-site colleagues, are increasingly required to carry the mission and goals of the corporation with them at all times. I have observed in another corporation,[11] which like

Hephaestus is implementing a new culture program based on the concepts of "total quality management," official encouragement of a "quality awareness" assessment among employees. Employees are expected to serve as "cultural ambassadors" who perform company duties outside regular working hours. The task of "bringing in business" is shared and performed by dedicated and company-identified employees wherever they they may be at any time. Their physically decentered workplaces remain, none the less, *psychically* centered in the corporation.

CONCLUSION

It may be, in the long run, that corporate culture will sustain post-industrialism for a long time to come. If it is successful in establishing a neo-Protestant bourgeois employee-self as its ideal employee, whose disenchantment is displaced in the promise of sexual or narcissistic gratification at work, production will be ensured under new conditions by a cohesive sociality of a revived and restored infrastructure of an old culture. The problem of the capitulated, pragmatic, strategic self may well be controlled and accommodated by wider corporate culture – the influences of the multi-national corporations on wider social events, values, practices across the world – in absorbing its disintegrative influence by ensuring that a population of consumers is maintained simultaneously with a population of "colluded" hard-working, self-denying producers. The dialectical tension between these opposing impulses may be managed sufficiently to ensure corporate cultural survival, albeit within a visibly polarized society in which those who work and "belong" one way or another to corporate society will be structurally privileged and disparate from those who do not work and who live on the margins of corporate social integration.

On the other hand, as I have indicated, the neo-Protestant bourgeois self is cheated of the other half of the bargain that Protestantism promised and delivered to its conformants: the psychic salvation of reparation, fellowship, righteous satisfaction of the fruits of one's labor, and in serving one's community and the reciprocity of interdependence. The bargain is further breached in that the spiritual satisfaction derived from, and the integrity ascribed to, living one's life according to the calling of one's occupation (vocation) is now denied. Instead, one must displace one's calling and its accompanying rules and ethics into the hands and direction of the company. The employee is called only to the service of the company, not to the keeping of occupational traditions and contributing to their repository of skills and knowledge, and sharing in their guild fellowship. A possible source of rupture in the new culture, and of the corporate self, may be in a recognition of that corporate breach of implied contract.

Under the present conditions of corporatism, there is little immediate

196

prospect of new forms of social, and self, alternatives. Capitulated selves are unlikely to create new forms of alliances and solidarities outside those formed in and by the corporation. The new corporate culture is a totalizing culture. It seeks to gain a pervasive influence in every area of the employee's life and to influence the wider culture of post-industrial capitalism. Post-occupational work is too closely bound by the requirements of corporate, advanced technological production for a new solidarity practice to emerge. Post-occupational solidarity is, so far, only a corporate appropriation of former industrial solidarity functions, and it does not yet herald a form of solidarity that extends beyond the primacy of production and work. As it is currently manifested, the new corporate culture is only an interim post-industrial culture. Its evangelical revivalism thwarts possibilities for nurturing embryonic forms of new social formations, other than the global corporation, and the conditions for self-transformation that will herald new forms of social life that are truly beyond industrialism. That, it seems, must wait until there is a social movement beyond productionism.

The great leaps forward that advanced electronic technologies have made in the second half of the twentieth century, seem paradoxically, for the moment, accompanied by a revivalist movement in the culture of post-industrial capitalism, as viewed through the corporation as a sign of this culture, in the resuscitation of the core of industrial cultural infrastructure. The new corporate self is a product of this movement. At its best, it is drawn toward possibilities of new ways of being in postmodern life beyond the iron-age compulsive differentiations and demarcations that constrained self and social life; at its worst, it is reduced to a narcissistic, confused, weak and diffuse self, drawn back into the iron embrace of the corporation and the restoration of an old ethic.

Perhaps the analyst and scribe of the end of industrialism needs to concede the possibility that apparently opposing forces are not incompatible. The complex operation of these movements in self, culture and technology may yet germinate social and cultural possibilities for self and society that we have not yet conceived in the knowledge traditions of our time. It may be that in society after industrialism human being will be liberated from domination by human doing. Self-constituting processes other than those of work and production will configure selves and collective social life that are qualitatively different from modern industrial configurations. And therein lie the elements of a social movement beyond productionism. The end of productionism, I hope, will make way for new forms of self and social life.

APPENDIX: THE FIELD STUDY

ON QUALITATIVE RESEARCH

I have been influenced first by the Frankfurt School's effort to go beyond the ahistorical aspirations of the project of universal, objectivist science, and more recently by the post-structural recognition of decentered subjectivity and multiple competing discourses. Scientific discourses we now know must put aside claims for universals and absolute truth. But like many contemporary social analysts, when confronted by the necessary task of putting aside universality, the reification of "facts" and the authoritative voice, *and* the task of conducting communicable research within a scientific community, I falter in enunciating my position in this dilemma. But I wish to suggest that recognizing the contingency and plurality of knowledge does not require the abandonment of systematic scientific methods including precision and reliability in communicating interpretive knowledge. At the same time these scientific methods must also be scrutinized along with the wider framework of enquiry in which they are employed. There is no final arbiter between particularity and universality, there is only a "good," persuasive, and by and large reasonable case to be offered. With this humble admission I none the less claim the academic privilege to analyze and interpret the lives of other human beings, in this case, at work.

THE FIELD STUDY AND METHODS

In the 1991-2 academic year I conducted a field study of work in a multinational corporation. The company, which I call Hephaestus Corporation, is engaged in the manufacture and use of advanced technological products and in organizational restructuring and cultural change. The method of the field study was that generally described as ethnography. Ethnographic studies have in the past been most commonly undertaken by anthropologists. Ethnography is no longer simply associated with the practice of merely seeking out the primitive and exotic "other" to describe and report on their foreign ways and values for the curiosity of the Western gaze. The

198

reasons for the ascendancy of ethnographic research in the social sciences more broadly, and its theoretical and methodological sophistication since colonial anthropology, have been explored elsewhere (Atkinson 1990, Clifford and Marcus 1986, Geertz 1973, Tyler 1986). For many contemporary social scientists, especially those from the traditions of feminism, phenomenology, Marxism and interpretive anthropology, subscribing to a rejection of positivist science and caught in the theoretical uncertainties surrounding the decline in grand theory and the emergence of postmodernism, ethnographic methods have become attractive and appropriate. Critical ethnographic methods that allow for micro-social contextuality and self-reflexivity are now offering some contestation to much traditional empirical research.

Similarly, my own theoretical location in critical social theory renders an adoption of a qualitative method of enquiry in a study of the effects of the discursive practices work on the self in post-industrial society both appropriate and practical. The study I conducted was an exploration of symbolic interactions and processes that occur in the everyday institutional social practices of work. The study is not a "radical ethnography" in the sense that it disavowed any theoretical construction from the outset, for this study is embedded in a set of theoretical constructs and beliefs, primarily about work and about post-industrial society. My effort is, though, a critical ethnography in that it recognizes the discursive construction of knowledge, and that the cultural construction of meaning is always a matter of political and economic interest. It is somewhat modestly critical, however, in that its concern with excavating dominant social constructions about work and the self, and studying society in the hope that advanced knowledge might enhance possibilities for changing it, holds only the hope of social transformation, not its programmatic certainty that is evocative of an older, modern radicalism. Neither is there a pretension on my part that my research is catalytic or "action" oriented toward change in the site under study. That is neither my task, nor my business. In that sense then, this is a postmodern critical ethnography, a method and orientation that is both a product of, and I believe most appropriate for, this post-industrial juncture.

Clifford (1986) refers to ethnographic writing as "ethnographic fictions" that are crafted by the writer as an artisan. The result, therefore, is not an objective report, but a "persuasive fiction" (Geertz 1973), a narrative woven around the "data" of actual excerpts from informants and corroborative episodes in their daily lives, which the ethnographic writer selects, construes and interprets. At best, therefore, I construct myself as a credible witness, wishing by systematic description and reporting to convey the authenticity of my account and to invite the credibility of the interpretations and theoretical analyses I subsequently draw. However, in retreating somewhat from Clifford's (and others: see Clifford and Marcus (1986)) vigilance against authority (and a protracted apology for the legacy of anthropological colonialism) I prefer to admit the inevitability of the author's perspective and judgment, no matter how well reflected upon, and the power inherent in the researcher's gaze transposed into writing. While the archetypical modern scientist denied his subjectivity in the clinical observation of agreed-upon "facts," the apparently more modest and self-reflective critical ethnographer can similarly risk denying the continuing inherent relation of privilege and of authority implicit in her inevitable claim to veracity and credibility.

The site and the subjects

The study investigated the practices of work and the everyday working lives of a large selected group of mostly technological and professional workers (as they now comprise the majority of Hephaestus Corporation employees) in a product development division at Hephaestus Corporation in the city of Rusty River in the north eastern United States. Hephaestus Corporation is popularly known as a company that has introduced and pioneered many of the new forms of work organization currently much debated in business and industry circles. The corporation employs more than 100,000 workers worldwide, with about 25,000 working in the industrial city of "Rusty River." The employee figures are lower than those of a decade ago and production and revenue figures are greater than those of the mid-1980s. I was granted approval for access and to conduct the research project by the Chief Engineer (responsible for the Iris (a pseudonym) product and its product development team) of the building in which I spent most of my time.

Like all new employees I completed an orientation and security course that was conducted by a centralized Hephaestus Corporation department and I was granted the status of a "contract employee." (I was never employed by Hephaestus Corporation. The status of "contract employee" was the best way for the company to accommodate me and to grant me virtually unrestricted access to the site during weekdays.) I was "badged," that is, I received a photograph identification card to be displayed at all times, and subsequently, my entry to Building 700 and most other Hephaestus Corporation buildings in Rusty River was unrestricted. With the Chief Engineer's sanction I was permitted to go anywhere in the buildings, talk to anyone and attend any meetings.

Hephaestus Corporation, like other large technological and manufacturing operations, is a high-security site. Each building has security entrances and guards. Some buildings have further internal security procedures of number-coded security doors that admit only certain personnel. I was granted such access in a building housing a research team (not part of Iris) where I spent some time. Non-employees and visitors are required to be signed in and accompanied while on site. I experienced few field research problems once my access was confirmed. As time passed and people became familiar with me, and came to trust and respect me, and I them, I was soon regarded as part of the scenery. During the many all-day meetings I attended in which lunch was catered for, I was always generously invited to share in the fare, the social conversation and workplace humor.

The layout of the building is in the style of partitioned cubicles joined by a network of narrow corridors. The seven-foot high dividing walls, decorated in soft tones of gray and pink, are movable and allow for easy workspace reorganization. A few of the Iris team members occupy small individual offices without windows but with doors but most occupy shared cubicles. The more senior managers occupy offices located around the periphery of the blocks of cubicles where their employees are easily seen and readily summoned. Pictures, photographs, cartoons and memorabilia are displayed in an effort to personalize work stations. Employees with patents or Hephaestus awards display them on the walls of their offices. The senior executives have larger offices, often with windows and with status-bearing wood furniture. There are few books displayed. Coke cans and coffee pots are a much more common feature of office decor. An intercom public address system operates constantly, accompanying the sound of the heating and air-conditioning systems that provide the aural backdrop. Similarly, the sounds of conversations in neighboring cubicles ensure a constant level of background noise. Lighting is fluorescent and centralized, although I noticed that two or three individuals had brought in their own soft-toned desk lamps.

Doing the research

I spent a great deal of time lingering around individual people, observing them work outside of meetings, at their work stations, in their cubicles or in small interactions with one another: on the phone, e-mail communications, talking to one another in their cubicles and around the vending machines and cafeterias. I also observed various training sessions of technical representatives, customer-service representatives and trainers of these groups. I toured the vast manufacturing production sites, talked to and observed the manufacturing line workers, chemical workers, zinc platers, supervisors, packers, and metal craftsmen and electricians of the model shops, test operators and research scientists and technicians working on new projects, possible new products. I visited, observed and interviewed specialist groups of physicists and research computer scientists working on advanced technology and specialized customer projects. I talked with secretaries and clerical workers, with cleaners and security officers, with retired line workers who are now employed as perimeter controllers who plow snow and jump-start cars. I had lunch with many of them, on and off site, and I visited some in their homes and after hours. I met with marketing people and financial analysts, and with public-relations people.

The subjects of the study were workers in a variety of occupational groupings including engineers, computer professionals, scientists, technical analysts, financial analysts, administrators, managers and manufacturing workers. From this group I interviewed 60 people who were selected in the effort to gain a wide sample of occupation, rank, tenure, and demographic features such as gender, race, ethnicity and regional origin. Some were also chosen on the basis of their strategic location in the team or in the broader division of Hephaestus, i.e. Vice-President, union representative (among the manufacturing workers), returned retiree, new entry employee. I also interviewed the spouses of some employees and some former Hephaestus employees. The interviews (lasting 1.5–3.5 hours) consisted of open-ended questions about working lives, thoughts and feelings about work, workmates, the company and the products. Most of them were recorded and transcribed. All interviewees were assured of confidentiality and anonymity. No-one I approached declined to be interviewed. Many people volunteered without my invitation and some were disappointed that I did not interview them. Almost all of them were followed up by subsequent conversations and encounters at meetings, lunches or in corridors.

As part of my daily observations and research routines I also studied formal company documents including "Hephaestus Today" a daily news release, other employee news bulletins, management memoranda, promotional materials and training materials. I read some of the electronic mail of specialist interest groups – a regular and increasingly important form of social interaction among employees in the corporation.

I spent many hours in the Hephaestus Corporation Library. I attended and observed training seminars and courses, and studied visual and printed curricula. I attended hundreds of hours of meetings to listen, observe and record what went on there and the relations among the people. I found that after the initial introductions my presence in the Iris Team meetings was largely taken for granted. While I never spoke in these meetings, even if invited to comment, I was regarded as a legitimate "extra" member of the team and privy to information and the discussions that transpired. I noticed that when visitors from out of state attended these meetings they assumed I was an Iris Team member and would introduce themselves to me accordingly.

Writing it up

I kept substantive fieldnotes that recorded chronological events, places, people, conversations, meetings and observations of the workplace site and the subjects. I also kept a private field-research journal in which I recorded my own experiences, reflections, analyses and emerging theoretical insights. Notwithstanding the vast bulk of my notes, transcripts and copies of company documents, I have condensed much of the "thick description" (Lincoln and Guba 1985) usually expected of ethnographic research in the narrative I have constructed. My project is to analyze and understand what is happening in this corporate organization (and in others) and to draw interpretive schema largely, but I hope not only, of interest to other critical social analysts. Ethnographers generally describe their task as to formulate insights, to explain and interpret events and to seek understanding (see Anderson 1989, Geertz 1973, Lather 1991, Lincoln and Guba 1985, Lofland and Lofland 1984, Thompson 1981). They also recognize that the informant's perceptions of social reality are themselves theoretical constructs. Each of my interviewees constructed a narrative about their experiences of their work, and about themselves. I, in turn, have interpreted these narratives in a way that I believe makes deeper theoretical sense of their collective world. That is the privileged assertion of the academic researcher.

The interpretations and analyses are my constructions, they are not some effort to "give voice" to other voices, although that clearly does occur as I report, albeit highly selectively, their own words. My subjects neither invited, nor accorded to me, the role of spokesperson. They can, indeed, speak for themselves. What they did accord me, with warmth and generosity, was a role of witness, scribe, analyst, and vicariously, therapist. None of them regarded me as some cold-blooded scientist, and neither did I presume to be unaffected by my months among them and in sharing the buildings, the environment, the food and daily life of Hephaestus Corporation. I did not discourage the therapeutic role. Not only did it avail me of considerable data and insights, it provided some catharsis for employees trying, variously, to make sense of their lives in the institution of corporate work.

The narrative that I have constructed from my extensive observations, interviews and analyses of the workplace site has necessarily been written from my strategically located point of view. There is no illusion that my selection of data and that which I have constructed and interpreted as knowledge is either objective or definitive. Critical social theorists eschew certainties and absolutes, but endeavor to practice systematic reflexivity and to construct rational analyses and interpretations. A claim to validity and reliability is thereby justifiable. The result, I would argue, is that this work, necessarily a narrative fiction, invites credibility from the "natural" validity of the data and its rendering in theory.

Finally, on a more personal note, the completion of my field work was fraught with ambivalence about walking away and writing about the lives of people who had for a year been my "subjects." As a member of the academic community I assume the validity of our endeavor to contribute to knowledge about what is going on in the world, and yet I am positioned, too, as a corporate employee. My own project of self creation is enacted within and against my particular experiences of corporate culture. There is, then, not as much distance in my positioning *vis-à-vis* Hephaestus Corporation selves as my formal academic voice might suggest.

NOTES

1 CRITICAL ANALYSIS AND THE PROBLEM OF WORK

1 There are various views concerning why French post-structuralism has become popular in the United States. Huyssen (1984) points out that the more politically intended projects of Foucault and Baudrillard, and I would add Lyotard, have been overshadowed by the politically averse body of French writing such as that of Derrida and Barthes. Foucault advocated practices of uncovering power in its "specific technologies" and building "strategic knowledge" as political practice, and argued for the practice of politics as ethics. (See the collections of papers in Foucault 1980, and in Kritzman 1988 in particular.)

   Feminists are divided on their appropriation of post-structuralism and post-modernism, even as many feminist theorists reject the modern theorists as masculinist and patriarchal.

2 Foucault had sought to study the "subjugated knowledges" of modern discourses and to explore that which Reason had excluded from according a history: madness, chance, discontinuity, sexuality, discipline. Developments in these areas "did not obey the same laws" as the dominant knowledge system had recorded (Foucault 1972, see also 1973, 1980). The interest of some contemporary analysts in specificities of subjective experience and cultural products without seeking to articulate connections with other experiences of phenomena is a product of such a reading of Foucault.

3 In referring to discursive practices I am emphasizing a distinction between the materiality of production (other than the economic) that includes: the physical plant and production technologies, the conditions of labor such as noise, electromagnetic emissions, climate, workspace, heaviness, hygiene, and material product; and discursive, that is, communicational and symbolic elements in production and work organization. These discourses include the corporate workplace culture, the myths, beliefs, norms and customs, attitudes and behavior and the new cultural practices of "team," "family" and "customer," the character values of leadership, excellence, dedication and so forth, that are elaborated in Chapter 5. Although ultimately materiality, especially the relations of ownership and control, is also mediated discursively, for analytic purposes (following Foucault 1972) they are held distinct from the discursive practices under study here.

4 The sociology of work has followed the influence of the grand theories of Marx, Durkheim and Weber and their various traditions as well as thinkers including Pareto, Sorokin, Mayo, Parsons, Mills. A range of applied interests has produced voluminous studies in labor economics, labor relations, management and orga-

nizational studies, industrial psychology. The Durkheimian approach is characterized by a functionalist orientation to work and organizations and an interest in social integration and solidarity. It influenced the Human Relations school that was interested in scientific management and social integration. The Weberian approach followed Weber's own earlier work in the 1920s "on the individual personality, the career and the extra-occupational style of living of the workers" (Weber [1908] 1971:104). The Goldthorpe and Lockwood (1968, 1969) studies and those of Baldamus (1961) are among the most well-known of this approach. The Weberian notion of a "social action frame of reference" emphasized the systemic aspects of social and economic life. Marxist approaches are characterized by an interest in worker alienation, exploitation, the social relations of work in capitalist conditions and power. Harry Braverman's (1974) *Labor and Monopoly Capital*, launched an influential wave of Marxist approaches to the study of industrial work and the labor process debate (Aronowitz 1983, Burawoy 1979, Gallie 1978, Knights and Willmott 1990, Littler 1982, Salaman 1986, Wood 1982, Zimbalist 1979). Feminist theorists emerged in the 1970s bringing new critical approaches to the dominant schools and to the question of the labor process. Ann Oakley's *The Sociology of Housework* in 1974 launched a series of subsequent studies on the division of labor and the feminization of domestic work (Hartmann 1976, Middleton 1988, Kamerman and Kahn 1981). Rosabeth Moss Kanter (1977) studied professional and middle-ranking clerical women in corporate industries Feminists also identified the phenomenon of "emotional labor" (Hochschild 1983). Feminist studies included empirical accounts of the structure of male and female workforces in the primary and secondary sectors (Frank Fox and Hesse-Biber 1984, Stromberg and Harkess 1978), the male/female earnings gap and occupational stratification (e.g. Corcoran and Duncan 1979, Treiman and Hartman 1981, Sawhill 1973), discriminatory industrial and domestic-relations legislation and practices (Baer 1978, Sachs and Wilson 1978) and poor and professional working women (Epstein 1970, 1974, 1975). Ethnographic studies of working-class women's lives (Rubin 1976, Kessler-Harris 1981) their marriages and families, their aspirations (Frank Fox and Hesse-Biber 1984) followed.

5 In traditional preindustrial society where there was little differentiation and specialization of labor, social order and cohesion were maintained through "mechanical solidarity." Mechanical solidarity, or "solidarity by similarities" (Durkheim [1933] 1984) as the basis for social cohesion, is characterized by social conduct that is controlled by shared values and beliefs. The collective dominates the individual and there is only a rudimentary development of individual self-consciousness. Solidarity derives from communality of sentiment and belief. It is an aggregation in which the parts are connected "mechanically," rather than a system of mutually dependent elements that form an "organic" unity akin to a differentiated biological system (an analogy that Parsons keenly developed in the 1950s).

6 See also the general occupations, professions, and organizations literature such as: Bledstein 1976, Dubin 1976, Freidson 1973, Glaser 1964, Kanter 1977, 1983, Salaman 1974, Van Maanen and Barley 1985, Van Maanen and Schein 1979, and the journals *Work and Occupations, Administrative Science Quarterly, American Journal of Sociology, Journal of Industrial Relations*, for example.

7 There have been, though, some studies of work and organization that included a focus on people's experiences at work (Becker *et al.* 1961, Fraser 1968, Kanter 1977, Maccoby 1976, Merton 1957, Turkel 1974, Valli 1986, Whyte 1956). But

an emphasis on work as constitutive of self processes was seldom explored, notwithstanding the exceptional work of Everett Hughes (1951, 1958, 1971).

2 THE TRANSFORMATION OF WORK

1 For a comprehensive review of the literature see, for example: Appelbaum 1992, Arendt 1959, Heilbroner 1985, Joyce 1987, Tilgher 1930, Thompson 1963, 1967, Pahl 1988.

2 Early "new" technologies were those of the post-World War II decades of the 1950s and 1960s that involved linked machines, simple automation and Numerically Controlled Machine Tools (NCMT) (see Noble 1978 and 1984) in manufacturing and heavy industry. Following the development in the early 1970s of the micro-processor (computer "chip") a second generation of electronic mechanical controls and electronic data processing was launched. It made possible vast increases in production, information generation and processing capacity, continuous capital and labor savings, the miniaturization and cheapening of electronics goods and components, and extensive innovation in new product developments.

3 See especially Aronowitz 1973, 1981, Bell 1973, Drucker 1993, Gorz 1980, 1989, Gershuny 1978, Harrison and Bluestone 1988, Piore and Sabel 1984, Reich 1991, Toffler 1980, Touraine 1971, 1981.

4 Lash and Urry (1987),and other European analysts, make special note of the the growing unemployment resulting from changes in manufacturing operations and organizational restructuring. In the US, analysts such as Harrison and Bluestone 1988, and Reich 1991, consider the problem of unemployment to be due largely to the current recession. Harrison and Bluestone predict that there will be a skills shortage in the US in the 1990s. Harrison and Bluestone and Reich take the views, respectively, that an expanding service sector, and the rise of the "symbolic analyst," will mitigate present unemployment trends. Furthermore, there are differences in the absolute numbers of unemployed in industrialized regions. The US figures at 8.9 percent remain lower than those of Europe at 10.8 percent and Australia at 12.4 percent (1992), for instance. But the upward trend is common to all of these regions.

5 Scientific Management, also known as "Taylorism," was formulated by an industrial engineer Frederick Winslow Taylor (1911) in the 1900s. The basic principles were to reduce labor to its simplest tasks thereby reducing waste and gaining economy of time and motion and preventing "soldiering" on the part of workers. It was believed more efficient to remove the tasks of conception, planning and decision-making from the workers who would be employed to carry out scientifically designed tasks eliminating conflict and other inefficiencies, and preventing the sabotage of continuous, efficient operations which was possible when workers retained some control over the production process and the exertion of their energies. Taylorism exercised considerable influence over modern management practices and work organization notwithstanding some challenges from industrial and humanistic psychology in the 1950s.

6 Aronowitz 1983, Baran and Sweezy 1966, Braverman 1974, Burawoy 1985, Fraser 1968, Kessler-Harris 1981, Rubin 1976, Turkel 1974, *Work in America*, Task Force Report to the US Government, 1973.

7 After the well-known Hawthorne investigations in Chicago (Roethlisberger and Dickson 1939) a number of subsequent studies and workplace reform efforts were instigated (Mayo 1949 on work teams in the factory – revived in the 1980s and 1990s) and improvements in satisfying workers' needs in the

207

workplace (Argyris 1964, Herzberg *et al.* 1959, Kornhauser 1965, McGregor 1960, Silverman 1970).

8 See Ayres and Miller 1983, Hirschhorn 1984, Howard 1985, Kochan 1986, Noble 1984, Piore and Sabel 1984, Shaiken 1984, Sorge *et al.* 1983, for studies of the early effects of automation technologies on production, labor and work. More recent works include Block 1990, Jaikumar 1987, Zuboff 1988. Studies on the effects of advanced technologies on office work include Castells 1985, Garson 1988, Hartmann 1987, Wright 1987.

9 See Aronowitz 1983, Braverman 1974, Burawoy 1985, Gallie 1978, Knights *et al.* 1985, Kochan *et al.* 1986, Littler 1982, Littler and Salaman 1984, Robertson 1985, Noble 1978, 1984, Wood 1982, Zimbalist 1979.

10 Although traditional men's work still attracts most attention from analysts – see, notably, Drucker's recent book (1993) that does not address traditional and typical women's work at all.

11 The old manual typewriter, for instance, could not outpace the typist's manual ability. Electronic keyboards no longer exert a physical limitation on the operator and high levels of production are possible, as are new occupational hazards such as repetitive strain injuries and eye strain.

3 DISCOURSES OF THE SELF

1 In the course of normal psychological development, libido is concentrated on different parts of the body. The early infantile stages of oral and anal satisfaction or frustration are succeeded in the process of psycho-sexual maturation by the phallic stage that occurs from about the fourth year of a child's life. At this stage, the genitalia become the focal zone, representing for the child competence, physical prowess and worth.

2 In the Oedipus complex, the triangular relationship between the parents and the child as experienced by the little boy (for Freud, only the boy) is critical. The complex is precipitated by the child's growing awareness of the disparity between his wish for sexual union with the mother and the impossibility of carrying it out. The child loves his mother and wishes to possess her, and he hates his father and wishes to kill him. At the same time the child fears the father and the threat of castration. The child therefore renounces his incestuous wishes for his mother and internalizes the paternal authority that demands this renunciation (Freud [1915–17] 1966 Lecture XXII: 257–8). The renunciation is also an insistence that the child has become autonomous – a severing of the primary maternal bond.

3 Symbolic interactionism influenced the sociological studies of work of Everett Hughes (1951, 1958, 1971) and H.S. Becker *et al.* (1961, 1968) who studied the "social drama" of the interactions that take place at work.

4 For the critical theorists, the idea of a value-free science and social science was an "objectivist illusion" – that there can be perception without a perspective from which perception takes place. For Adorno, the belief in the value-neutrality of one's perspective simply means that one has no categories with which to recognize that perspective (Adorno 1982, Gebhardt 1982, Held 1980). The critical theorists argued that the combination of formal logic and empiricism constituted a working framework that resisted inquiring into its own social and ideological functions. Rules of inference became facts, and as such irreducible "givens," not proper objects of investigation.

4 THE WORKING SELF: SOCIALIZATION AND LEARNING AT WORK

1 See, for example, the work of: Apple 1979, 1982, Apple and Weis 1983, Aronowitz and Giroux 1986, Bernstein 1975, Giroux 1981, 1983, Persell 1977, Wexler 1976, 1981, 1982, Young 1971.
2 Inkeles (1968) defined socialization as a set of processes that occur through: explicit instruction; conditioning and innovation; and role modeling.
3 See, for example, Dreeben 1968, Inkeles 1968, Merton 1957, Parsons 1951, 1964.
4 Studies in the 1960s studies produced empirical evidence of the state of workers' needs and satisfactions in the workplace (e.g. Argyris 1964, Herzberg *et al.* 1959, Kornhauser 1965, McGregor 1967, Silverman 1970). These studies demonstrated that workers' lack of feelings of competence led to lower levels of self-esteem, poorer psychological health and diminished job involvement. Blauner's (1964) well-known study of alienation at work later influenced experiments in organizational design.
5 Perception of locus of control affects the psychological functioning of the person including their activities, their cognitions and their emotions (Bandura 1981), their sense of "life satisfaction" (Fawcett, Stonner and Zepelin 1980, Gerrard, Reznikoff and Riklan 1982), their mental health (Hale, Hedgepeth and Taylor 1985–6), their physical health (Wallston and Wallston 1981) and their achievement (Connell 1985, Deci and Ryan 1991).
6 This learning-generalization process is crucial. People who do intellectually demanding work tend to exercise their intellectual abilities in their non-occupational activities as well as on the job (Kohn and Schooler 1983). They also tend to seek out intellectually challenging leisure-time pursuits. Furthermore, people who perform self-directed work come to value self-direction more highly, both for themselves and for their children, and to have self-conceptions consonant with such values (Coburn and Edwards 1976, Kohn 1969, Slomczynski *et al.* 1981).
7 For instance, a self-directed orientation and intellectual flexibility in the job lead to gaining more responsible jobs that allow for even greater latitude and opportunity for self-direction.

5 DISCOURSES OF PRODUCTION

1 The literature on organizational culture and the management of organizational change includes Deal and Kennedy (1982), Deming (1986), Drucker (1993), Garvin (1988), Handy (1985), Kanter (1983, 1989), Kunda (1992), Martin (1992), Schein (1985). In addition various scholarly publications including the *Administrative Science Quarterly* (1983) and the *Journal of Management Studies* (1986) have devoted special issues to the discussion of questions in corporate culture and change.
2 Contributions include a number of popular "how to" works such as Ouchi (1981), Peters and Waterman (1984), Naisbitt and Aburdene (1985), Wilkins (1989) as well as management academic analyses: Kanter (1983), Kilman and Covin (1988), Smith (1990). Critical interest is represented by Powell and DiMaggio (1991), Kunda (1992) and Martin (1992).
3 These works include Howard (1985), Piore and Sabel (1984), Zuboff (1988) and Harrison and Bluestone (1988), and the more theoretical works of Bell (1973), Lasch (1984) and Gorz (1989).

4 Hephaestus was the Greek god of fire with dominion over the industry of the forge. Son of Zeus and Hera, Hephaestus was a master craftsman constructing many magical toys and novelties for the gods. Hephaestus Corporation is the fictional name for the company I studied. The names of its employees have all been changed, as have the names of its products, teams, divisions, buildings and location.

5 Howard (1985), LaBier (1986), Wright (1987), Zuboff (1988) for example, emphasize the problems of adaptation to the use of new technologies in the workplace.

6 The rhetoric and sentiment of family-style employee involvement and paternalistic company care for its employees is not new (having been introduced in industry in the early twentieth century and re-invoked again in the 1950s). But the structural change that the more comprehensive new culture program of Hephaestus, and other "progressive" corporations, requires was not implemented in earlier efforts. Importantly, the new culture and organizational change is not only a management strategy – it is precipitated and required by the new flexibilities and informating capacities of advanced electronic technologies.

7 The new culture, although it was designed by Hephaestus' own team of specialists, resembled the archtypical "Theory Z" culture expounded by Ouchi a decade ago and reiterated in other influential management guide books such as Peters and Waterman (1984), Kanter (1989).

8 These manufacturing workers, such as Doreen and Betty, are none the less organized in a production factory with traditional industrial forms of discipline and control and supervisory hierarchies still in place. The Just-In-Time operation these workers are referring to increases the workers' job flexibility and their grasp of the wider process, at the same time that it places clear restrictions on their time and motion economies and attempts to limit and control the worker's initiative and judgement in performing her duties.

9 My view differs from the conventional view retained, for example, in the work of Kohn (1983, 1990) and Derber et al. (1990) and their associates, who hold the modern categories of occupation and profession to be central to social structure and character.

10 Derber et al. (1990) makes such an analysis. The analysis of professionals as a class, rather than as occupational specialists, is commensurable with the propositions I make here.

11 For instance: Bahro (1984), Bellah et al. (1985), Bell (1973), Harvey (1989), Lasch (1978, 1984), Roszak (1972), Sennett (1977), Slater (1970).

12 The control over which had been earlier a matter of more visible contestation by the relatively stronger labor movement in the USA (see United Steel Workers of America 1960) as well as in Europe. The new technologies posed a threat to industrial bureaucratic organizations and social systems facing the revolutionary potential of the new electronic automation technologies, information technologies and biotechnologies.

13 With the low-skilled, casualized and contract employees at one pole and a multi-skilled, highly trained and benefitted group at the other.

6 DESIGNER EMPLOYEES: CORPORATE CULTURE AND THE PRODUCTION OF SELF

1 The notion of "depth" in psychic structures and processes is, of course, central to classical psychodynamic thought, and implicitly taken for granted in modern

empirical psychology too. While it may be interpreted to imply a modernist "essentialism" – that there is some inner core beneath the depths – I wish to address this problem by suggesting that depth remains useful in referring to unconscious processes that may operate like a language (as Lacan theorizes) and that does not necessarily predicate a unified, essentialist, inner core. I am invoking an idea of fluid or atomic depths, rather than a fixed or mechanistic core that operates at some irreducible inner realm.

2 Industrial bureaucratic rationality has been described by the critical literature on institutional culture which includes LaBier (1986), Baum (1987) and Hirschhorn (1988). These works explore the effects of bureaucratic institutions on the person and stress the assault on the self and the concomitant costs to psychic health.

3 This reference, and all subsequent references to Protestantism, refer to a particularly Calvinist tradition within Protestantism. The differences of view and style inspired by later Protestant thinkers and expressed within some branches of Protestantism are not elaborated or evoked here. I am emphasizing the Calvinist theologies and teachings that continued to exert a defining influence within Protestantism even after some of Calvin's teachings had been reconsidered. Importantly, his views on the spiritual value of work, and the moral sanctions to which it gave rise, remain significant and prevalent both within Protestantism and in its secular manifestations.

4 This anxiety is not recognized by LaBier (1986) who identifies and focuses on the anxieties caused by adaptation to the new technologies and increased demands of work output. He suggests, in (unintentional) agreement with official discourse on the new culture, that improved participative and team structures will diminish such conflicts and anxieties. My data and analyses claim that not only is this not necessarily the case, but the embedded and denied contradictions in the new culture actually contribute to new and complex work anxieties which significantly affect the character of the corporate self.

5 Compare with Wexler (1991b). Wexler, following Alberoni (1984), suggests that "intensified ambivalence is the trigger for a collective, socially shared and communicated self transformation" (248). That may indeed eventuate. But it will require that the trigger for collectivizing the currently deeply privatized ambivalence, manifested among Hephaestus employees, is located and activated. The present corporate cultural conditions mitigate against such activation.

6 Formal employee review procedures are still in place, as are other organizational mechanisms to prevent internal fraud and corruption. But their use belies the informal and growing provision for nepotist-style favoritism to covertly undermine or override the formal procedures.

7 The Weberian schema of "ideal-types" (see Parsons 1968) is adopted in my construction of self types. These self-styles, of course, do not actually exist. They represent clusters of tendencies among employees experiencing the conditions of the new corporate culture. Some psychoanalytic concepts are used in this analysis of self-strategies but a fuller psychoanalytic treatment is not developed or intended.

8 These self strategies may be compared with Wexler's (1992) self types developed from his ethnographic study of social life in American high schools. His categories of *defensive*, *divided*, *depressed* and *displayed* selves, are class-specific (as shaped by the institutional processes of class-differentiated schooling), yet their composite, he argues, is the modern self.

9 The demise of other forms of social cohesion including traditional religion, family and community life are part of the process of the erosion of social

solidarities. The main focus here is on the particular forms of industrial solidarities associated with occupation and class.

10 The latter characteristics may be construed, following Hochschild's (1983) schema, as "deep acting" by the employee, i.e., the employee acts the institutionally prescribed role and emotion. My suggestion here is that over time the effects of the daily pedagogical program of the "new culture" and the predilection of some employees (because of psychic biographical and other pre-work influences) toward collusion, the boundaries between acting and owning the roles collapse. The colluded self thus avoids cognitive and emotional dissonance as she/he becomes what others seek only to appear.

11 It is possible that for some, although in my "sample" of Hephaestus employees only one (Vinny) exhibited such prospects, capitulation may enable a process of negotiated co-habitation for the more aware and assertive. Vinny, to recall, had forged a stronger sense of self through prior life experience and was inclined to treat Hephaestus as yet another obstacle on the road. Under these rarer conditions it is possible for employees like Vinny to negotiate a more psychically healthy strategy not just for survival, but for sources of more self-determined satisfaction in their work. But these people are a minority, and they tend to be younger and strongly influenced by events outside the corporation.

7 REVIVALISM, SELF AND SOLIDARITY

1 I refer to Hewitt's (1989) *Dilemmas of the American Self*, and not for instance, to Gergen's (1991) *The Saturated Self*, as the former is more exemplary among contemporary studies on the self in contemporary society, to indicate not just the points of difference but the limits of my study's focus.

2 Similarly, the feminist theorists (Benjamin 1987, Chodorow 1979, Probyn 1993, for example) argue that the biological condition is socially mediated: sex is biological, gender is socially ascribed. A gendered self is a further refinement of a theory of a "new self" that I have not attempted in this study.

3 Furthermore, Hewitt's bipolar thesis in which he describes oppositional pair-groupings of optimism and pessimism, tradition-centered and future-seeking, conformity and rebellion, security-conscious and freedom-loving, dependence and independence (Hewitt 1989: 192) as the basis of his theory of personal and social identity, may be accounted for in psychoanalytic theory. A psycho-analytic theory of identity proposes that the infantile crises of separation and individuation lay the primary patterns of all self-development and social interaction, and are replicated repeatedly throughout human life. However, the tension and ambivalence Hewitt observes around these bipolar themes, which he too recognizes as recurrent patterns in individual and social life, may support in my analyses the variation in individual "choice" of self strategy.

4 As, for example, in the USA-headquartered Pizza Hut's red gingham blouse and black skirt that I have worn in an Antipodean city.

5 Among them, Geertz 1973, Clifford 1986, Marcus 1986, Atkinson 1990, Burawoy (ed.) 1991.

6 The pre-industrial (and early industrial) occupations of, for example, weaver, sawyer, blacksmith, cartwright, being already rendered obsolete by mechanized industrial technologies.

7 At the same time there appears to be a rise in the numbers and varieties of professional and trade qualifications. These assertions in credentialed expertise may represent a reinvigorated attempt to recover professionalism from its

corporate assault. An exploration of that question is not undertaken in this book.

8 I refer to "neo-Protestant" because I wish to draw the distinction between traditional Protestantism (in its Church manifestation) in which the "bargain" was by and large kept for individual adherents to the faith, and in its secular manifestation in which the civic bargain was by and large kept for bourgeois citizens of broader Protestant culture – and the current corporate manifestation of the (secular) tradition in which the implied "salvation" is incompletely honored, even for colluded selves, and breached at the corporation's decree.

9 See in particular Kanter (1977) who describes adjustment and coping patterns for secretarial, clerical and middle-management employees in response to their experiences of work in a large corporation. Kanter does not develop a social psychology of work and does not refer to defensiveness or offer a typology of corporate selves.

10 For those who have retained a greater sense of self constituted by other identity loci and woven into a coherent autobiographical self-narrative – if such has withstood the pathologies of secondary narcissism embedded in the culture of late capitalism – it is a wearied, reluctant surrender.

11 I refer here to a multi-national telecommunications corporation in which I have conducted some informal research.

BIBLIOGRAPHY

Abercrombie, N. and Urry, J., 1983, *Capital, Labour and the Middle Classes*, London: Allen and Unwin.

Adler, Alfred, 1927, *The Practice and Theory of Individual Psychology*, New York: Harcourt, Brace and World.

Adler, Alfred, 1928, *Understanding Human Nature* (trans. W.B. Wolfe), London: Allen and Unwin.

Adorno, Theodor, 1968, "Sociology and psychology – II", *New Left Review* 47: 79–97.

Aglietta, Michel, 1979, *A Theory of Capitalist Regulation: The US Experience* (trans. David Fernbach), London: New Left Books.

Ainsworth, M.D. 1969, "Object relations, dependency, and attachment", *Child Development* 40: 969–1025.

Alberoni, F., 1984, *Movement and Institution* (trans. Arden Delmoro, P.C.), New York: Columbia University Press.

Alic, John A. and Harris, Martha Caldwell, 1988, "Employment lessons from the US electronics industry" in R.E. Pahl, (ed.), *On Work*, Oxford: Basil Blackwell.

Allport, G.W., 1954, *Becoming: Basic Considerations for a Pyschology of Personality*, New Haven: Yale University Press.

Allport, G.W, 1961, *Pattern and Growth in Personality*, Holt, New York: Rinehart and Winston.

Anderson, Gary, 1989, "Critical ethnography in education: origins, current status and new directions", *Review of Educational Research* 59(3): 249–70.

Anderson, Perry, 1976, *In the Tracks of Historical Materialism*, London: Verso.

Anderson, Perry, 1984, "Modernity and revolution", *New Left Review* 144.

Apple, Michael, 1979, *Ideology and Curriculum*, London: Routledge & Kegan Paul.

Apple, Michael (ed.), 1982, *Cultural and Economic Reproduction in Education*, London: Routledge & Kegan Paul.

Apple, Michael, and Weis, Lois (eds), 1983, *Ideology and Practice in Schooling*, Philadelphia: Temple University Press.

Applebaum, Herbert, 1992, *The Concept of Work*, New York: SUNY Press.

Arendt, Hannah, 1959, *The Human Condition*, New York: Doubleday & Co.

Argyris, C. 1964, *Integrating the Individual and the Organization*, New York: Wiley.

Armistead, N. (ed.), 1974, *Reconstructing Social Psychology*, Baltimore: Penguin.

Aronowitz, Stanley, 1973, *False Promises: The Shaping of the American Working Class*, New York: McGraw Hill.

Aronowitz, Stanley, 1981, *The Crisis in Historical Materialism*, South Hadley, Massachusetts: Bergin and Garvey Publishers.

Aronowitz, Stanley, 1983, *Working Class Hero: A New Strategy for Labor*, New York: Pilgrim Press.

Aronowitz, Stanley, 1992, *The Politics of Identity*, London and New York: Routledge.

Aronowitz, Stanley and Giroux, Henry, 1986, *Education Under Seige*, South Hadley, Massachusetts: Bergin and Garvey Publishers.

Atkinson, Paul, 1990, *The Ethnographic Imagination*, London: Routledge.

Augustine, [4th century AD] 1958, *The City of God* (Introduction by Etienne Gilson), New York: Image Books.

Ayres, Robert U. and Miller, Steven, 1983, *Robotics: Applications and Social Implications*, Cambridge, Massachusetts: Ballinger.

Baer, Judith A., 1978, *The Chains of Protection: The Judicial Response to Women's Labor Legislation*, Westport, Connecticut: Greenwood Press.

Bahro, Rudolf, 1978, *The Alternative*, London: New Left Books.

Bahro, Rudolf, 1984, *From Red to Green*, London: Verso.

Baldamus, W., 1961, *Efficiency and Effort*, London: Tavistock Publishing Co.

Baltes, P.B., 1979, "Life-span developmental pyschology" in P.B. Baltes and C.G. Brim (eds), *Life-span Development and Behavior*, 2, New York: Academic Press.

Bamber, Greg and Lansbury, Russell D. (eds), 1989, *New Technology: International Perspectives on Human Resources and Industrial Relations*, Sydney: Allen & Unwin.

Bandura, A., 1981, "Self-referent thought: a developmental analysis of self-efficacy", in J.H. Flavell and L. Ross (eds), *Social Cognitive Development: Frontiers and Possible Futures*, New York: Cambridge University Press.

Bandura, A., 1989, "Human agency in social cognitive theory", *American Psychologist* 44: 1175–84.

Baran, Barbara, 1988, "Office automation and women's work: the technological transformation of the insurance industry" in R.E. Pahl (ed.), *On Work*, Oxford: Basil Blackwell.

Baran, Paul and Sweezy, 1966, *Monopoly Capitalism*, Harmondsworth: Penguin.

Barclay, Craig, 1990, "The remembered self and autobiographical remembering: composing protoselves through improvisation", unpublished manuscript, New York: University of Rochester.

Barclay, Craig and Smith, Thomas, 1993 "Autobiographical remembering and self-composing", *International Journal of Personal Construct Psychology* 6 (1): 1–25.

Baron, Ava, 1987, "Contested terrain revisited: technology and gender definitions of work in the printing industry" in Barbara Drygulski Wright (ed.), *Women, Work and Technology*, Michigan: University of Michigan.

Baudrillard, Jean, [1981] 1988, "For a critique of the political economy of the sign", in Mark Poster (ed.), *Jean Baudrillard: Selected Writings*, Stanford: Stanford University Press.

Baudrillard, Jean, 1983, *In the Shadow of the Silent Majorities . . . or the End of the Social, and Other Essays*, New York: Semiotext(e).

Baum, Howell S., 1987, *The Invisible Bureaucracy: The Unconscious in Organizational Problem Solving*, New York: Oxford University Press.

Becker, Howard S., 1963, *Outsiders: Studies in the Sociology of Deviance*, New York: Free Press.

Becker, Howard, Greer, Blanche, Hughes, Everett and Strauss, Anselm, 1961, *Boys in White: Student Culture in Medical School*, Chicago: University of Chicago Press.

Becker, Howard, Greer, Blanche, Riesman, David and Weiss, Robert (eds), 1968, *Institutions and the Person*, Chicago: Aldine.

Bell, Daniel, 1973, *The Coming of Post-industrial Society*, Harmondsworth: Penguin.

Bell, Daniel, 1976, *The Cultural Contradictions of Capitalism*, New York: Basic Books.

Bell, Daniel, 1988, *The End of Ideology*, Cambridge, Massachusetts: Harvard University Press.

Bellah, Robert, Madsen, R., Sullivan, W., Swidler, A., Tipton, S., 1985, *Habits of the Heart*, California: University of California Press.

Bellin, Seymour and Miller, S.M., 1990, "The split society" in Kai Eriksen, and Stephen Peter Vallas (eds), *The Nature of Work: Sociological Perspectives*, New Haven: Yale University Press.

Beniger, James R., 1986, *The Control Revolution*, Cambridge, Mass.: Harvard University Press.

Benjamin, Jessica, 1987, "The decline of the Oedipus Complex", in John Broughton (ed.), *Critical Psychological Theories of Development*, New York: Plenum.

Benjamin, Jessica, 1988, *The Bonds of Love: Psychoanalysis, Feminism and the Problem of Domination*, New York: Pantheon Books.

Bensman, David and Lynch, Roberta, 1987, *Rusted Dreams: Hard Times in a Steel Community*, Los Angeles: University of California Press.

Berg, Ivar, 1970, *Education and Jobs: The Great Training Robbery*, New York: Praegar.

Berger, P.L. and Luckman, T. 1966, *The Social Construction of Reality*, New York: Doubleday.

Berlyne, D.E., 1971, *Aesthetics and Psychobiology*, New York: Appleton-Century-Crofts-Beniger.

Berman, Marshall, 1983, *All That is Solid Melts into Air*, London: Verso.

Berman, Marshall, 1992, "Why Modernism still matters", in Scott Lash and Jonathan Friedman (eds), 1992, *Modernity and Identity*, Oxford: Basil Blackwell.

Bernstein, Basil, 1975, *Class, Codes and Control: Toward a Theory of Educational Transmissions*, London: Routledge & Kegan Paul.

Best, Fred (ed.), 1973, *The Future of Work*, Englewood Cliffs, New Jersey: Prentice Hall.

Blauner, R. 1964, *Alienation and Freedom*, Chicago: University of Chicago Press.

Bledstein, B.J., 1976, *The Culture of Professionalism*, New York: Norton.

Block, Fred, 1990, *Postindustrial Possibilities: A Critique of Economic Discourse*, Berkeley, California: University of California Press.

Bluestone, Barry and Harrison, Bennett, 1982, *The Deindustrialization of America*, New York: Basic Books.

Bourdieu, Pierre and Passeron, Jean-Claude, 1977, *Reproduction In Education, Society and Culture*, London: Sage.

Boutlier, R.G., Roed, J.C. and Svenson, A.C., 1980, "Crisis in the two social psychologies: A critical comparison", *Social Psychology Quarterly* 43: 5–17.

Bowers, K.S., 1973, "Situationism in pyschology: an analysis and a critique", *Psychological Review* 80: 506–20.

Bowles, Samuel and Gintis, Herbert, 1976, *Schooling in Capitalist America*, New York: Basic Books.

Braverman, Harry, 1974, *Labor and Monopoly Capital*, New York: Monthly Review Press.

Buck-Morss, Susan, 1987, "Piaget, Adorno and dialectical operations" in J. Broughton, (ed.), *Critical Psychological Theories of Development*, New York: Plenum.

Bulmer, M. 1984, *The Chicago School of Sociology: Institutionalization, Diversity, and the Rise of Sociological Research*, Chicago: University of Chicago Press.

Burawoy, Michael, 1979, *Manufacturing Consent*, Chicago: University of Chicago Press.

Burawoy, Michael, 1985, *The Politics of Production*, London: Verso.

Burawoy, Michael, 1989, "Marxism, Philosophy and Science", *Berkeley Journal of Sociology* 34.

Burawoy, Michael (ed.), 1991, *Ethnography Unbound: Power and Resistance in the Modern Metropolis*, Berkeley, California: University of California Press.

Butler, Judith, 1990 "Gender Trouble, Feminist Theory, and Psychoanalytic Discourse", in Linda Nicholson (ed.), *Feminism/Postmodernism*, London and New York: Routledge.

Callahan, R.E., 1962, *Education and the Cult of Efficiency*, Chicago: Chicago University Press.

Callinicos, A., 1989, *Against Postmodernism: A Marxist Critique*, Cambridge: Polity Press.

Carter, Valerie, 1987, "Office Technology and Relations of Control in Clerical Work Organization", in Barbara Drygulski Wright (ed.), *Women, Work and Technology*, Ann Arbor: University of Michigan Press.

Castells, Manuel (ed.), 1985, *High Technology, Space and Society*, Newbury Park, California: Sage.

Cherryholmes, Cleo H., 1988, *Power and Criticism: Poststructural Investigations in Education*, New York: Teachers College Press, Columbia University.

Chodorow, Nancy, 1979, "Difference, relation and gender in psychoanalytic perspective", *Socialist Review* 9 (4): 51–70.

Chrichlow, Warren, 1991, "A social analysis of commitment and disaffection among black youth in an urban school", unpublished Ed.D. dissertation, University of Rochester, New York.

Clifford, James and Marcus, George E. (eds), 1986, *Writing Culture: The Poetics and Politics of Ethnography*, Berkeley, California: University of California Press.

Coburn, David and Edwards, Virginia, 1976, "Job control and child-rearing values", *Canadian Review of Sociology and Anthropology* 13 (3): 337–44.

Cohen, A., 1919, *The Teaching of Maimonides*, London: Routledge.

Cohen, Stephen and Zysman, John, 1987, *Manufacturing Matters: The Myth of the Post-Industrial Economy*, New York: Basic Books.

Coleman, J.S., 1966, *Equality of Educational Opportunity*, Washington DC: National Center for Educational Statistics.

Connell, James P., 1985, "A New Multidimensional Measure of Children's Perceptions of Control", *Child Development* 56: 1018–41.

Connell, J.P., 1991, "Context, self and action: A motivational analysis of self-system processes across the life-span" in D. Chiccheti (ed.), *The Self in Transition*, Chicago: University of Chicago Press.

Connell, J.P. and Ryan, R.M., 1984, "A developmental theory of motivation in the classroom", *Teacher Education Quarterly 11*, 64–77.

Cooley, Charles Horton, 1902a, *Social Organization*, New York: Scribner and Sons.

Cooley, Charles Horton, 1902b, *Human Nature and the Social Order*, New York: Scribner and Sons.

Corcoran, Mary and Duncan, Gregory, 1979, "Work history, labor force attachment, and earnings differences between the races and sexes", *Journal of Human Resources* 14: 3–20.

Dannefer, Dale, 1984, "Adult development and social theory: a paradigmatic reappraisal", *American Sociological Review* 49: 100–16.

Dannefer, Dale and Perlmutter, Marion, 1990, "Development as a multi-dimensional process: individual and social constituents", *Human Development* 33: 108–37.

Deal, T.E. and Kennedy, A.A., 1982, *Corporate Cultures*, Reading, Massachusetts: Addison-Wesley.

de Beauvoir, Simone, 1953, *The Second Sex*, New York: Alfred Knopf.

Deci, E.L., 1971, "Effects of externally mediated rewards on intrinsic motivation", *Journal of Personality and Social Psychology* 18: 105–15.

Deci, E.L., 1972, "Intrinsic motivation, extrinsic reinforcement, and inequity", *Journal of Personality and Social Psychology* 22: 113–20.

Deci, E.L, and Ryan, R.M., 1985, *Intrinsic Motivation and Self-determination in Human Behavior*, New York: Plenum.

Deci, E.L and Ryan, 1991, "A motivational approach to self: integration in personality" in R. Dienstbier (ed.), *Nebraska Symposium on Motivation Vol. 38. Perspectives on Motivation*, Nebraska: University of Nebraska Press.

de Keyser, Veronique, Qvale, Thoralf, Wilpert, Bernhard, Quintanilla, S. Antonio Ruiz, (eds), 1988, *The Meaning of Work and Technological Options*, London and New York: John Wiley & Sons.

Deleuze, G. and Guattari, F., 1979, *Anti-Oedipus: Capitalism and Schizophrenia*, New York: Viking.

Derber, Richard, Schwartz, William, Magrass, Yale, 1990, *Power in the Highest Degree: Professionals and the Rise of a New Mandarin Order*, New York: Oxford University Press.

Derrida, Jacques, 1982, *Margins of Philosophy* (trans. Alan Bass), Chicago: University of Chicago Press.

Didsbury, Howard (ed.), 1983, *The World of Work*, Baltimore, Maryland: World Future Society.

Dobert, Rainer, Habermas, Jurgen, Nunner-Winkler, Gertrud, 1987, "The development of the self" in John Broughton (ed.), *Critical Psychological Theories of Development*, New York: Plenum.

Dreeben, Robert, 1968, *On What is Learned in School*, Reading, Massachusetts: Addison-Wesley.

Drucker, P.F., 1960, *Concept of the Corporation*, Boston: Beacon Press.

Drucker, Peter, 1973, "Evolution of the knowledge worker" in Fred Best (ed.), *The Future of Work*, Englewood Cliffs, New Jersey: Prentice-Hall.

Drucker, Peter, 1993, *Post-Capitalist Society*, New York: Harper.

Dubin, R. (ed.), 1976, *Handbook of Work, Organization and Society*, Chicago: Rand McNally.

Durkheim, Emile, [1915] 1965, *The Elementary Forms of the Religious Life*, New York: Free Press.

Durkheim, Emile, [1933] 1984, *The Division of Labor in Society* (trans. W.D. Halls), New York: Free Press.

Edwards, Richard, 1979, *Contested Terrain: The Transformation of the Workplace in the Twentiety Century*, New York: Basic Books.

Ehrenreich, Barbara, 1989, *Fear of Falling: The Inner Life of the Middleclass*, New York: Pantheon.

Ehrenreich, Barbara and Ehrenreich, John, 1979, "The professional managerial class" in Pat Walker (ed.), *Between Labor and Capital: The Professional Managerial Class*, Boston: Southend Press.

Elder, G.H., 1979, "Historical change in life patterns and personality", in P.B. Baltes and O.G. Brim (eds), *Life-span Development and Behavior* 2, New York: Academic Press.

Epstein, Cynthia Fuchs, 1970, *Woman's Place: Options and Limits in Professional Careers*, Berkeley, California: University of California Press.

Epstein, Cynthia Fuchs, 1974, "Bringing women in: rewards, punishments and the structure of achievement" in Ruth B. Kundsin (ed.), *Women and Success: The Anatomy of Achievement*, New York: Morrow, pp. 13–21.

Epstein, Cynthia Fuchs, 1975, "Institutional barriers: what keeps women out of the executive suite?" in Francine E. Gordon and Myra H. Strober (eds.), *Bringing Women into Management*, New York: McGraw-Hill, pp. 7–21.

Erikson, Kai, 1990, "On work and alienation", in Kai Erikson and Steven Peter Vallas (eds), *The Nature of Work*, New Haven: Yale University Press.

Erikson, Kai and Vallas, Steven Peter (eds), 1990, *The Nature of Work*, New Haven: Yale University Press.

Erikson, Erik H., 1958, *Childhood and Society*, New York: W.W. Norton.

Fantasia, Rick, 1988, *Cultures of Solidarity: Consciousness, Action and Contemporary American Workers*, Los Angeles: University of California Press.

Fawcett, G., Stonner, D., Zepelin, H., 1980, "Locus of control, perceived constraint and morale among institutionalized aged", *International Journal of Aging and Human Development* 11: 13–23.

Feldman, Richard and Betzold, Michael (eds), 1990, *End of the Line: Autoworkers and the American Dream*, Illinois: University of Illinois Press.

Festinger, L.A., 1957, *A Theory of Cognitive Dissonance*, Illinois: Row, Peterson & Co.

Finlay-Pelinski, Marike, 1982, "Semiotics or history: from content analysis to contextualized discursive praxis", *Semiotica* 40 (314).

Finlay-Pelinski, Marike, 1987, *Powermatics: A Discursive Critique of New Communications Technology*, London: Routledge & Kegan Paul.

Flax, Jane, 1989, "Postmodernism and gender relations in feminist theory" in Micheline Mason, Jean O'Barr, Saral Westphal-Wihl, Mary Myer, (eds), *Feminist Theory in Practice and Process*, Chicago: University of Chicago Press.

Foss, Daniel and Larkin, Ralph, 1986, *Beyond Revolution: A New Theory of Social Movements*, South Hadley, Massachusetts: Bergin and Garvey Publishers.

Foster, H. (ed.), 1985, *Postmodern Culture*, London: Pluto Press.

Foucault, Michel, 1972, *The Archeology of Knowledge*, New York: Tavistock Publications.

Foucault, Michel, 1973, *The Order of Things: An Archeology of the Human Sciences*, New York: Vintage.

Foucault, Michel, 1980, *Power/Knowledge: Selected Interviews and Other Writings, 1972–1977*, ed. Colin Gordon, New York: Pantheon Books.

Foucault, Michel, 1988a, *Care of the Self: The History of Sexuality, Vol. 3* (trans. Robert Hurley), New York: Vintage Books.

Foucault, Michel, 1988b *Technologies of the Self*, ed. L. Martin, H. Gutman and P. Hutton, Amherst: University of Massachusetts Press.

Foucault, Michel, 1989, *Foucault Live: Interviews 1964–1984*, ed. Sylvere

Cotringer (trans. John Johnston), New York: Semiotext(e): Foreign Agents Series.

Frank Fox, Mary and Hesse-Biber, Sharlene, 1984, *Women at Work*, Mountain View, California: Mayfield Publishing Company.

Frank, Andre Gunder, 1980, *Crisis in the World Economy*, London: Heinemann.

Frankel, Boris, 1987, *The Post-industrial Utopians*, Wisconsin: University of Wisconsin Press.

Fraser, Nancy, 1989, *Unruly Practices: Power, Discourse and Gender in Contemporary Social Theory*, Minneapolis: University of Minnesota Press.

Fraser, Nancy, and Nicholson, Linda, 1990, "Social criticism without philosophy", in Nancy Fraser and Linda Nicholson (eds), *Feminism/ Postmodernism*, New York and London: Routledge.

Fraser, Nancy and Linda Nicholson (eds), 1990, *Feminism/ Postmodernism*, New York and London: Routledge.

Fraser, Ronald (ed.), 1968, *Work: Twenty Personal Accounts*, Vols. 1 and 2, London: Penguin Books.

Freidson, Eliot (ed.), 1973, *The Professions and their Prospects*, Beverly Hills, California: Sage.

Freud, Sigmund, [1923] 1962, *The Ego and the Id*, New York: W.W. Norton.

Freud, Sigmund, [1915–17] 1966, *Introductory Lectures on Psycho-analysis* (trans. James Strachey), New York: W.W. Norton.

Fromm, Erich, 1947, *Man for Himself*, New York: Rinehart.

Fromm, Erich, 1955, *The Sane Society*, New York: Rinehart.

Fukuyama, F. 1989, "The End of History?", *The National Interest* 16, Summer.

Gallie, Duncan, 1978, *In Search of the New Working Class*, Cambridge: Cambridge University Press.

Garber, J. and Seligman, M. (eds), 1980, *Human Helplessness: Theory and Applications*, New York: Academic Press.

Gardell, B. and Johansson, G. (eds), 1981, *Working Life*, Chichester: Wiley and Sons.

Garson, Barbara, 1988, *The Electronic Sweatshop: How Computers are Transforming the Office of the Future into the Factory of the Past*, New York: Simon and Schuster.

Garvin, David, 1988, *Managing Quality: The Strategic and Competitive Edge*, New York: Free Press.

Gebhardt, Eike, 1982, "A critique of methodology" in Andrew Arato and Eike Gebhardt (eds), *The Essential Frankfurt School Reader*, New York: Continuum.

Geertz, Clifford, 1973, *The Interpretation of Culture*, New York: Basic Books.

George, Charles and George, Katherine, 1968, *The Protestant Ethic and Modernism*, New York: Basic Books.

Gergen, Kenneth, 1971, *The Concept of the Self*, New York: Holt, Reinhart and Winston.

Gergen, Kenneth, 1991, *The Saturated Self: Dilemmas of Identity in Contemporary Life*, New York: Basic Books.

Gergen, Kenneth and Gergen, Mary, 1988, "Narrative and the self as relationship", *Advances in Experimental Social Psychology* 21: 17–56.

Gerrard, C.K., Reznikoff, M. and Riklan, M., 1982, "Level of aspiration, life satisfaction and locus of control in older adults", *Experimental Aging Research* 8: 119–21.

Gershuny, Jonathan, 1978, *After Industrial Society?*, Atlantic Highlands, New Jersey: Humanities Press.

Giedion, Sigfried, 1948, *Mechanization takes Command*, New York: W.W. Norton.

Giddens, Anthony, 1987, *Social Theory and Modern Sociology*, Cambridge: Polity Press.

Giddens, Anthony, 1991, *Modernity and Self-Identity: Self and Society in the Late Modern Age*, Cambridge: Polity Press.

Giddens, Anthony and Mackenzie, Gavin, (eds), 1982, *Social Class and the Divisions of Labour*, Cambridge: Cambridge University Press.

Gill, Colin, 1985, *Work, Unemployment and the New Technology*, Cambridge: Polity Press.

Giroux, Henry, 1981, *Ideology, Culture and the Process of Schooling*, Philadephia: Temple University Press.

Giroux, Henry, 1983, *Theory and Resistance in Education*, South Hadley, Massachusetts: Bergin and Garvey Publishers.

Glaser, B.G., 1964, *Organizational Scientists*, Indianapolis: Bobbs-Merill.

Goffman, E., 1959, *The Presentation of Self in Everyday Life*, New York: Doubleday.

Goffman, E., 1961, *Asylums*, New York: Doubleday.

Goffman, E., 1967, *Interaction Ritual*, New York: Doubleday.

Goffman, E., 1974, *Frame Analysis*, New York: Harper and Row.

Goldthorpe, J.H., 1968, *The Affluent Worker: Industrial Attitudes and Behaviour*, Cambridge: Cambridge University Press.

Goldthorpe, John, Lockwood, David, Bechhofer, Frank, Platt, Jennifer, 1969, *The Affluent Worker in the Class Struggle*, Cambridge: Cambridge University Press.

Gorz, Andre, 1982, *Farewell to the Working Class* (trans. Michael Sonenscher) Boston: South End Press.

Gorz, Andre, 1989, *Critique of Economic Reason* (trans. Gillian Handyside and Chris Turner), London and New York: Verso.

Gouldner, Alvin, 1970, *The Coming Crisis of Western Sociology*, New York: Avon.

Gouldner, Alvin, 1976, *The Dialectic of Ideology and Technology*, New York: Oxford University Press.

Gouldner, Alvin, 1979, *The Future of Intellectuals and the Rise of the New Class*, New York: Seabury/Continuum.

Gramsci, Antonio, 1971, *Selections from the Prison Notebooks*, ed. Quintan Hoare and Geoffrey Nowell Smith, New York: International Publishers.

Grossberg, Lawrence and Nelson, Cary (eds), 1988, *Marxism and the Interpretation of Culture*, Chicago: University of Illinois Press.

Grossberg, Lawrence, Nelson, Cary and Treichler, Paula (eds), 1992, *Cultural Studies*, New York: Routledge.

Habermas, Jurgen, 1970, *Toward a Rational Society*, Boston: Beacon Press.

Habermas, Jurgen, [1973] 1989, "Toward a reconstruction of historical materialism" in Steven Seidman (ed.), *Jurgen Habermas on Society and Politics*, Boston: Beacon Press.

Habermas, Jurgen, 1981, "Modernity versus postmodernity", *New German Critique* 22, Winter.

Habermas, Jurgen, 1984, *The Theory of Communicative Action, Vol. 1: Reason and the Rationalization of Society* (trans. Thomas McCarthy), Boston: Beacon Press.

Habermas, Jurgen, 1987a, *The Theory of Communicative Action, Vol. 2: Lifeworld and System: A Critique of Functionalist Reason* (trans. Thomas McCarthy), Boston: Beacon Press.

Habermas, Jurgen, 1987b, *The Philosophical Discourses of Modernity*, Cambridge, Mass.: MIT Press.

Hale, W.D., Hedgepeth, B.E., Taylor, E.B., 1985–6, "Locus of control and psychological distress among the aged", *International Journal of Aging and Human Development* 21: 1–8.

Hall, Stuart, 1980, "Cultural Studies: Two Paradigms", *Media, Culture and Society* 2: 57–72.

Hall, Stuart, 1987, "Minimal Selves", *The Real Me: Postmodernism and the Question of Identity*, ICA Documents No. 6, London: Institute of Contemporary Arts.

Hall, Stuart, 1990 "Cultural Identity and Diaspora", in Jonathon Rutherford (ed.), *Identity, Community, Culture, Difference*, London; Lawrence & Wishart.

Handy, Charles, 1985, The Gods of Management: the Changing Work of Organizations, London: Pan Books.

Handy, Charles, 1989, *Age of Unreason*, London: Business Books.

Handy, Charles, 1990, *Inside Organizations: 21 Ideas for Managers*, London: BBC Books.

Harding, Sandra, 1990, "Feminism, science, and the anti-Enlightenment critiques", in Nancy Fraser and Linda Nicholson (eds), *Feminism/Postmodernism*, New York and London: Routledge.

Harlow, H.F., 1953, "Motivation as a factor in the acquisition of new response", *Current Theory and Research on Motivation*, Lincoln, Nebraska: University of Nebraska Press, pp. 24–49.

Harre, R. and Secord, P.F., 1972, *The Explanation of Social Behavior*, Totowa, New Jersey: Rowman and Littlefield.

Harrison, Bennett, and Bluestone, Barry, 1988, *The Great U-Turn: Corporate Restructuring and the Polarizing of America*, New York: Basic Books.

Hartmann, Heidi, 1976, "Capitalism, patriarchy, and job segregation by sex", *Signs* 1 (2): 137–69.

Hartmann, Heidi (ed.), 1987, *Computer Chips and Paper Clips: Technology and Women's Employment*, Washington DC: National Academy Press.

Harvey, David, 1989, *The Condition of Postmodernity*, Oxford: Basil Blackwell.

Hebdige, Dick, 1989, *Hiding in the Light: On Images and Things*, London: Comedia/Routledge.

Heckscher, Charles, 1988, *The New Unionism: Employee Involvement in the Changing Corporation*, New York: Basic Books.

Heider, F. 1958, *The Psychology of Interpersonal Relations*, New York: John Wiley.

Heilbroner, Robert, 1985, *The Act of Work*, Washington DC: Library of Congress.

Held, David, 1980, *Introduction to Critical Theory*, California: University of California Press.

Henderson, Hazel, 1978, *Creating Alternative Futures: The End of Economics*, New York: Berkeley Publishing Corp.

Herzberg, F., Mausner, B., Snyderman, B., 1959, *The Motivation to Work*, New York: Wiley.

Herzberg, R., 1966, *Work and the Nature of Man*, Cleveland, Ohio: World Press.

Hewitt, John P., 1989, *Dilemmas of the American Self*, Philadelphia: Temple University Press.

Hirschhorn, Larry, 1984, *Beyond Mechanization: Work and Technology in a Postindustrial Age*, Cambridge, Mass.: MIT Press.

Hirschhorn, Larry, 1988, *The Workplace Within: Psychodynamics of Organizational Life*, Cambridge, Mass.: MIT Press.

Hochschild, Arlie, 1983, *The Managed Heart: Commercialization of Human Feeling*, Berkeley, California: University of California Press.

Hochschild, Arlie, 1989, *The Second Shift*, New York: Avon Books.

Hoggart, Richard, 1957, *The Uses of Literacy*, London: Penguin.

hooks, bell, 1990, *Yearning: Race, Gender, and Cultural Politics*, Toronto: Between the Lines.

hooks, bell, 1992, "Representing whiteness in the black imagination", in Larry Grossberg, Cary Nelson and Paula Treichler (eds), 1992, *Cultural Studies: An Introduction*, London and New York: Routledge.

Horkheimer, Max, [1941] 1982, "The end of reason", in Andrew Arato and Eike Gebhardt (eds), *The Essential Frankfurt School Reader*, New York: Continuum.

Horkheimer, Max and Adorno, Theodor, 1972, *The Dialectic of Enlightenment*, New York: Herder and Herder.

Horney, Karen, 1942, *Self-analysis*, New York: W.W. Norton.

Horney, Karen, 1950, *Neurosis and Human Growth*, New York: W.W. Norton.

Howard, Robert, 1984, *Brave New Workplace*, New York: Viking.

Hughes, Everett C., 1951, "Work and self" in J. Rohrer and M. Sherif (eds), *Social Psychology at the Crossroads*, New York: Harper and Row.

Hughes, Everett C., 1958, *Men and their Work*, Chicago: Free Press.

Hughes, Everett C., 1971, *The Sociological Eye: Selected Papers on Work, Self and the Study of Society*, Chicago: Aldine.

Hunt, H. Allan and Hunt, Timothy, 1983, *Human Resource Implications of Robotics*, Michigan: Upjohn.

Huyssen, Andreas, 1984, "Mapping the Postmodern", *New German Critique* 33: 5–52.

Illich, Ivan, 1972, *Tools for Conviviality*, London: Fontana Books.

Inkeles, Alex, 1968, *Socialization and Society*, New York: Little Brown & Co.

Inkeles, Alex, and Smith, D., 1974, *Becoming Modern: Individual Change in Six Developing Countries*, Cambridge, Mass.: Harvard University Press.

Jacoby, R., 1975, *Social Amnesia: A Critique of Social Psychology from Adler to Laing*, Boston: Beacon Press.

Jaikumar, Ramachandran, 1987, "Post-industrial manufacturing", *Harvard Business Review* 64 (6) Nov/Dec.: 69–76.

James, William, 1892, *Principles of Psychology*, New York: Holt.

Jameson, Frederic, 1981, *The Political Unconscious*, New York: Cornell University Press.

Jameson, Frederic, 1984a, "The politics of theory: ideological positions in the postmodern debate", *New German Critique* 32.

Jameson, Frederic, 1984b, "Postmodernism, or the cultural logic of late capitalism", *New Left Review* 146, July/August.

Joyce, Patrick, (ed.), 1987, *The Historical Meanings of Work*, Cambridge: Cambridge University Press.

Jung, Carl, [1921] 1971, *Psychological Types*, New York: Harcourt.

Jung, Carl, 1961, *Memories, Dreams, Reflections*, ed. Aniela Jaffe, New York: Pantheon.

Kamerman, Sheila B. and Kahn, Alfred J., 1981, *Child Care, Family Benefits, and Working Parents: A Study in Comparative Policy*, New York: Free Press.

Kanter, Rosabeth Moss, 1977, *Men and Women of the Corporation*, New York: Basic Books.

Kanter, Rosabeth Moss, 1983, *The Changemasters*, New York: Simon and Schuster.

Kanter, Rosabeth Moss, 1989, *When Giants Learn to Dance: Mastering the Challenge of Strategy, Management and Careers in the 1990s*, New York: Simon and Schuster.

Kanter, Rosabeth Moss, 1992, *The Challenge of Organizational Change*, New York: Free Press.

Karabel, Jerome and Halsey, A.H. (eds), 1977, *Power and Ideology in Education*, New York: Oxford University Press.

Kassalow, Everett, 1989, "Technological change: American unions and employers in a new era", in Greg Bamber and Russell D. Lansbury (eds), *New Technology: International Perspectives on Human Resources and Industrial Relations*, Sydney: Allen & Unwin.

Kayser, Thomas, 1990, *Mining Group Gold*, El Segundo, California: Sherif Publishing Co.

Kellner, Douglas, 1989, *Critical Theory, Marxism and Modernity*, Baltimore: Johns Hopkins University Press.

Kessler-Harris, Alice, 1981, *Women Have Always Worked: An Historical Overview*, New York: Feminist Press.

Kessler-Harris, Alice, 1982, *Out to Work: A History of Wage-earning Women in the United States*, New York: Oxford University Press.

Kilman, Ralph, 1989, *Gaining Control of the Corporate Culture*, San Francisco: Jossey Bass.

Kilman, Ralph and Covin, Theresa (eds), 1988, *Corporate Transformations: Revitalizing Organizations for a Competitive World*, San Francisco: Jossey Bass.

Kleindorfer, Paul (ed.), 1985, *The Management of Productivity and Technology in Manufacturing*, New York: Plenum.

Knights, David, Willmott, Hugh and Collinson, David, 1985, *Job Redesign: A Critical Perspective on the Labour Process*, Aldershot: Gower Press.

Knights, David and Willmott, Hugh (eds), 1990, *Labor Process Theory*, London: Macmillan.

Kochan, D. (ed.), 1986, *CAM: Developments in Computer Integrated Manufacturing*, New York: Springer Verlag.

Kochan, Thomas (ed.), 1986, *Challenges and Choices Facing American Labor*, Cambridge, Mass.: MIT Press.

Kochan, Thomas, Katz, Harry C. and McKersie, Robert, 1986, *The Transformation of American Industrial Relations*, New York: Basic Books.

Kohlberg, Lawrence, 1969, "Stage and sequence: the cognitive-development approach", in D.A. Goslin (ed.), *Handbook of Socialization Theory and Research*, Chicago: Rand McNally.

Kohlberg, Lawrence, 1981, *The Philosophy of Moral Development*, San Francisco: Harper and Row.

Kohn, Melvin, 1990, "Unresolved issues in the relationship between work and personality", in Kai Erikson and Steven Peter Vallas (eds), *The Nature of Work: Sociological Perspectives*, New Haven: Yale University Press.

Kohn, Melvin and Schoenbach, Carrie, 1983, "Class, stratification and psychological functioning" in Kohn and Schooler, *Work and Personality*, New Jersey: Ablex Publishing Co.

Kohn, Melvin, and Schooler, Carmi, 1973, "Occupational experience and psychological functioning: an assessment of reciprocal effects", *American Sociological Review* 38: 97–118.

Kohn, Melvin L. and Schooler, Carmi, 1983, *Work and Personality: An Inquiry into the Impact of Social Stratification*, New Jersey: Ablex Publishing Co.

Kondo, Dorinne K., 1990, *Crafting Selves: Power, Gender and Discourse of Identity in a Japanese Workplace*, Chicago: University of Chicago Press.

Kornhauser, A., 1965, *Mental Health of the Industrial Worker*, New York: Wiley.

Kristeva, Julia, 1980, *Desire in Language: A Semiotic Approach to Literature and Art*, New York: Columbia University Press.

Kritzman, Lawrence, 1988, *Michel Foucault: Politics, Philosophy and Culture*, London: Routledge.

Kroker, Arthur and Cook, David, 1986, *The Postmodern Scene: Excremental Culture and Hyper-Aesthetics*, New York: St Martin's Press.

Kunda, Gideon, 1992, *Engineering Culture: Control and Commitment in a High-Tech Corporation*, Philadelphia: Temple University Press.

LaBier, Douglas, 1986, *Modern Madness: The Hidden Link Between Work and Emotional Conflict*, New York: Simon and Schuster.

Lacan, Jacques, 1981, *Speech and Language in Psychoanalysis*, Baltimore: Johns Hopkins University Press.

Laclau, E. and Mouffe, C., 1985, *Hegemony and Socialist Strategy: Towards a Radical Democratic Politics*, London: Verso.

Laclau, E. and Mouffe, C., 1987, "Post-Marxism without apologies", *New Left Review* 166.

Langman, Lauren, 1991, "From pathos to panic: American character meets the future", in Philip Wexler (ed.) *Critical Theory Now*, London and New York: Falmer Press.

Lasch, Christopher, 1978, *The Cultural of Narcissism*, New York: Warner Books.

Lasch, Christopher, 1984, *The Minimal Self: Psychic Survival in Troubled Times*, New York: W.W. Norton.

Lasch, Christopher, 1991, *The True and Only Heaven: Progress and its Critics*, London and New York: W.W. Norton.

Lash, Scott and Urry, John, 1987, *The End of Organized Capitalism*, Madison, Wisconsin: University of Wisconsin Press.

Lash, Scott and Friedman, Jonathan (eds), 1992, *Modernity and Identity*, Oxford: Basil Blackwell.

Lather, Patricia, 1991, *Getting Smart: Feminist Research and Pedagogy with/in the Postmodern*, New York: Routledge.

Lefcourt, H.M., 1976, *Locus of Control*, New York: Wiley.

Lefebvre, Henri, 1976, *The Survival of Capitalism*, New York: St Martin's Press.

Leontief, Wassily and Duchin, Faye, 1986, *The Future Impact of Automation on Workers*, Oxford: Oxford University Press.

LePlay, P.G. Frederick, (1858), *Les Ouvriers Europeens*, Paris: Imprimeries Imperiale, cited in Silver, Catherine Bodard, 1982, *Frederick LePlay – On Family, Work and Social Change*, Chicago: University of Chicago Press.

Lennerlof, L. 1986, "Psychology at work: behaviour science in work environment research", *International Review of Applied Psychology* 35: 79–99.

Lens, S., 1966, *Radicalism in America*, New York: Crowell.

Lerner, Richard and Hultsch, D.F., 1983, *Human Development: A Life-span Perspective*, New York: McGraw-Hill.

Levinson, D., 1978, *The Seasons of a Man's Life*, New York: Knopf.

Lewin, Kurt, 1935, *A Dynamic Theory of Personality*, New York: McGraw Hill.

Lewin, Kurt, 1951, *Field Theory in Social Science*, New York: Harper.

Leymann, Heinz and Kornbluh, Hy (eds), 1989, *Socialization and Learning at Work*, Aldershot: Avebury Press.

Lincoln, Yvonna and Guba, Egon, 1985, *Naturalistic Inquiry*, London: Sage Publications.

Littler, C.R., 1982, *The Development of the Labour Process in Capitalist Societies: A Comparative Study of the Transformation of Work Organization in Britain, Japan and the USA*, London: Heinemann.

Littler, C.R. and Salaman, G., 1984, *Class at Work: The Design, Allocation and Control of Jobs*, London: Batsford Academic.

Livingston, David (ed.), 1987, *Critical Pedagogy and Cultural Power*, South Hadley, Massachusetts: Bergin and Garvey.

Lofland, John and Lofland, Lyn, 1984, *Analyzing Social Settings: A Guide to Qualitative Observation and Analysis*, Belmont, California: Wadsworth Publishing Co.

Lukacs, Georg, [1923] 1971, *History and Class Consciousness*, Cambridge, Mass.: MIT Press.

Luke, Timothy, 1991, "Touring hyperreality: critical theory confronts informational society", in Philip Wexler (ed.), *Critical Theory Now*, London and New York: Falmer Press.

Lumer, Hyman, 1962, *Is Full Employment Possible?* New York: New Century Publishers.

Lyotard, Jean-François, 1984, *The Postmodern Condition*, Minneapolis: University of Minnesota Press.

Maccoby, Michael, 1976, *The Gamesman*, New York: Simon and Schuster.

Maccoby, Michael, 1981, *The Leader: A New Face for American Management*, New York: Simon and Schuster.

Maccoby, Michael, 1988, *Why Work: Leading the New Generation*, New York: Simon and Schuster.

McGregor, David, 1960, *The Human Side of Enterprise*, New York: McGraw-Hill.

McGregor, David, 1967, *The Professional Manager*, New York: McGraw-Hill.

MacKinnon, Catherine, 1979, *Sexual Harassment of Working Women*, New Haven: Yale University Press.

Mandel, Ernest, 1978, *Late Capitalism*, London: Verso.

Mann, Eric, 1987, *Taking On General Motors: A Case Study of the UAW Campaign to Keep GM Van Nuys Open*, Los Angeles, California: University of California.

Marcus, George E., 1986, "Contemporary problems of ethnography in the modern world system", in James Clifford and George E. Marcus (eds), *Writing Culture: The Poetics and Politics of Ethnography*, Berkeley, California: University of California Press.

Marcuse, Herbert, 1962, *Eros and Civilization: A Philosophical Inquiry into Freud*, New York: Vintage Press.

Marcuse, Herbert, 1964, *One-Dimensional Man*, New York: Abacus.

Marks, Elaine and de Courtivron, Isabelle (eds), 1981, *New French Feminisms*, New York: Schocken Books.

Martin, Joanne, 1992, *Cultures in Organizations: Three Perspectives*, New York: Oxford.

Marx, Karl, [1844] 1978, *Economic and Philosophical Manuscripts*, in Robert Tucker (ed.), *The Marx–Engels Reader*, New York: W.W. Norton.

Marx, Karl, [1846] 1983, *The German Ideology*, in Eugene Kamenka (ed.), *The Portable Karl Marx*, New York: Penguin.

Marx, Karl, [1852] 1978, *The Eighteenth Brumaire of Louis Bonaparte*, in Robert Tucker (ed.), *The Marx–Engels Reader*, New York: W.W. Norton.

Marx, Karl, [1859] 1983, *A Contribution to Political Economy*, in Eugene Kamenka (ed.), *The Portable Karl Marx*, New York: Penguin.

Marx, Karl, [1867] 1978, *Capital Vol. 1*, in Robert Tucker (ed.), *The Marx–Engels Reader*, New York: W.W. Norton.

Marx, Karl, [1888] 1983, *Theses of Feuerbach, VI*, in Eugene Kamenka (ed.), *The Portable Karl Marx*, New York: Penguin.

Marx, Karl and Engels, Friedrich [1888] 1968, *The Communist Manifesto*, ed. A.J.P. Taylor, London: Penguin.

Maslow, A.H., 1943, "A theory of human motivation", *Psychological Review* 50: 370–96.

Maslow, A.H. 1954, *Motivation and Personality*, New York: Harper.

Maslow, A.H. 1965, *Eupsychian Management*, Homewood, Illinois: R.D. Irwin.

Mayo, Elton, 1949, *The Social Problems of Industrial Civilization*, London: Routledge & Kegan Paul.

Mead, George Herbert, 1934, *Mind, Self and Society*, ed. Charles Morris, Chicago: University of Chicago Press.

Melucci, Alberto, 1980, "The New Social Movements: a theoretical approach", *Social Science Information* 19 (2): 199–226.

Merton, Robert, 1957, *Social Theory and Social Structure*, Chicago: Free Press.

Merton, R.K., Reaer, G.G. and Kendall, P.L., 1957, *The Student Physician*, Cambridge, Mass.: Harvard University Press.

Middleton, Chris, 1988, "The familiar fate of the famulae: gender divisions in the history of wage labour" in R.E. Pahl (ed.), *On Work*, London: Basil Blackwell.

Miller, Karen, Kohn, Melvin and Schooler, Carmie, 1986, "Educational Self-Direction and Personality", *American Sociological Review* 51: 372–90.

Mills, C. Wright, 1956, *White Collar*, New York: Basic Books.

Mills, C. Wright, 1959, *The Sociological Imagination*, New York: Oxford University Press.

Mills, C. Wright, 1973, "The meanings of work throughout history", in Fred Best (ed.), *The Future of Work*, New Jersey: Prentice-Hall.

Mischel, Walter, 1968, *Personality and Assessment*, New York: Wiley.

Mischel, W. and Mischel, H., 1977, "Self-control and the self", in T. Mischel (ed.), *The Self: Psychological and Philosophical Issues*, Totowa, New Jersey: Rowman and Littlefield.

Mitchell, Juliette, 1974, *Pyschoanalysis and Feminism*, New York: Vintage Books.

Modleski, Tania, 1991, *Feminism Without Women: Culture and Criticism in a 'Postfeminist' Age*, New York and London: Routledge.

Montgomery, David, 1979, *Workers' Control in America*, Cambridge: Cambridge University Press.

Montgomery, David, 1987, *The Fall of the House of Labor*, Cambridge: Cambridge University Press.

Murray, H.A., 1938, *Explorations in Personality*, New York: Oxford University Press.

Naisbitt, John and Aburdene, Patricia, 1985, *Re-inventing the Corporation*, New York: Warner Books.

Neisser, U., 1990, *Modes of Perception and Forms of Knowledge*, Paper presented to Japanese Psychological Association, Tokyo.

Nelson, D., 1975, *Managers and Workers: Origins of the new factory system in the United States, 1880–1920*, Madison, Wisconsin: University of Wisconsin Press.

Neugarten, Bernice Levin (ed.), 1968, *Middle Age and Aging*, Chicago: University of Chicago Press.

Nicholson, Linda (ed.), 1990, *Feminism/Postmodernism*, New York: Routledge.

Noble, David, 1978, "Social choice in machine design: the case of automatically controlled machine tools, and a challenge for labor", *Politics and Society* 8 (3–4): 313–47.

Noble, David, 1984, *Forces of Production: A Social History of Industrial Automation*, New York: Knopf.

Oakley, Ann, 1974, *Images of Housework*, London: Martin Robertson.

O'Brien, Gordon, 1984, "Locus of control, work and retirement", in *Research with the Locus of Control Construct, Vol.3, Extensions and Limitations*, New York: Academic Press.

O'Brien, Gordon, 1986, *Psychology of Work and Unemployment*, New York: John Wiley & Sons.

O'Connor, James, 1973, *The Fiscal Crisis of the State*, New York: St Martin's Press.

Offe, Claus, 1985, *Disorganised Capitalism*, Cambridge: Polity Press.

Offe, Claus, 1992, *Beyond Employment: Time, Work and the Informal Economy*, (trans. Alan Braley), Cambridge: Polity Press.

Ouchi, William, 1981, *Theory Z: How American Business Can Meet the Japanese Challenge*, Reading, Massachusetts: Addison-Wesley.

Pahl, R.E. (ed.) 1988, *On Work: Historical, Comparative and Theoretical Approaches*, Oxford: Basil Blackwell.

Palloix, Christian, 1976, *The Labor Process and Class Struggles*: London: CSE Pamphlet no.1

Pareto, Vilfredo, 1935, *The Mind and Society*, Vol. 1, ed. Arthur Livingston (trans. Andre Bongiorno and Arthur Livingston), New York: Harcourt Brace.

Parker, Jane and Slaughter, Mike, 1988, *Choosing Sides: Unions and the Team Concept*, Boston: South End Press.

Parsons, Talcott, 1951, *The Social System*, Chicago: Free Press.

Parsons, Talcott, 1959, "The school class as a social system: some of its functions in American society" in *Harvard Education Review* 29 (4): 292–318.

Parsons, Talcott, 1964, *Essays in Sociological Theory*, Chicago: Free Press.

Parsons, Talcott, 1968, *American Sociology: Perspectives, Problems, Methods*, New York: Basic Books.

Persell, C.A., 1977, *Education and Inequality*, New York: Free Press.

Peters, Tom, 1991, *Beyond Hierarchy Organizations in the 1990s*, New York: Knopf.

Peters, Tom, 1992, *Liberation Management: Necessary Disorganization for the Nanosecond Nineties*, London: Macmillan.

Peters, Tom and Waterman, Robert, 1982, *In Search of Excellence: Lessons from America's Best-Run Companies*, New York: Warne Books.

Piaget, Jean, 1932, *The Origins of Intelligence in Children*, New York: International Universities Press.

Piore, Michael and Sabel, Charles, 1984, *The Second Industrial Divide: Possibilities for Prosperity*, New York: Basic Books.

Pipan, Richard, 1989, "Towards a curricular perspective of workplaces" in Leymann and Kornbluh (eds), *Socialization and Learning at Work*, Aldershot: Avebury.

Pollard, Sydney, 1965, *The Genesis of Modern Management*, Cambridge, Mass.: Harvard University Press.

Popkewitz, Thomas (ed.), 1987, *The Formation of the School Subjects*, London and New York: Falmer Press.

Poulantzas, Nicos, 1975, *Classes in Contemporary Capitalism*, London: New Left Books.

Powell, Walter P. and DiMaggio, Paul (eds), 1991, *The New Institutionalism in Organizational Analysis*, Chicago: University of Chicago Press.

Probyn, Elspeth, 1993, *Sexing the Self: Gendered Positions in Cultural Studies*, London and New York: Routledge.

Reich, Charles, 1970, *The Greening of America*, New York: Random House.

Reich, Wilhelm, 1966, *Sex-Pol: Essays 1924–1934*, New York: Random House.

Reich, Robert, 1991, *The Work of Nations : Preparing Ourselves for 21st Century Capitalism*, New York: Alfred Knopf.

Riesman, David, with Glazer, Nathan and Denny, Reul, 1950, *The Lonely Crowd: A Study of the Changing American Character*, New Haven: Yale University Press.

Rinehart, James W., 1985, *The Tyranny of Work*, New York: Academic Press.

Robertson, J., 1985, *Future Work: Jobs, Self-Employment and Leisure after the Industrial Age*, Aldershot: Gower.

Roethlisberger, F.J. and Dickson, W.J., 1939, *Management and the Worker*, Cambridge, Mass.: Harvard University Press.

Rogers, Carl, 1951, *Client-centered Therapy: its Current Practice, Implications and Theory*, Boston: Houghton.

Rorty, Richard, 1989, *Contingency, Irony, and Solidarity*, Cambridge: Cambridge University Press.

Rose, Nikolas, 1990, *Governing the Soul: The Shaping of the Private Self*, London: Routledge.

Rosow, I., 1974, *Socialization to Old Age*, California: University of California.

Roszak, T., 1972, *Where the Wasteland Ends: Politics and Transcendance in Postindustrial Society*, New York: Doubleday.

Rotter, J.B., 1954, *Social Learning and Clinical Pyschology*, Englewood Cliffs, New Jersey: Prentice Hall.

Rotter, J.B., 1960, "Some implications of social learning theory for the prediction of goal directed behavior from testing procedures", *Psychological Review* 67: 301–16.

Rotter, J.B., 1966, "Generalized expectancies for internal versus external control of reinforcement", *Psychological Monographs* 80: 1–28.

Rozen, Frieda S., 1987, "Technological advances and increasing militance: flight attendants in the jet age" in Barbara Drygulski Wright (ed.), *Women, Work and Technology*, Ann Arbor, Michigan: University of Michigan Press.

Rubin, Lillian, 1976, *Worlds of Pain: Life in the Working Class Family*, New York: Basic Books.

Ryan, R.M. and Lynch, J., 1989, "Emotional autonomy versus detachment: revisiting the vicissitudes of adolescence and young adulthood", *Child Development* 60: 340–56.

Sachs, Albie and Wilson, Joan Hoff, 1978, *Sexism and the Law: A Study of Male beliefs in Britain and the United States*, Oxford: Robertson.

Said, Edward, 1993, *Culture and Imperialism*, New York: Knopf.

Salaman, Graeme, 1974, *Community and Occupation*, Cambridge: Cambridge University Press.

Salaman, Graeme, 1979, *Work Organizations, Resistance and Control*, Harlow: Longman.

Salaman, Graeme, 1986, *Working*, London: Tavistock Publications.

Sawhill, Isabel, 1973, "The economics of discrimination against women: some new findings", *Journal of Human Resources* 8: 383–96.

Sayers, Sean, 1988, "The need to work: A perspective from philosophy" in R.E. Pahl (ed.), *On Work*, Oxford: Basil Blackwell.

Schein, Edgar, 1985, *Organizational Culture and Leadership*, San Francisco: Jossey-Bass.

Schumacher, E.F., 1974, *Small is Beautiful*, London: Abacus.

Seeman, Melvin, 1959, "On the Meaning of Alienation", *American Sociological Review* 24: 783–91.

Seeman, Melvin, 1972, "Alienation and Engagement", in Angus Campbell and

Philip E. Converse (eds), *the Human Meaning of Social Change*, New York: Russell Sage Foundation.

Seeman, Melvin, 1975, "Alienation Studies", in Alex Inkeles, James Coleman and Neil Smelser (eds), *Annual Review of Sociology* 2: 91–123.

Seidman, Steven, 1989, *The Habermas Reader*, Boston: Beacon Press.

Seligman, Martin, 1975, *Helplessness: On Depression, Development and Death*, San Francisco: Freeman.

Senge, Peter, 1990, "The leader's new work", *Sloan Management Review*, Fall.

Sennett, R., 1977, *The Fall of Public Man*, New York: Alfred Knopf.

Shaiken, Harley, 1984, *Work Transformed: Automation and Labor in the Computer Age*, New York: Holt, Reinhart and Winston.

Sharp, Rachel, 1980, *Knowledge, Ideology and the Politics of Schooling: Towards a Marxist Analysis of Schooling*, Boston: Routledge & Kegan Paul.

Sheridan, Susan (ed.), 1988, *Grafts: Feminist Cultural Criticism*, London: Verso.

Shipley, T.E. and Veroff, J., 1952, "A projective measure of need for affiliation", *Journal of Experimental Psychology* 43: 349–56.

Shotter, J., 1990, "The social construction of remembering and forgetting" in D. Middleton and D. Edwards (eds), *Collective Remembering*, London: Sage Publications, pp. 120–39.

Shumway, David R., 1989, "Reading rock'n'roll in the classroom: a critical pedagogy", in Henry Giroux and Peter McLaren (eds), *Critical Pedagogy, the State, and Cultural Struggle*, Albany, New York: State University of New York Press.

Silverman, Bertram and Yanowitch, Murray (eds), 1974, *The Worker in " Post-industrial" Capitalism: Liberal and Radical Responses*, New York: Free Press.

Silverman, D., 1970, *The Theory of Organisations*, London: Heinemann.

Skinner, B.F., 1938, *The Behavior of Organisms: An Experimental Analysis*, New York: Appleton-Century-Crofts.

Skinner, B.F., 1953, *Science and Human Behavior*, New York: Macmillan.

Skinner, B.F., 1971, *Beyond Freedom and Dignity*, New York: Knopf.

Skinner, B.F., 1974, *About Behaviorism*, New York: Knopf.

Skocpol, Theda, 1990, "Brother, can you spare a job? Work and welfare in the United States" in Kai Eriksen and Steven Peter Vallas (eds), *The Nature of Work*, New Haven: Yale University Press.

Slater, Philip, 1970, *The Pursuit of Loneliness*, Boston: Beacon Press.

Sleeter, Christine E. and Grant, Carl A., 1988, *Making Choices for Multi-cultural Education*, London: Merrill Publishers.

Slomczynski, Kazimierz, Miller, Joanne, Kohn, Melvin, 1981, "Stratification, work and values: a Polish-United States comparison", *American Sociological Review* 46: 720–44.

Smart, Barry, 1992, *Modern Conditions, Postmodern Controversies*, London and New York: Routledge.

Smelser, Neil and Smelser, William (eds), 1963, *Personality and Social Systems*, New York: John Wiley and Sons.

Smith, Adam [1776]1974, *The Wealth of Nations*, New York: Penguin.

Smith, Vicki, 1990, *Managing in the Corporate Interest*, California: University of California Press.

Sorge, Arndt *et al.*, 1983, *Microelectronics and Manpower in Manufacturing: Applications of Computer Numeric Control in Great Britain and West Germany*, Aldershot: Gower.

Sorokin, Pitirim, 1927, *Social Mobility*, New York: Harper and Bros.

Spivak, Gayatri Chakravorty, 1990, *The Post-Colonial Critic: Interviews, Strategies, Dialogues*, ed. Sarah Harasym, London: Routledge.

Stinchcombe, Arthur L., 1990, *Information and Organizations*, Berkeley, California: University of California.

Strassman, Paul, 1985, *Information Payoff: The Transformation of Work in the Electronic Age*, New York: Free Press.

Stromberg, Ann H. and Harkess, Shirley (eds), 1978, *Working Women: Theories and Facts in Perspective*, California: Mayfield.

Taylor, Charles, 1989, *Sources of the Self: the Making of Modern Identity*, Cambridge: Cambridge University Press.

Taylor, Frederick, [1911] 1967, *The Principles of Scientific Management*, New York: W.W. Norton.

Thompson, E.P., 1963, *The Making of the English Working Class*, New York: Random House.

Thompson, E.P., 1967, "Time, work discipline and industrial capitalism", *Past and Present* 38: 56–103.

Thompson, John B., 1981, *Critical Hermeneutics*, Cambridge: Cambridge University Press.

Tilgher, Adriano, 1930, *Work: What it has Meant to Men Through the Ages*, New York: Harcourt, Brace and Co.

Toffler, Alvin, 1971, *Future Shock*, London: Pan Books.

Toffler, Alvin, 1980, *The Third Wave*, London: Pan Books.

Touraine, Alain, 1971, *The Post-industrial Society*, New York: Random House.

Touraine, Alain, 1981, *The Voice and the Eye*, New York: Cambridge University Press.

Treiman, Donald and Hartmann, Heidi, 1981, *Women, Work and Wages: Equal Pay for Jobs of Equal Value*, Washington DC: National Academy Press.

Trilling, Lionel, 1972, *Sincerity and Authenticity*, Cambridge, Mass.: Harvard University Press.

Turkel, Studs, 1974, *Working*, New York: Avon Books.

Turner, Ralph, 1976, "The real self: from institution to impulse", *American Journal of Sociology* 81: 989–1016.

Tyler, Stephen A., 1986, "Post-modern ethnography: from document of the occult to occult document", in James Clifford and George E. Marcus *Writing Culture: The Poetics and Politics of Ethnography*, California: University of California Press.

United Steel Workers of America, 1960, *An Experiment in Education*, No. PR–108 United Steel Workers of America, Pennsylvania: Pittsburgh.

Vallas, Steven Peter, 1988, "New technology, job content and worker alienation: a test of two rival perspectives", *Work and Occupations* 15(2): 148–78.

Valli, Linda, 1986, *Becoming Clerical Workers*, Boston: Routledge.

Van Maanen, John and Barley, Stephen, 1984, "Occupational communities: culture and control in organizations", in B. Staw (ed.), *Research in Organizational Behavior*, Vol. 6, Greenwich, CT: Jai Press.

Van Maanen, John and Schein, E.H., 1979, "Toward a theory of organizational socialization", in B. Staw (ed.), *Research in Organizational Behavior*, Vol. 1, Greenwich, CT: Jai Press.

Walker, Charles, 1957, *Toward the Automated Factory*, New Haven: Yale University Press.

Walkerdine, Valerie, 1986, "Post-structuralist theory and everyday social practices: the family and the school" in Sue Wilkinson, (ed.), *Feminist Social Psychology*, Milton Keynes: Open University Press.

Wallace, Michele, 1990, *Invisibility Blues: From Pop to Theory*, London: Verso.

Wallston, K.A., Wallston, B.S., 1981, "Health locus of control scales", in H.M. Lefcourt (ed.), *Research with the Locus of Control Construct*, Vol. 1, New York: Academic Press.

Walton, Richard and Lawrence, Paul (eds), 1985, *Human Resources Management: Trends and Challenges*, Boston: Harvard Business School.

Waring, Marilyn, 1988, *Counting for Nothing: What Men Value and What Women are Worth*, Wellington, New Zealand: Allen and Unwin.

Waring, Marilyn, 1989, *If Women Counted: A New Feminist Economics*, London: Macmillan.

Watson, J.B., [1925] 1930, *Behaviorism*, New York: W.W. Norton.

Watson, Tony J., 1980, *Sociology, Work and Industry*, London: Routledge & Kegan Paul.

Weber, Max, [1930] 1958, *The Protestant Ethic and the Spirit of Capitalism*, New York: Charles Scribner Sons.

Weber, Max, [1908] 1971, "A Research Strategy for the Study of Occupational Careers and Mobility Patterns", in *Max Weber: the Interpretation of Social Reality*, ed. J.E.T. Eldridge, New York: Charles Scribner Sons.

Weber, Max, [1919] 1946, *Science as a Vocation*, in Hans Gerth and C. Wright Mills, (eds), *From Max Weber: Essays in Sociology*, New York: Oxford Unversity Press.

Webster, F. and Robins, K., 1986, *Information Technology: A Luddite Analysis*, Norwood, New Jersey: Ablex.

Weis, Lois, 1990, *Working Class Without Work: High School Students in a De-Industrializing Economy*, New York and London: Routledge.

Wexler, Philip, 1976, *The Sociology of Education: Beyond Equality*, Indianapolis: Bobbs-Merill.

Wexler, Philip, 1981, "Body and Soul: sources of social change and strategies of education", *British Journal of Sociology of Education* 2 (3).

Wexler, Philip, 1982, "Ideology and education: from critique to class action", *Interchange* 13 (3): 390–4.

Wexler, Philip, 1983, *Critical Social Pyschology*, Boston and London: Routledge & Kegan Paul.

Wexler, Philip, 1987, *The Social Analysis of Education*, London and New York: Routledge & Kegan Paul.

Wexler, Philip (ed.), 1991a, *Critical Theory Now*, London and New York: Falmer Press.

Wexler, Philip, 1991b, "Afterword. Collective/Self/Collective: a short chapter in the professional middle class story", in Philip Wexler (ed.), *Critical Theory Now*, London and New York: Falmer Press.

Wexler, Philip, 1992, *Becoming Somebody: Toward a Social Psychology of School*, London and New York: Falmer Press.

Wheelis, Allen, 1958, *Quest for Identity*, New York: W.W. Norton.

White, R.W., 1959, "Motivation reconsidered: the concept of competence", *Psychological Review*, 66: 297–333.

White, R.W., 1963, "Ego and reality in psychoanalytic theory", *Psychological Issues* III, 3 (Monograph 11).

Whyte, William, 1956, *The Organization Man*, New York: Simon and Schuster.

Wilkins, Alan, 1989, *Developing Corporate Character: How to Successfully Change an Organization Without Destroying it*, San Francisco: Jossey-Bass.

Wilkinson, Sue (ed.) 1986, *Feminist Social Psychology: Developing Theory and Practice*, Milton Keynes: Open University Press.

Williams, Raymond, 1961, *The Long Revolution*, New York: Columbia University Press.

Williams, Raymond, 1968, "The Meanings of Work", in Fraser (ed.), *Work: Twenty Personal Accounts, Volume 2*, London: Penguin Books.

Willis, Paul, 1977, *Learning to Labour: How Working Class Kids Get Working Class Jobs*, Westmead: Saxon House.

Winnicott, D.W., 1960, *The Maturational Process and the Facilitating Environment*, London: Penguin Press.

Wood, Stephen (ed.), 1982, *The Degradation of Work?* London: Hutchinson & Co.

Work in America, 1973, Report of a Special Task Force to the Minister of Health, Education and Welfare, Massachusetts: MIT Press.

Wright, Barbara Drygulski, (ed.), 1987, *Women, Work, and Technology*, Ann Arbor, Michigan: The University of Michigan Press.

Young, Michael F.D. (ed.), 1971, *Knowledge and Control: New Directions for the Sociology of Education*, London: Collier-Macmillan.

Zaretsky, E., 1976, *Capitalism, the Family and Personal Life*, New York: Harper & Row.

Zimbalist, Andrew (ed.), 1979, *Case Studies in the Labor Process*, New York: Monthly Review Press.

Zohar, Danah, 1990, *The Quantum Self: Human Nature and Consciousness Defined by the New Physics*, New York: Quill/ William Morrow.

Zuboff, Shoshana, 1988, *In the Age of the Smart Machine: The Future of Work and Power*, New York: Basic Books.

233

INDEX